Yale Publications in American
Studies, 15

Published under the Direction of
the American Studies Program

The Interpreted Design
as a Structural Principle
in American Prose

David L. Minter

New Haven and London Yale University Press
1969

1/1971
Am. Lit

Published with assistance from
the Mary Cady Tew Memorial Fund.

Library of Congress catalog card number:
69–15453
Designed by Marvin Howard Simmons,
set in Times Roman type,
and printed in the United States of America
by The Carl Purington Rollins Printing-Office
of the Yale University Press, New Haven,
Connecticut.
Distributed in Great Britain, Europe, Asia,
and Africa by Yale University Press Ltd.,
London; in Canada by McGill University
Press, Montreal; and in Latin America by
Centro Interamericano de Libros Aca-
démicos, Mexico City.

To the memory of
  my father
    Kenneth Cruse Minter (1889–1948)
  and my mother
    Frances Hennessy Minter (1892–1948)

Contents

Acknowledgments

I have tried in the usual ways to indicate my indebtednesses to the many scholars and critics from whose works I have benefited. I hope I have left no one out.

Several years ago four teachers and a friend helped me to a new start. To these men, Garrett Ballard, James Brown, George W. Linden, Martin S. Shockley, and Larry McMurtry, I remain deeply grateful.

More recently I have learned from acquaintances, friends, and teachers at Yale University, where an earlier version of this study was written as a dissertation. Don Summerhayes helped me in many ways to extend my thinking. A. N. Kaul read an earlier draft of this study and made several helpful suggestions. Sydney E. Ahlstrom and Edmund S. Morgan guided me in my study of Puritanism and other post-medieval intellectual developments; Charles Feidelson, Jr., Gordon Haight, R. W. B. Lewis, and Norman Pearson guided me in my study of modern literature. In addition, Mr. Lewis directed and encouraged me in my preparation of this study as a dissertation, and Mr. Feidelson helped me to develop the interests in American literature that give this study its shape and focus.

More recently still, Wayland Schmitt has given me expert editorial guidance, and several readers, anonymous except for Edwin Fussell, have made suggestions that enabled me to improve my work. I am grateful to all of them, especially to Mr. Fussell, who was kind to an unknown writer whom he has never met. My new academic home, Rice University, has given me research grants that have simplified and expedited my work.

My wife, Caroline Sewell Minter, has given, with the rarest generosity, to the progress and improvement of this work and to the encouragement of its author.

For permission to quote from copyrighted material I am indebted to the following authors and publishers:

Wallace Stevens, *Collected Poems,* Alfred A. Knopf, Incorporated;

Benjamin Franklin's Memoirs: Parallel Text Edition, University of California Press;

The Autobiography of Benjamin Franklin, Yale University Press;

Henry Adams, *The Education of Henry Adams,* Houghton Mifflin Company;

R. P. Blackmur, ed., *The Art of the Novel: Critical Prefaces by Henry James,* Henry James, *The Novels and Tales of Henry James,* and F. Scott Fitzgerald, *The Great Gatsby,* Charles Scribner's Sons;

W. H. Auden, *Collected Shorter Poems, 1927–1957,* and William Faulkner, *Absalom, Absalom!,* Random House, Inc.

A portion of "Extension of the Form: Henry James, and F. Scott Fitzgerald's *The Great Gatsby*" appeared previously in a slightly different form in *Twentieth Century Interpretations of The Great Gatsby,* ed. Ernest Lockridge (Englewood Cliffs, N.J., 1968), and is reprinted here through assignment of copyright by Prentice-Hall, Inc.

. . . the poem makes meanings of the rock,
Of such mixed motion and such imagery
That its barrenness becomes a thousand things

And so exists no more.

Wallace Stevens, "The Rock"

Introduction

This study began as an effort to define a particular kind of intellectual hero—one distinguished less by capacity of mind or originality of thought than by his being, in Henry James' description of Nathaniel Hawthorne's Miles Coverdale, "half a poet, half a critic, and all a spectator."[1] Soon after I began seriously to concentrate on Miles Coverdale in *The Blithedale Romance* and Quentin Compson in *Absalom, Absalom!* as instances of this kind of intellectual hero, I began to see that, beyond sharing a certain disposition to life, they inhabited similarly textured worlds. In the days that followed I made what I proudly conceived as "a discovery": that the worlds to which Miles Coverdale and Quentin Compson respond as spectators and critics are not only deeply problematical but are rendered so chiefly because the men (Hollingsworth in *The Blithedale Romance,* Thomas Sutpen in *Absalom, Absalom!)* who dominate their action meet with problematical fates in their efforts to realize grand designs.

The focus of my study accordingly shifted from a kind of intellectual hero to a prose form, the development of which I have tried to trace from colonial beginnings to William Faulkner's *Absalom, Absalom!* The term *interpreted design* is intended, and will I hope be taken, as a kind of metaphor for the works on which this study focuses—works structured by juxtaposition of two characters, one a man of design or designed ac-

1. Henry James, *Hawthorne*, English Men of Letters Series (London, 1879), p. 129. See Victor Brombert, *The Intellectual Hero: Studies in the French Novel, 1880–1955* (Philadelphia, Lippincott, 1961), pp. 12–13.

tion, a Hollingsworth, who dominates the action of his world, the other a man of interpretation, a Coverdale, through whose interpreting mind and voice the story of the man of design comes to us. My study is, in short, basically a genre study, the purpose of which is to describe the way certain prose pieces work, the way they unfold. In the second part of the study the focus is on autobiographies; in the third, on novels. In the first part I seek to locate, in sermonic literature and historical narratives of the seventeenth and early eighteenth centuries, anticipations of the themes and structures of the autobiographies discussed in the second part of the study and the novels discussed in the third.

Informing the study, therefore, in addition to a general chronological development, with some overlap between parts two and three, is a move from less to more thoroughly imaginative prose works. Within parts two and three, however, there is also a move toward works of increasing richness and complexity. In short, the more important, and perhaps at first glance less obvious, sequential development is thematic and formal. Like the focus of the study, this development is dual. On the "design" side we move from the early Puritans' collective, public design for founding an exemplary city through Jonathan Edwards' private plan for attaining salvation to Benjamin Franklin's dual, private and public, plan—first for attaining personal moral perfection, and second for establishing in world society an international party of virtue. Franklin's dual plan prepares, in turn, both for the experiment that Thoreau first privately conceived and lived and then publicly published, and for the intention of attaining high public office that Adams inherited from his family but perforce followed in public. *The Blithedale Romance* is to the third part of the study what Franklin's *Autobiography* is to the second: it is built around both the Blithedalers' public plan, a plan that in its collective aspect recalls the Puritans' design, and Hollingsworth's private (even secret) design. Hawthorne's allusions to the early

Puritans define the antecedents of the Blithedalers' group plan for founding an idyllic community. Hollingsworth's secret plan for reclaiming criminals is, on the other hand, very much his own. Together the two designs of *The Blithedale Romance* prepare not only for the astonishing variety (ranging from Kate Croy's secret scheme to Adam Verver's plan for building a palace of art in American City) of plans, schemes, and designs that we see in James' fiction, but also for the plan of Jay Gatsby and for the proliferation of designs in *Absalom, Absalom!* On the interpretive side the study moves from the Puritans' public response to public failure (their making of the various "small memorials," to use Cotton Mather's term, that are scattered through their sermons and histories) to Edwards' effort to combine interpretation of his own unworthy human plan with interpretation of the more than worthy divine plan of God. From Edwards we move to Franklin, who can conceive no plan worthier than his own, and who insists that his failure to realize his plan has resulted rather from his having been distracted by other duties than from his having inadequately executed his plan or from his having undertaken a task impossible of execution, and who insists, second, that since his is therefore not true failure at all, simple narrative record and simple assertion of his plan's practicability will suffice to reclaim it. Franklin's rather simple narrative in turn gives way to the more sophisticated, more thoroughly symbolistic works of Thoreau and Adams, who, because they take the problem of their failure more seriously than Franklin had taken his, must seek to discover more complex, more truly redemptive, modes of interpretation. Far more than Thoreau, however, Adams makes virtually unlimited claims for the exemplary aspect, the analogical possibilities, interpretively available in his own experience. In fiction we make a similar, though of course far from identical, journey: we move from the timid, partial, apologetic interpretive effort of Miles Coverdale to the fuller, more confident effort of Nick Carraway, to the far more troubled and deeply problematic but far more imaginative and creative interpretation of Quentin and Shreve in *Absalom, Absalom!*

The primary burden of the pages through which these developments are traced is definition, in relation to American literature, of the interpreted design as a prose form. Works shaped as interpreted designs are linked, first, by the shared structural conventions that I more fully outline in the first section of my initial chapter. But they also share the thematic and analogical concerns that I discuss in the second and third parts of the first chapter. In the second part to that chapter I suggest that the works on which I focus are linked to certain aspects of modern, and especially American, history. The man of design participates in modern man's continuing faith in design, in careful planning and concerted devotion as means of assuring success; the man of interpretation participates, on the other hand, in modern man's tendency, especially in his art, to make interpretation—both as historical recounting (historical narrative) and as imaginative translation (artistic narrative)—a means of taming unexpected and unacceptable failure. I want to stress, however, here as well as in my initial chapter, that my concern (and responsibility) is not with history per se, but rather with the uses to which history has been put, or the ways in which history has entered, the works I discuss. In the third and final section of my first chapter I try, first, to define the aesthetic implicit in the works I examine, and second, to link that aesthetic to modern notions about the genesis and nature of literature. In several of the more sophisticated of the works examined in this study, there is present a concern for "design" as suggesting a kind of architectural or intentional principle, according to which a work of art is to be viewed as an artifact constructed by design; and "interpretation" as suggesting a kind of organic or developmental principle, according to which a work of art is to be viewed as an artifact discovered, as an aesthetic possibility come upon, explored, and realized, during an act of creation.

The thematic and analogical concerns here sketched become complex, multilayered, and at times somewhat cumbersome. But they are important: they not only enrich the form; they also link it to recent cultural and intellectual developments that are modern rather than merely American. Indeed, it is the presence of these concerns that makes the interpreted design, in the ways I try to indicate at the end of the first chapter, relevant to one's understanding of modern literature in general.

The shift in focus from a kind of intellectual hero to works that unfold as interpreted designs introduced, necessarily, very different problems of selectivity and procedure. The effort to define the genre's immediate literary context took me beyond fiction, first to autobiographies and then to some Puritan literature of the seventeenth and early eighteenth centuries. Beyond this I was tempted to broaden the study in one of two ways: either to make it a study of the interpreted design and American literature, including some poetry, especially, of Walt Whitman, Hart Crane, and Wallace Stevens; or to make it a study of the interpreted design and modern fiction.

The first of these alternatives—that of including American poetry—would have involved me in treating works related thematically but not formally. There is, in short, no exact parallel, even in the poetry of the poets closest to my study, to the structuring roles of my men of design and interpretation. I decided, therefore, to limit myself to suggesting (with allusions to and borrowing from American poetry) a few of the more important thematic links that I observed.

The second alternative—that of including non-American autobiographical and fictional prose—would, in a very different way, have taken me almost as far afield, and would in addition have made the study impossibly large. I want, however, to stress that, while it is my intention to trace the American version of the interpreted design, it is not my intention to claim that the

8 Introduction

interpreted design is peculiarly American. Even as originally conceived, the purpose of this study was not to separate American literature from Western literature but, rather, by relating and distinguishing American and French intellectual heroes, to define an American version of a Western type. Readers familiar with French fiction will see links not only between some of the heroes of Proust and Malraux and my men of interpretation, but also between some of Stendhal's and Balzac's young men from the provinces and a man of design like Jay Gatsby.[2] The works I treat have moreover, in English literature, an antecedent in Shakespeare's *Hamlet,* near parallels in Charles Dickens' stories of men of great expectations and James Joyce's stories of young artists, and rather exact parallels in Joseph Conrad's *Heart of Darkness* and *Lord Jim.*[3] Again, however, I decided

2. See Brombert, pp. 165–80, on Malraux. And see Lionel Trilling, "The Princess Casamassima," *The Liberal Imagination: Essays on Literature and Society* [1950] (Garden City, New York, Doubleday, 1957), pp. 55–88, on the young man from the provinces.

3. A part of what we observe in Shakespeare's *Hamlet* is Hamlet's move from bafflement to planned action. Hamlet discovers in the first scene of the play that his world has become, as a result of the death of his father, a baffling scene—"an unweeded garden" (I.2.135). In its new condition his world requires that he give up being an observer & critic and become a man of action, that he accept responsibility for reclaiming his world (see I.5.187–89). His triumph, at least in part, consists in his ability finally to act, in a rather traditional Christian sense, in faith: his refusal, despite his longing for certitude, to be rendered impotent by the dark uncertainty that shrouds his world. Hamlet's penultimate words—

> If thou didst ever hold me in thy heart,
> Absent thee from felicity awhile,
> And in this harsh world draw thy breath in pain,
> To tell my story. (V.2.349–52)

which he speaks to Horatio and which I quote as an epigraph to Chapter 8, for my study of *The Great Gatsby,* are the words of a man of failed action to a potential man of interpretation, the words of a Gatsby to a Carraway.

that, in order to do something like full justice to the turns and
twists American writers have given the genre, I would have to
limit myself to suggesting, in various ways and places, a few
of the genre's more important moments in the broader literary
context in which I have tried to write and in which I hope the
reader will try to read.

Within my chosen context of American prose, I have opted
rather for full treatment of "representative cases" than for
encyclopedic survey of a potentially very large range of works.
With the models I provide the reader should be able to relate
the interpreted design to other American and non-American
works that I merely mention or lightly touch, as well as to
whatever other unmentioned works may seem to him relevant.
My choice of cases will, I know, trouble some readers. But the
choice was necessarily determined, first by a need for works
that would clearly and fully represent the form, for rather pure
cases, as it were, and second by a need for works that would
suggest the variety of modes the form has taken. Applied

In Joseph Conrad's *Heart of Darkness* Kurtz is not only "gifted creature" (Joseph Conrad, *Heart of Darkness* [1902], in *Youth and Two
Other Stories* [Garden City, New York, Doubleday, Page, 1925], p. 113);
he is also a man of "immense plans," a man whose action is controlled
by devotion to a "cause" and a "purpose" (pp. 143, 79; cf. pp. 53–55).
Kurtz' effort to master and overcome the darkness within and without
him meets, however, not with success but with "innumerable defeats"
(p. 151), including the big defeat of his last vision of ultimate horror.
Yet Kurtz' "gift of expression" (p. 113), including the expression he
gives to his final vision, and his capacity for devotion, including his
determination to "return" from his illness and "carry [his] ideas out
yet" (p. 137), meet with "a victory" that lies beyond his "innumerable
defeats" (p. 151). Of this strange victory, this "affirmation" (p. 151),
Marlow, Kurtz' interpreter, is the agent. Marlow so shares with Kurtz
the gift of expression that he is able to find words adequate even for
"inconclusive experiences" (p. 51). By becoming another voice in the
darkness, Marlow is able to remain "loyal to Kurtz to the last," and
not simply to Kurtz, but to the "magnificent eloquence" of voice and
vision that Kurtz represents (pp. 151–52, 113).

loosely, the interpreted design touches a large—even inexhaustible—range of works; applied strictly to works structured
by juxtaposition of a man of design who controls the action of
the work and a man of interpretation who controls the thought
and language of the work, it touches fewer cases. To the former
and larger range, the form is relevant—and I hope illuminating;
to the latter, it is, I believe, essential.[4]

4. In Chapter 8, I discuss several of Henry James' works, including
The Wings of the Dove and *The Golden Bowl*. The interpreted design
is also "relevant" to *The Portrait of a Lady,* in which several of the
motifs, devices, and conventions that I discuss are prominent even
though they do not finally define the structure of the work. In Isabel
Archer we have a heroine who is "always planning out her development, desiring her perfection, observing her progress" (*The Portrait of a
Lady* [1881], *The Novels and Tales of Henry James* [New York Edition,
26 vols. New York, Scribner, 1907–17], *3,* 72). In Ralph Touchett we
have a hero who, "being ill and disabled and restricted to mere spectator-
ship at the game of life," takes his pleasure in "the thrill of seeing"
what Isabel Archer will do (*3,* 209–12). To Ralph the drama of Isabel is
"an entertainment of a high order." What he sees quite clearly is that
"Isabel's originality" consists in her "having intentions of her own." It
is this knowledge, as well as his own attenuated role, that makes Ralph
a dedicated observer of Isabel's progress: "Whenever she executes them,"
Ralph says of Isabel's intentions, "may I be there to see!" (*3,* 86–87).
In fact, however, Isabel's intentions are as vague as they are grand.
Success means to her seeing "some dream of one's youth come true"
(*3,* 286). But what dream it is her intention to live, she does not say.
She conveys to others the sense of having high intentions and great
possibilities, but since she limits herself to vague references to her wish
to meet her "fate" (*3,* 185–86, 212–14), she tends to inspire intentions in
them: in particular, in characters as different as Mr. Touchett, Henrietta
Stackpole, and Madame Merle, each of whom becomes something of a
matchmaker. Not Isabel's vague intentions but Madame Merle's specific
ones emerge to shape both the novel's action and Isabel's fate: it is they
that Ralph sees executed. Nor does Ralph, in the course of his observing, ever really move beyond being an observer to become an interpreter:
his manner remains too passive, too free of any interpretive edge; and
his role remains too freely shared, too undifferentiated, too clearly not
our only perspective. He is in short only a cousin to the interpreters.

The principle according to which I chose between near and pure cases can be illustrated with my choice of *The Blithedale Romance,* which it is probably fair to say present consensus holds to be a trivial novel.[5] Even if the work is, as I think, Hawthorne's second best novel, it is clearly and substantially inferior to *The Scarlet Letter,* which I treat only in relation to the controversial "Custom House" introduction, and which, moreover, though Hawthorne's finest long work, is not in my opinion, in the context of world literature, a masterpiece. Which is to say that to my own view I have discussed at length a lesser novel by a writer who failed to compose a masterpiece in the novel form. I have done so, however, because the writer and the work are important not only generally but specifically to the subject of my study. It is my hope that my treatment of *The Blithedale Romance* may contribute to revision of its present status, but I have discussed it primarily because it (and not *The Scarlet Letter,* to which the interpreted design is merely relevant) is a pure instance of one mode of the interpreted design. To those readers for whom *The Blithedale Romance* is hopelessly inferior and uninteresting, I should like to stress, by way of placation I suppose, that it is only a starting point. The culminating cases of both the second and third parts of my study (in autobiography *The Education of Henry Adams;* in fiction *Absalom, Absalom!)* are literary masterpieces.

I do not anticipate general rejoicing at the appearance of yet another broad-gauged study of American literature. The

5. This is not to say that all critics dismiss *The Blithedale Romance.* See Daniel G. Hoffman, *Form and Fable in American Fiction* (New York, Oxford University Press, 1961), pp. 202–18; Frederick C. Crews, "A New Reading of *The Blithedale Romance,*" *American Literature, 29* (1957–58), 147–70, and *The Sins of the Fathers* (New York, Oxford University Press, 1966), pp. 194–212; and A. N. Kaul, *The American Vision* (New Haven, Yale University Press, 1963), pp. 196–213.

proliferation of such studies already has inspired at least one "big idea" about the susceptibility of American literature to "big ideas."[6] No interested party can attend such a development with unruffled equanimity. As one of those obliged by internal logic, if not request of friends, to plow an overplowed field, however, I take consolation in knowing that the works I have tried to interpret will survive it all, that they cannot be violated "by a little scratching."[7] And I should like to make clear at the outset the spirit in which my work is intended.

The serious study of American literature began with the work of men like Moses Coit Tyler and W. C. Brownell and continued in the 1920s, with notable shifts in focus, in the work of men like D. H. Lawrence and Lewis Mumford. More recently, beginning with Yvor Winters' fine study, *Maule's Curse* (1938), and F. O. Matthiessen's great work, *American Renaissance* (1941), the study of American literature has issued a series of fine broad-gauged studies. To Henry Nash Smith's *Virgin Land* (1950), Charles Feidelson's *Symbolism and American Literature* (1953), R. W. B. Lewis' *The American Adam* (1955), Marius Bewley's *The Eccentric Design* (1959), Leslie A. Fiedler's *Love and Death in the American Novel* (1960), Daniel G. Hoffman's *Form and Fable in American Fiction* (1961), and A. N. Kaul's *The American Vision* (1963), as well as to several of Perry Miller's works on Puritan New England, my debts are large, as they would also have been to Edwin Fussell's *Frontier: American Literature and the American West* (1965) and Richard Poirier's *A World Elsewhere: The Place of Style in American Literature* (1966), had these works not appeared after the relevant portions of my work had been written. It would, in some ways at least, be

6. R. W. B. Lewis, "Literature and Things," *The Hudson Review, 7* (1954–55), 311–12.

7. I have borrowed here from Alexander Pope, "Epistle to Dr. Arbuthnot" [1735], 1. 44. The quoted phrase is from William Empson, *Seven Types of Ambiguity* [1930] (New York, Meridian, 1955), p. 13.

satisfying to me to believe that my ideas and approach would displace the ideas and approaches of these men. In fact, however, and this fortunately has satisfactions of its own, I conceive my work as moving at times beyond but basically beside these studies, and others, of course, as well. "The house of fiction," Henry James once remarked, has "not one window, but a million"; so too, for several reasons, has the house of criticism.[8] The task of critics is after all to place works of literature in as many illuminating contexts as they can discover, remembering all the while that in humanistic studies even a genuinely new context need not necessarily displace other contexts. It is, of course, my hope that the context I try here to establish will revise and extend the reader's understanding of literature. But I do not recommend it to him as displacing other contexts.

8. R. P. Blackmur, ed., *The Art of the Novel: Critical Prefaces by Henry James* (New York and London, Scribner, 1934), p. 46.

Part One: Literary and Historical Background

Here was prose
More exquisite than any tumbling verse:
A still new continent in which to dwell.
What was the purpose of his pilgrimage,
Whatever shape it took in Crispin's mind,
If not, when all is said, to drive away
The shadow of his fellows from the skies,
And, from their stale intelligence released,
To make a new intelligence prevail?

Wallace Stevens, "The Comedian as
the Letter C"

1 The Interpreted Design as a Prose Form

> *When we mean to build,*
> *We first survey the plot, then draw the model;*
> *And when we see the figure of the house,*
> *Then we must rate the cost of the erection;*
> *Which if we find outweighs ability,*
> *What do we then but draw anew the model,*
>
> . . . .
> *or else*
> *We fortify in paper and in figures,*
> *Using the names of men instead of men . . .*
>
> William Shakespeare, King Henry IV,
> Part 2

Projects and plans, schemes and designs have of course played roles in numerous literary works. Within works shaped as interpreted designs, however, designs make themselves felt with peculiar intensity, not by mere prominence but because of the grounds from which they spring and the action to which they lead. Anterior to the designs stands a definition of reality that gives large place to man's ability to shape his world according to his thought and his desire. Given such definition, given insistence that with careful planning and high devotion man can construct a worthy edifice or achieve a worthy end, there is almost a "coinstaneity of the plan and the execution":[1] the ideal constructs, the visions, initiate confident endeavors to translate them into achieved actualities.

1. See Samuel Taylor Coleridge, "Poesy or Art," *Coleridge's Miscellaneous Criticism,* ed. Thomas M. Raysor (London, Constable, 1936), p. 209. Cf. the discussion of William James, below, n. 2.

——The term *interpreted design* is intended to suggest in its second part a recurring story and in its first a recurring strategy. The story of course permits variety of detail and incident; for, like all good stories, it is many stories. In outline, however, it is the story of a man dedicated to realizing a grand design, a man of action who gives himself to erecting a magnificent edifice, establishing a new dynasty, or attaining a high office. By asserting himself, the man of design seeks to shape his world according to a vision or model; he seeks to make something that corresponds to his notion of what will suffice. His failure to do precisely what he intends to do provides the core of the interpreted design.[2]

There is, as Kenneth Burke once noted, "a radical difference . . . between building a house and writing a poem about building a house."[3] The strategy that defines the interpreted design consists of juxtaposing to a man engaged in the first of these pursuits (the man of designed action) a man engaged in the

2. As John E. Smith has noted in *The Spirit of American Philosophy* (New York, Oxford University Press, 1963), p. 43, "the belief that the face of nature can be civilized through the ingenuity and effort of man" lies "at the heart of the American experience." As Smith's discussion makes clear, and as James' notion of "ideas" as "plans of action" suggests, William James was *the* philosopher of the man of design. If for Aristotle man is a rational animal, and if for Ernst Cassirer he is a symbolic animal (Cassirer being really the philosopher of the man of interpretation), for James he is an intentional animal. For to James, man's capacity for intentional activity is the token of his freedom. Indeed, that man is an intentional animal within a malleable and unfinished universe is what for James makes life hopeful and adventurous. For relevant context and perspective, see Walter Pater, *Marius the Epicurean: His Sensations and Ideas* (London and New York, 1893), pp. 111–12; and Northrop Frye, *The Educated Imagination* (Bloomington, Indiana University Press, 1964), pp. 19–22.

3. *The Philosophy of Literary Form: Studies in Symbolic Action* [1941] (2d ed. Baton Rouge, Louisiana State University Press, 1967), pp. 8–9. See Stanley Edgar Hyman's discussion of this phrase in *The Armed Vision* (rev. ed. New York, Vintage, 1955), pp. 332–34.

second (a man of interpretation). The interpreter is concerned not with building a house but with interpreting another man's building, both as activity and as edifice, and in all its aspects, comic, ironic, and tragic. The muddled life and problematic fate of a man of design constitute the donnée with which an interpreter begins, the barren "rock" whose meaning he seeks first to discover (or create) and then relate.

Interpreted designs accordingly focus on the dramas of two very different men or, more precisely, on the dramatic interaction of those dramas; they are dialectical in structure. The move to interpretation is derivative: it represents one man's response to another man's fate. Yet only what follows from that move gives meaning to that fate. Without the man of interpretation, the man of action would remain captive to the consequences of the faulty conception and inadequate execution of his design. Pragmatically considered, to be sure, the act of interpretation is "quite useless"; it does not help to implement the design; it "makes nothing happen." But it nonetheless represents one man's "revolt against [another] man's fate."[4]

In a man like Thomas Sutpen, who is in American fiction the man of design par excellence, we witness the drama of the human will engaged in a crucial instance of grand, visionary action. Beginning with consternation and need born of deep personal affront, Sutpen becomes first a visionary (a man who envisages a condition, a possible context, that will meet his need and assuage his affront), and second a man of designed action (a man devoted without stint or thought of compromise to a course of action conceived and pursued in order to realize that

4. I have borrowed one phrase from Oscar Wilde, Preface, *The Picture of Dorian Gray* (New York, Dodd, Mead, and London, John Lane, 1925), p. xvi; another from W. H. Auden, "In Memory of W. B. Yeats," *Collected Shorter Poems, 1927–1957* (New York, Random House, 1967), p. 142; and another from André Malraux, *The Voices of Silence*, trans. Stuart Gilbert (Garden City, New York, Doubleday, 1953), p. 639.

envisaged condition).[5] Within his world, Sutpen is significant because, in seeking to establish his plantation, build his mansion, and found his dynasty, he instigates and dominates the action of his world. But he is also significant because, since he pursues a specific design, his success or unsuccess can be measured.

In the man of interpretation—Quentin Compson in *Absalom, Absalom!*—we witness the drama of man "in his aspect of bafflement" as he engages "in a crucial act of knowledge."[6] Moved by the baffling fate of a man of design, by failure of considerable magnitude and uncertain causes and significance, the man of interpretation dedicates his rational and imaginative faculties and his linguistic resources to recounting a story so dominated by failure that it requires an act of interpretation to define and perhaps reclaim it. Himself a visionary of sorts, the man of interpretation responds to the failed visionary activity of another man by trying to tame, by trying to make coherent, "huge incoherent failure."[7] The man of interpretation seeks, in short, to master a story that, in its outline, deeply threatens not simply faith in design, in careful planning and concerted devotion as means of assuring success, but even more faith in all intentional endeavors, including his own deliberate effort at understanding. Which is to say that the interpreter is moved by a particularly disconcerting kind of human failure. In interpreted designs, the interpreter acts in faith that narration (whether as rather simple recounting or as rather thoroughgoing imaginative rearranging and creating) will provide a way of mastering unexpected and unacceptable fail-

5. See John E. Smith, pp. 38–79 and as discussed above, n. 2. On the term *visionary,* cf. Northrop Frye, *Fearful Symmetry: A Study of William Blake* (Princeton, Princeton University Press, 1947), pp. 7–8, 11–14, 91–92.

6. Maynard Mack, "The World of *Hamlet,*" *Yale Review, 41* (1952), 507. Charles Feidelson, Jr., *Symbolism and American Literature* (Chicago, University of Chicago Press, 1953), p. 5.

7. F. Scott Fitzgerald, *The Great Gatsby* (New York, Scribner, 1925), p. 181.

ure. Within his world, therefore, a man of interpretation is significant only in part because it is through his performance of the essential tasks of investigating and knowing and telling that his world comes to us. He is significant, too, because the adequacy of his performance can be tested against the ideal (of rich and fully ordered knowledge) to which the work that at once includes and transcends him is implicitly dedicated. Moved as he is by his own need (of understanding), his own affront (at bafflement), his own vision (of understanding as the condition that for him will suffice), and his own faith (that narration will bring understanding), the man of interpretation, no less than the man of action, is vulnerable to failure, albeit of a different sort. Whereas the man of design, who characteristically moves from dream to design, from vision to an effort to realize that vision, may fail in his effort to build something that corresponds to it, the man of interpretation may fail in his effort to shape a reclaiming narrative, to build a poem. In short, though "radically different," the pursuits of the man of design and the man of interpretation are more than interlaced and interrelated; the interpretive act reverses the direction of the designed act, yet is analogous to it: the man of design moves from affront to vision, and then seeks to move from vision to achieved construct; the man of interpretation moves from bafflement before a botched construct and muddled fate toward ordered narrative; but both men seek to move from what can only affront them toward what will for them suffice. Readers acquainted with either the timid, apologetic, ever-hesitating Miles Coverdale, or the deeply haunted and finally ambivalent Quentin Compson will know that failure of one sort or another is almost as frequently the fate of the man of interpretation as of the man of design.

In autobiographical works the characteristic dialectic is between older (investigating-interpreting) and younger (designing-acting) versions of the same man. In Henry Adams' *Education,* to take the finest case, self-examination, self-discovery, and self-portraiture represent an older man's effort, through language, to get at the meaning of a younger man's effort, through action, to build according to his design. It is to the fact of the younger man's failure that the older man addresses himself; he seeks to redefine that failure.[8] In auto-biographical contexts, the comic rather than the tragic potential of the genre is developed. In Thoreau's *Walden,* for instance (and even in Adams' *Education,* where the theme of failure bulks so large), the missing of a grand self-designation is seen as ironic transcendence, not as tragic fall.

In fiction, however, where the dialectic characteristically is established by juxtaposing different characters, the interpreted design characteristically recalls the action of classical tragedy of antiquity. It provides a way of shaping and thereby master-ing disaster. In its most enriching moments, moreover, the form's parts are so balanced that its dialectical movement is sustained throughout, enforcing interaction of contrasting no-tions of the pursuit of meaningful order. In *The Blithedale Romance,* for example, Hollingsworth, who seeks to build ac-cording to the specifications of an envisaged design, is set against Coverdale, who seeks through investigation and narra-tion to give form to a part of the world of action. Whereas Hollingsworth is bound to prosecution of his grand design, Coverdale is bound to interpretation of Hollingsworth's fate; whereas the former depends upon visionary, technical intelli-gence coupled with faith in action, the latter depends upon ana-lytic and critical understanding coupled with faith in thought and language; whereas the former moves from the world of imagination into the world of action, the latter translates the world of action into the world of imagination.

The story of American history is in considerable measure "a success story," a story defined by growth to enormous afflu-

8. Cf. this with André Gide, *Journals,* trans. Justin O'Brien (4 vols. New York, Knopf, 1947–51), *1,* 18–19.

ence and power.[9] Yet despite her long and serious affair with success America, particularly in her imaginative literature, has been preoccupied with what Melville called the blackness of darkness and with what Reinhold Niebuhr has called the ironies of her history.[10]

A part of what has troubled America is closely related to themes central to the interpreted design: namely that in building, perhaps grandly and at least stupendously, her builders have succeeded only by failing; that they have built as they have only by failing repeatedly to build as they had intended. New England Puritans, who were the first Americans to know and explore this strange kind of success, promptly labeled it sad and inadequate. When, almost three centuries later, F. Scott Fitzgerald recalled in the concluding lines of *The Great Gatsby* what fabulous things man had wrought with the new world, he echoed the Puritans' judgment.[11]

The sad and inadequate fate we encounter in *The Great Gatsby* is, in its beginnings at least, personal. Jay Gatsby participates in America's faith in a fluid world that invites man to shape his fate: to make or remake himself. *The Great Gatsby* is in part the story of the effort of James Gatz, the

9. C. Vann Woodward, *The Burden of Southern History* (New York, Vintage, 1961), p. 18.

10. Herman Melville, "Hawthorne and His Mosses" [1850], in Edmund Wilson, ed., *The Shock of Recognition: The Development of Literature in the United States Recorded by the Men Who Made It* (2 vols. Garden City, New York, Doubleday, Doran, 1943), *1*, 192. Reinhold Niebuhr, *The Irony of American History* (New York, Scribner, 1952), pp. 204, 7–8, and passim. Cf. Leslie A. Fiedler, *Love and Death in the American Novel* [1960] (rev. ed. New York, Stein and Day, 1966), p. 27: "In our most enduring books, the cheapjack machinery of the gothic novel is called on to represent the hidden blackness of the human soul and human society."

11. See William Stoughton, *New-Englands True Interest* (Cambridge, Mass., 1670), pp. 21–22; Fitzgerald, *The Great Gatsby*, p. 182.

son of "shiftless and unsuccessful farm people," to become Jay Gatsby, a man of "phantom millions" with a colossal mansion and a beautiful bride.[12] At least officially America has promulgated belief in the possibility of this kind of translation: I always thought, said Benjamin Franklin, that "one Man of tolerable Abilities may work great Changes, and accomplish great Affairs . . . if he first forms a good Plan, and, cutting off all . . . that would divert his Attention, makes the Execution of that same Plan his sole Study and Business."[13]

These are a few of the "lost words" that Nick Carraway, Gatsby's interpreter, hears but cannot locate behind Gatsby's strange and finally catastrophic effort to work his own great changes and accomplish his own great affairs.[14] In Franklin's conception, however, there were public and collective as well as private and individual possibilities. And faith in these possibilities antedated Franklin; it has in fact persisted in America since the days of the Bay Colony experiment, or rather, as we shall see, at least since the day John Winthrop delivered his sermon on board the *Arbella* en route to that colony. Franklin himself, who was nothing if not founder of clubs and societies, as well as author of plans and schemes, engaged in various social experiments. It is, moreover, as descendants of both Winthrop and Franklin, both Puritanism and the Enlightenment, that Hawthorne's Blithedalers engage in their "scheme for beginning the life of Paradise anew."[15]

Even before Cotton Mather began making, in histories and

12. Fitzgerald, *The Great Gatsby,* pp. 99, 149; see p. 5.

13. Benjamin Franklin, *Autobiography,* ed. Leonard W. Labaree and others (New Haven, Yale University Press, 1964), p. 163. See below, n. 48, Chap. 2; and n. 17, Chap. 9.

14. Fitzgerald, *The Great Gatsby,* p. 112.

15. Nathaniel Hawthorne, *The Blithedale Romance* [1852], *The Centenary Edition of the Works of Nathaniel Hawthorne,* ed. William Charvat and others (3 vols. to date, Columbus, Ohio State University Press, 1962–), *3, 9.* On Winthrop see Chap. 2, and on Franklin Chap. 4, of this study.

biographies, "small Memorials" of New England's story, second and third generation Puritans had responded to what seemed to them the sad fate of the New England experiment, not merely with lamentation, but also with salvaging stories, with narratives that celebrate the deeds of their fathers.[16] They thus established, in response to their own experience with inadequate success, a pattern that has survived them by three centuries and that has become, in *Absalom, Absalom!* for example, a way of mastering great failure as well as unsuccess.

Like her complicity in the "great" and "irresistible revolution" that has dominated the social development of the West during the last eight hundred years, America's uneasiness with her success is significant less for its singularity than for its modernity.[17] Not only socially but intellectually America has become "a kind of epitome of modern . . . conditions," a distinctly "modern instance," a kind of "test case of life in the 'new' (that is, post-medieval) world."[18] In her participation in man's "experience of radical solitude" and "spiritual isolation," in her involvement in man's entangled efforts to master and control his environment—again and again America has met with sad and inadequate success.[19] The deep and varied

16. See the concluding pages of Chap. 3 of this study.

17. Alexis de Tocqueville, *Democracy in America* [1835–1840], trans. Henry Reeve, ed. Phillips Bradley (2 vols. New York, Vintage, 1954), *1*, 14, 7, 5. Compare Karl Marx and Friedrich Engels, *Communist Manifesto,* trans. Samuel Moore, ed. Harold J. Laski (London, Allen and Unwin, 1948), p. 126.

18. Feidelson, *Symbolism and American Literature,* p. 105; and *"The Scarlet Letter,"* in *Hawthorne Centenary Essays,* ed. Roy Harvey Pearce (Columbus, Ohio State University Press, 1964), p. 32. Cf. Roy Harvey Pearce, *The Continuity of American Poetry* (Princeton, Princeton University Press, 1961), pp. 4–5, and esp. p. 5, where Pearce states that "The 'Americanness' of American poetry is, quite simply, its compulsive 'modernism.' " Cf. also D. H. Lawrence's *The Rainbow* [1915], where the "new world" is not only post-medieval but post-industrial and is obviously not peculiarly American.

19. Feidelson, *"The Scarlet Letter,"* p. 32.

uneasiness with self and world thus fostered, far from being peculiar to America, bespeaks anxieties borne by many. And those anxieties bespeak more than nerves congenitally weak, all too ready to fail. Provocations have proved perplexing and legion: in addition to hiding any God that may exist from "our gross eyes," recent intellectual developments have shrouded man's image of himself and unsettled even his rules of spelling, leaving him confident of pieces, not of coherent pattern, nor even of the meaning of meaning.[20] Developments that, for at least six centuries now, have made for an increasingly anthropocentric world, forcing man to bear the burden as well as accept the grandeur of being the center (the one source of meaning, coherence, and authority) for his world, also increasingly have revealed to him both how integrally he is a part of that world and how infinitesimally small are the dimensions not only of himself within his world but of his world within the cosmos. Analytic powers that have enabled him to penetrate

20. Emily Dickinson, "I know that He exists," *Complete Poems,* ed. Thomas H. Johnson (Boston, Little, Brown, 1960), p. 160. See J. Hillis Miller, *The Disappearance of God: Five Nineteenth-Century Writers* (Cambridge, Mass., Harvard University Press, 1963); and Erich Heller, *The Disinherited Mind* (New York, Meridian, 1959); and cf. Bertrand Russell, "The Free Man's Worship" [1903], in *Mysticism and Logic and Other Essays* (London, Allen and Unwin, 1917), pp. 46–57, and esp. the following from pp. 47–48: "That Man is the product of causes which had no prevision of the end they were achieving; that his origin, his growth, his hopes and fears, his loves and beliefs, are but the outcome of accidental collocations of atoms; that no fire, no heroism, no intensity of thought and feeling, can preserve an individual life beyond the grave; that all the labours of the ages, all the devotion, all the inspiration, all the noonday brightness of human genius, are destined to extinction in the vast death of the solar system, and that the whole temple of Man's achievement must inevitably be buried beneath the débris of a universe in ruins—all these things, if not quite beyond dispute, are yet so nearly certain, that no philosophy which rejects them can hope to stand."

innumerable mysteries of the universe, increasing his knowledge and power inestimably, have unsettled "the old verities and truths of the heart": powers that have disclosed to man the wonders of nuclear physics also have taught him to see process as reality and stability as illusion.[21]

During this exquisite initiation into modernity, man has learned again and again that "viewed realistically" history is "a series of *disorders*."[22] Tension between imagination and reality has of course all along been a part of the grandeur and misery of man, but recent experience surely has redoubled it, making it a defining problem of our time.[23] For again and

21. The quoted phrase is from William Faulkner, "Nobel Prize Address" [1950], *The Faulkner Reader* (New York, Random House, 1954), p. 3. See also Alfred North Whitehead, *Science and the Modern World* (New York, Macmillan, 1925); and Mileč Čapek, *The Philosophical Impact of Contemporary Physics* (Princeton, Princeton University Press, 1961).

Poetic apprehension of modernity as I am here discussing it has of course been many-sided. For D. H. Lawrence in *The Rainbow* [1915] it is beautiful: with the disappearance of the old world everything is lost; but with the discovery of the new world, everything is found. For others varied loss is dominant. "*Religion* blushing veils her sacred fires, / And unawares *Morality* expires," Pope writes in the concluding lines of the *Dunciad*. But the "universal darkness" Pope sees in his great poem is only partially defined by the disappearance of moral and religious order; it is also defined by the disappearance of needed wonder and beauty—by seeing "*Mystery* to *Mathematics* fly!" or as a very different poet, E. E. Cummings, later put it (in "you shall above all things be glad and young," *Poems, 1923–1954* [New York, Harcourt, Brace, 1954], p. 345), by seeing ourselves "teach ten thousand stars how not to dance."

22. E. M. Forster, "Art for Art's Sake," *Two Cheers for Democracy* (London, Edward Arnold, 1951), p. 99.

23. See Blaise Pascal, *Pensées,* trans. Martin Turnell (New York, Harper and Brothers, 1962), pp. 130, 144, 166, 172; and cf. Naphta's words in Thomas Mann, *The Magic Mountain,* trans. H. T. Lowe-Porter (New York, Knopf, 1944), p. 507: "You see, what perplexes the

again man has been compelled to acknowledge that the powers
with which he bravely endeavored to conquer his new world
have brought forth newness of which he had never dreamed
nor, to paraphrase Henry Adams, had ever much cared to
dream.[24] Modern man's great experiments have fulfilled his
dream of ever-increasing control over his environment only
in the same motion to enlarge the regions of the problematic
and create the possibility of nuclear holocaust. At least as
seen in the major works of modern literature, the great expectations, explorations, and adventures of modern times have delivered man not to a delectable mountain but to a wasteland.

Henry James once cataloged "the items of high civilisation
. . . absent from the texture of American life." The "flower of
art," he insisted, "blooms only where the soil is deep"; "it takes
a great deal of history to produce a little literature."[25] Yet as
James elsewhere noted about Hawthorne and indeed as the case
of James himself suggests, it has been possible for an American
to become an artist "just by being American *enough*."[26]
America's brief hour has proved stimulating because disturbing. And no aspect of American experience has proved more
disturbing (and therefore more stimulating) than the danger
of having transformed the "new world" into a "non-world,"
the disaster of having discovered, perhaps for the last time in

---

world is the disparity between the swiftness of the spirit, and the immense unwieldiness, sluggishness, inertia, permanence of matter."

24. See Henry Adams, *The Education of Henry Adams* [1907] (Boston and New York, Houghton Mifflin, 1918), p. 499.

25. Henry James, *Hawthorne*, pp. 42–43 and 2–3. Cf. F. O. Matthiessen and Kenneth B. Murdock, eds., *The Notebooks of Henry
James* (New York, Oxford University Press, 1947), p. 14, where James
catalogs America's vacancies as a possible speech for "some one" in
"a story."

26. Henry James, *Notes of a Son and Brother* [1914], *Autobiography*,
ed. F. W. Dupee (New York, Criterion, 1956), p. 480.

history, a green world commensurate with man's capacity to
envisage, only to invade it and build, not a city upon a hill,
a model of ordered richness and open community, but "a society of isolatoes," a model of purposeless wealth and spiritual
isolation.[27] If, moreover, as James once suggested, an "American as cultivated as Hawthorne" would inevitably be somewhat
"Europeanised in advance," and if, as T. S. Eliot later observed
in an essay on James, "It is the final perfection, the consummation of an American to become" European, perhaps it is in
part because inadequate success, dispossession, deprivation,
and isolation are Western and modern no less than American.[28]

In any case, whatever the complex history lying behind and
informing the works examined in the pages that follow, in the
worlds of those works we meet both Franklin's faith in success and Gatsby's experience of failure. History enters literature subtly, to be sure; but it is always newly constituted in
literary art by the "manipulation of language within [a] peculiarly poetic context." Here we are concerned with history
primarily as it has been manipulated in poetic contexts, as it has
been reordered and newly constituted in imaginative prose.
Such constitution and manipulation are after all not only the
defining tasks of the poet but by extension the primary concerns of the critic. We, in short, have in this study primarily
to do with realities created by men out of words, not with the
often consonant and always informing historical reality that
lies behind those realities. Such created realities are, to be sure,

27. Feidelson, *"The Scarlet Letter,"* p. 32. See R. E. Watters, "Melville's 'Isolatoes,' " *PMLA, 60* (1945), 1138–48; and Oscar Handlin,
*The Uprooted: The Epic Story of the Great Migrations that Made the
American People* (Boston, Little, Brown, 1951), pp. 3–4, where we see,
first, that "the immigrants *were* American history," and second, that
"the history of immigration is a history of alienation and its consequences."

28. James, *Hawthorne,* p. 157. T. S. Eliot, "Henry James" [1918],
in Edmund Wilson, ed., *The Shock of Recognition, 2, 855.*

finally fictional, but in their own enduring way they exist, and it is to them that this study is responsible.[29]

Men of design reflect man's effort, particularly in America's version of the modern era, to master his world; his effort (in the twilight of his faith in the providential activity of God in history) intentionally to shape, according to programs, plans, and designs, his context. They are, to put the matter bluntly, surrogates for (American) formers and reformers dedicated to mastering and portioning out their natural and social environments. Men of interpretation seek, on the other hand, to understand man's curious failures in such endeavors. Put bluntly, and more specifically, men of interpretation are surrogates for those "poets" dedicated to singing of "human unsuccess, / In a rapture of distress."[30]

There is accordingly present in works that unfold as interpreted designs not only concern for tension between success and failure in modern history, but concern also for the relation of art to life. If we had life, Wagner said, we should have no need of art. In interpreted designs, active life is implicitly defined in terms of failure, of failed designs, of unsuccesses, and art is seen as redemptive interpretation. The dream that precedes and inspires Jay Gatsby's design corresponds to what Northrop Frye calls the phase of birth, its season being spring. The design that derives from that dream corresponds to what Frye calls the phase of growth, its season being summer. Interpretation, arising as it does out of failure, lies beyond the seasons of decline and death and dissolution, after autumn and after win-

29. Murray Krieger, *A Window to Criticism: Shakespeare's Sonnets and Modern Poetics* (Princeton, Princeton University Press, 1964), p. 54; see pp. 53–66. Cf. Fiedler, p. 27, where he notes that "The American writer inhabits a country at once the dream of Europe and a fact of history."

30. See Auden, p. 143, and especially as quoted in the epigraph to Chap. 9 of this study.

ter (the seasons of initial and final failure), and belongs to a phase of new birth and new growth, in word and myth, of life, its season being a new spring.[31] Thus seen as interpretation that redefines failure in life, poetry is derivative and limited (derivative because it is a response to life; limited because it makes nothing happen, because it does not bring forth, as actuality, ordered life from mere existence). Yet, even thus defined, poetry is also vital: it represents man's efforts imaginatively and verbally to order his efforts actively to order his life.

A final concern implicit in the interpreted design as a literary form has to do with the nature of art as determined by its genesis rather than as defined by its function. In *The Mirror and the Lamp,* in discussing various theories of art, M. H. Abrams moves from description of the "mimetic" theories of classical antiquity and the "pragmatic" theories of the Renaissance and the eighteenth century to a description of modern "expressive" theories. According to the basic "expressive" criterion, what is vital in art is the sincere, honest representation of the inner life of the artist; and what therefore is central is the artist's governing intent.

> The first test any poem must pass is no longer, "Is it true to nature?" or "Is it appropriate to the requirements either of the best judges or the generality of mankind?" but a criterion looking in a different direction; namely, "Is it sincere? Is it genuine? Does it match the intention, the feeling, and the actual state of mind of the poet while composing?" The work ceases then to be regarded as primarily a reflection of nature, actual or improved; the mirror held up to nature becomes transparent and yields

31. Northrop Frye, *Anatomy of Criticism* (Princeton, Princeton Univeristy Press, 1957), pp. 158–239; and "The Archetypes of Literature" [1951], *Fables of Identity: Studies in Poetic Mythology* (New York, Harcourt, Brace, and World, 1963), pp. 7–20.

the reader insights into the mind and heart of the poet himself.[32]

One of the dominant themes of twentieth-century criticism is revision of this "expressive" theory. We now "know" that preoccupation with an author's intention is a mistake: "that the design or intention of the author"—that is, the "design or plan in the author's mind"—"is neither available nor desirable as a standard for judging the success of a work of literary art."[33] Works of art possess, we insist, independent existence, and they reside in the public domain. Concomitantly, we "know" that, far from being "merely a means" of "organizing material . . . 'given' " to it, literary technique provides a way of exploring "content" and discovering the values and significance of experience.[34] We accordingly insist that, because language is shaping, linguistic formulation is perpetual creation: "it is only as the brute given . . . actualizes or expresses itself in language that this given becomes, in any meaningful and intelligible sense, reality. Language . . . is not moulded on reality. It is rather the mould in which reality as signficant is first given."[35]

32. Meyer H. Abrams, *The Mirror and the Lamp: Romantic Theory and the Critical Tradition* (New York, Oxford University Press, 1953), p. 23.

33. William K. Wimsatt, Jr., *The Verbal Icon: Studies in the Meaning of Poetry* (Lexington, University of Kentucky Press, 1954), pp. 3, 4, 3.

34. Mark Schorer, "Technique as Discovery," *Hudson Review, 1* (1948), 68; see pp. 67–69.

35. Wilbur M. Urban, *Language and Reality: The Philosophy of Language and the Principles of Symbolism* (London, Allen and Unwin, 1939), p. 375. See Feidelson, *Symbolism and American Literature,* pp. 44–76 and 253–70; and Wallace Stevens, *The Necessary Angel: Essays on Reality and the Imagination* (New York, Knopf, 1951).

The point of view I am trying here very briefly to characterize is one of the main points of view of our time, but it is by no means unanimously held. For a very pointed and powerful critique, see Eric Donald Hirsch, *Validity in Interpretation* (New Haven, Yale University Press, 1967).

In its implicit grappling (through concern with getting at the meaning of the fate of the man of design) with various aspects of what philosophers know as the "genetic fallacy" and what literary critics call the "intentional fallacy," the interpreted design reflects the context of modern criticism's quarrel with "expressive" theories. More complexly, however, it reflects the artist's implicit concern with tension between his impulse to make his work according to a preconceived design and his urge to trust his technique to explore and alter, to reshape and re-define his plan. Poetry is born, after all, in part of man's desire intentionally to build, word by word, verbal emblems that achieve beauty by coupling order with magnitude, precise arrangement with infinite fecundity. "The dramatist," James said, "has verily to *build,* is committed to architecture, to con-struction at any cost."[36] By mirroring artists' concern with the possibility of intentional human building on a grand scale, men of design reflect artists' concern with themselves as builders of artifacts produced by intentional activity. But art also is born, in part, as Edgar Allan Poe once noted, of man's "un-conquerable desire—*to know,"* or more accurately perhaps, his desire to permit germs of perception to grow, according to what James called the "law of fructification," into a new "vision."[37] By mirroring artists' concern with themselves as discoverers of order and knowledge, men of interpretation reflect artists' concern with works of art not only as visions born of organic process but also as artifacts discovered through literary "technique."[38]

In and through the recurring themes of this study—the na-ture of the innocence present in the conception and execution of the designs; the contrast between the intent of the designs and the results of the actions; and the relation between the intent

36. Blackmur, ed., *The Art of the Novel,* p. 109.
37. James Harrison, ed., *The Complete Works of Edgar Allen Poe* (17 vols. New York, Crowell, 1902), *8,* 283. Matthiessen and Murdock, eds., *Notebooks,* p. 111. Blackmur, ed., *The Art of the Novel,* p. 45.
38. See Schorer, pp. 67–69.

and the results of the interpretation—attention accordingly is given to an implicit, multilayered analogy: first, between the effort of the man of designed action to build meaningfully (that is, in strict compliance and fulfillment of his design) and the effort of the man of interpretation, with words and through investigation and imagination, to discover meaning in the story of the man of design; and second, between each of these endeavors and the corresponding impulses of the artist, the impulses through which his work has become whatever it is. The visionary and active pursuits of the men of designed action and the intellectual and imaginative pursuits of the men of interpretative narration are of course very different. Within works in which each has its place, however, these pursuits are more than interlaced and interdependent; shared consecration to the cause of order and meaning makes them analogous. Through them, moreover, the complex needs of the artist are refracted. Together the man of design and the man of interpretation represent the artist's effort, through powers of mind, fecundity of imagination, and resources of craft, to order action and interpretation in art. The interpreted design is art become, or at least becoming, not only self-conscious but self-critical.

Although the interpreted design is a live tradition, its origins can be delineated and its properties defined. Furthermore, in both the autobiography and the novel its development can be traced from inchoate beginnings to achieved perfection. In part a shaper of style, in part a source of thematic and analogical concerns, in part a determinant of structure, the interpreted design as a prose form, at least in American literature, is archetypal; in that young literature it has been a molding force. The focus here is on the turns and twists American prose writers have given that form; those turns and twists are interesting and illuminating. It would be difficult, moreover, to find in other Western literatures, despite in several cases greater reach and density of achievement, a comparable appropriation of this form. But the interpreted design is neither an exclusively American nor an exclusively prose form. Nor is it without historical antecedents not examined in this study. However interesting and illuminating the American turns may be, and however much experience of them may contribute to understanding of American moments of modern life and art, the interpreted design is significant, before and after all, because it has to do with man's existence and life and art.

2 The Origins of Design: Aspects of the Colonial Experience

> *Lands found and nations born, thou born America,*
> *For purpose vast, man's long probation fill'd,*
> *Thou rondure of the world at last accomplish'd.*
>
> Walt Whitman, "Passage to India"

Columbus' rediscovery of the New World led to extravagant statements. Some viewed it as a howling wilderness where there was "nothing but wild beasts and beastlike men"; others as a "vast and unpeopled" land "fruitful and fit for habitation"; still others as a "Paradise" of "Virgin Beauties" fit to be "described by a poetical pen."[1] Hope—hope that the new land would provide caches of riches or simply "a better . . . place of living"—proved mightier than terror, however, enabling patriotism, profit, and piety to move men to shores unknown and untamed.[2] Men of "very old" and "very enlightened" worlds journeyed, of course, from varied motives and with varied

1. The first description is from John Winthrop, *Journal: History of New England, 1630–1649*, ed. James K. Hosmer (2 vols. New York, Scribner, 1908), *2*, 83; the second from William Bradford, *Of Plymouth Plantation, 1620–1647*, ed. Samuel E. Morison (New York, Knopf, 1952), p. 25; and the third combines phrases from Robert Montgomery, *A Discourse concerning the Design'd Establishment of a New Colony to the South of Carolina* [1717], and from *A New and Accurate Account of the Provinces of South Carolina and Georgia* [1733], both as quoted in Daniel J. Boorstin, *The Americans: The Colonial Experience* (New York, Random House, 1958), pp. 75–76.

2. Bradford, p. 24.

visions of the "new and unbounded."[3] Some sought a place proper for adventuring, some a land suited to new beginnings, some a scene appropriate to new experiments. But because the "fresh, green breast of the new world" pandered to "human dreams," because it offered man "something commensurate to his capacity for wonder," it enticed and inspired.[4] America became, in Ralph Waldo Emerson's phrase, "a country of beginnings, of projects, of designs, of expectations."[5]

The great mistake of Christopher Columbus, with which the story of modern America began, was followed by other false starts. Humphrey Gilbert's visionary scheme for settling Englishmen permanently on the new continent aborted. But it stirred the imagination of Sir Walter Raleigh, and thereby prepared the way for Jamestown and for Captain John Smith (1580–1631). Like Raleigh, Smith was a man of considerable and diverse talents. In legend, however, he is an adventurer for whom America was a land of great "expectations."[6]

Although only twenty-seven when he first landed on Virginia's shores, Smith already had adventured in southern Europe, in Turkey, and in the East, and already was known in England as a footloose champion of the ladies, an authentic knight-errant. Less than one tenth of Smith's fifty-one years were spent in America; he was always on the move. Yet during his American years he made a place for himself in the New World's story. "[R]estless, vain, ambitious, overbearing, blustering," he not only adventured; he also named himself "resplendent and invincible" adventurer, thereby establishing himself as prototype of scores of men who, in seeking space and

3. Tocqueville, *Democracy in America*, 2, 36.
4. Fitzgerald, *The Great Gatsby*, p. 182.
5. Ralph Waldo Emerson, "The Young American," *The Complete Works of Ralph Waldo Emerson*, ed. Edward W. Emerson (12 vols. Boston, Houghton Mifflin, 1903–04), *1*, 371.
6. For Smith's own story, see Edward Arber and A. G. Bradley, eds., *The Travels and Works of Captain John Smith* (2 vols. London, 1910).

chance enough for adventure, have made America's adventure their own.[7]

The vast majority of America's settlers are not accurately termed adventurers, though adventure perforce they did. In increasing numbers, dispossessed seekers—men more uprooted than rootless—undertook the long, unsettling voyage to America.[8] Not the spirit of adventure, but despair for the old and hope for the new moved the already uprooted and dispossessed to suffer yet another uprooting, estranging process. Dreaming of new beginnings in a new land, they embraced America less as a place where chance might have sway than as a garden where the ancient practices of sinking roots and raising simple homes were likely to go better.

To disinherited seekers, America was a fresh, new world— the proper place, to continue with Emerson's terms, for "beginnings." After first moving from England to Holland, the Pilgrims journeyed across a sea that carried them not to Virginia but to the unsought shores of Massachusetts, where they submitted as to a decree and established Plymouth Plantation. Having crossed "the vast and furious ocean" to "firm and stable earth, their proper element," however, the Pilgrims found, as William Bradford makes clear, that their lonely struggle was not at an end. With "no friends to welcome them . . . no houses or much less towns to repair to, to seek for succour," they saw

7. Moses Coit Tyler, *History of American Literature, 1607–1765* [1878] (New York, Crowell-Collier, 1962), p. 46; cf. pp. 44–61. Of special interest to this study is Henry Adams, "Captain John Smith," *North American Review, 104* (1867), 1–30. Note that in Tyler's description Smith resembles both Cooper's Leatherstocking and Whitman's self-singing poet. See, for example, Cooper's reference to "the pursuit of adventures" in an "empty empire"—a "virgin territory"—in Chap. 1 of *The Prairie.*

8. See Handlin, *The Uprooted.* See also Ole E. Rølvaag, *Giants in the Earth* (New York, A. L. Burt, 1927), and Willa Cather, *My Antonia* (Boston, Houghton Mifflin, 1918).

on one side "a hideous and desolate wilderness" and on the other a great and mighty ocean "now . . . a main bar and gulf" separating "them from all the civil parts of the world."[9]

Time has doubly blessed the deprived Pilgrims. It has made their story America's favorite saga of settlement; and it has made them rich in spiritual progeny: their descendants include nomadic seekers who have left and yet leave dust bowls of deprivation and pockmarked hills of persecution, searching for golden "Californias" and open "Chicagos," as well as thousands of emigrants who have left and yet leave older worlds, seeking refuge and a new life. At present, however, both the adventurers (the men of great "expectations") and the seekers (the men of new "beginnings") are important for contrast and perspective. During the days of its settlement, the new continent also "offered a vague and nearly boundless arena for practical energies."[10] Its very "emptiness . . . made it the field for social experiment."[11] With rootless adventurers and uprooted seekers came a strong, able minority who saw in America, to use Emerson's remaining categories, a place proper for trying out "projects" or "designs."

To visionaries like John Winthrop the open wilderness seemed to invite attempts to realize grand designs: it presented itself as "a fair, blank page on which to write a new chapter in the story of man's struggle for a higher type of society."[12] At work was not merely a "great hope . . . of laying [a] good foundation," nor simply a dream of serving, by "propagating and advancing the gospel," as "stepping-stones" to some

9. Bradford, pp. 61–62. On the problem of the Puritans' intended course, see Morison's comments in Bradford, p. 39, n. 7, and p. 60, n. 6.

10. Daniel J. Boorstin, *The Lost World of Thomas Jefferson* [1948] (Boston, Beacon Press, 1960), p. 225.

11. Oscar Handlin, Editor's Preface to Edmund S. Morgan, *The Puritan Dilemma: The Story of John Winthrop*, Library of American Biography (Boston, Little, Brown, 1958), p. ix.

12. Frederick Jackson Turner, *The Frontier in American History* (New York, Holt, 1920), p. 261.

"great" future work, but explicit commitments to specific plans.[13] "In the early days of colonization," Henry Adams wrote, "every new settlement represented an idea and proclaimed a mission." Among those proclaiming missions, the Puritans of the Bay Colony are prominent. To these men of design we shall return. But as Adams suggested and as Daniel J. Boorstin has shown, other men burdened and blessed with plans and projects helped to shape life and events from New England to Georgia.[14]

Humble though they were, the Quakers of Pennsylvania were dedicated "perfectionists." In coming to Pennsylvania, they of course hoped to escape persecution and improve their lives. But the Quaker way was shaped by more than chance flight and vague hope, by more even than firm commitment to principles of equality, informality, simplicity, and to habits of toleration and peace. By settling a new land, a land free of established institutions and weighty traditions, American Quakers hoped to establish a perfect society. Their "Holy Experiment in Government" derived from deliberate dedication to building "outward plantations" that would foster rather than smother what George Fox called inward plantations of heart and spirit.[15]

South of Pennsylvania, in colonial Virginia, men scorned

13. Bradford, p. 25.

14. Henry Adams, *History of the United States during the Administrations of Thomas Jefferson and James Madison* (9 vols. New York, 1889–91), *1*, 177. Cf. Fiedler, *Love and Death in the American Novel*, as quoted above, n. 29, Chap. 1.

My treatment of America's colonial experience is frankly derivative. With regard to Pennsylvania, Virginia, and Georgia, I owe most to Boorstin, *The Americans*. I am also indebted to George Bancroft, *History of the United States from the Discovery of the American Continent* (10 vols. Boston, 1834–74); and Charles M. Andrews, *The Colonial Period of American History* (4 vols. New Haven, Yale University Press, 1934–37).

15. Boorstin, *The Americans*, pp. 33–69. See Andrews, *3*, 268–328; Bancroft, *2*, 326–404; Adams, *1*, 177–78; and Turner, pp. 261–63.

new schemes of ordering life. What the Pennsylvanians in considerable measure did, the Virginians consciously dedicated themselves to doing: transplanting the established virtues of rural England. Curiously, however, the Virginians looked rather to future than to past. They undertook the task of "transplantation" in faith that new soil would invigorate old ideals and fresh air purify old values. In the New World the life of the English squire and landed gentleman would recover its pristine purity and yet attain new maturity.[16]

In Georgia life was shaped by a design at once less traditional and more detailed than anything conceived in Virginia or Pennsylvania. Perhaps "the fabled lushness and tropical wealth of Georgia" moved its builders to extravagant and rigid plans.[17] In any case, the establishment of Georgia was the work of empire-builders. Like the founders of the Bay Colony, the architects of Savannah were "Men with empires in their purpose / And new eras in their brains."[18] In contrast to Massachusetts, however, the Georgia enterprise was an altruistic gesture. The colony may have become the scene of selfish "DESIGNING," as is charged in *The Castle-Builders . . . A Political Novel* (1759). But the design of the planners and sponsors was philanthropic, not selfish. The charter of the colony specified that no Trustee should hold any office, own any land, or make any profit.[19]

Like Sir Robert Montgomery's earlier unrealized plan for the territory that became Georgia—his "design" for "Setling . . . Margravate of Azilia"—the blueprint that guided building in

16. Boorstin, *The Americans,* pp. 97–143. See Bancroft, *1,* 118–235; and Adams, *1,* 177–78.

17. Boorstin, *The Americans,* p. 71. See Turner, pp. 261–63.

18. The lines of verse are from J. W. Foss' feeble poem, "The Coming American," *Whiffs from Wild Meadows* (Boston, 1898), p. 260.

19. [Thomas Stephens] *The Castle-Builders; or, the History of William Stephens . . . A Political Novel* (London, 1759), p. 191. See Boorstin, *The Americans,* pp. 71–96; and Bancroft, *3,* 416–48.

Georgia was detailed. Behind it stood General Oglethorpe, a man of action, and Lord Percival, an armchair visionary—the representatives and mobilizers of forces of piety and charity.[20] Philanthropy dictated not only that Georgia be settled with dispossessed, underprivileged people, but that specific regulations be made to protect them from further impoverishment; wherefore, the Trustees carefully controlled the distribution of land and explicitly prohibited traffic in rum and slaves. Similarly, patriotism dictated that Georgia practice be made to square with mercantile theory; wherefore the Trustees centered their economic policy on the cultivation of white mulberry trees and the production of silk. Finally, practicality dictated that Georgia be made a strong link in the defense line of the "Southern Frontier"; wherefore the Trustees adopted a policy of planned and compact settlement—a policy carried out, for example, in Savannah.[21]

Convinced that they could shape life in the New World at will, the builders of Georgia pursued a scheme matched in its detail of conception only by its inappropriateness to Georgia life. Their endeavor was, to be sure, both "pious and charitable."[22] But their "Design" for "Establishment" nevertheless initiated America's most comic settlement of errors.[23]

20. Robert Montgomery, *A Discourse concerning the Design'd Establishment of a New Colony to the South of Carolina* [1717], *American Colonial Tracts Monthly,* Vol. I (1897–98), No. 1, p. 4, and the plan and illustration between pp. 10–11. See Boorstin, *The Americans,* pp. 80–84.

21. See Verner W. Crane, *The Southern Frontier, 1670–1732* (Durham, North Carolina, Duke University Press, 1928), p. 324 and passim Chap. 13; Boorstin, *The Americans,* pp. 80–96; Sarah B. G. Temple and Kenneth Coleman, *Georgia Journey* (Athens, University of Georgia Press, 1961), pp. x-xviii.

22. John Burton, *A Sermon Preach'd before the Trustees for Establishing the Colony of Georgia in America* (London, 1733), p. 3.

23. *An Impartial Inquiry into . . . the Province of Georgia* (London, 1741), ed. P. Radin, *Occasional Papers,* California State Library, Re-

Like the Adam and Eve of John Milton, the Puritans who
journeyed to the New World felt not only loss but hope. Their
way was "solitary," and it took them from a land they had
learned to love. But "The world was all before them" and
Providence was "their guide." The lost land they were leaving
they yet hoped to see redeemed. It was "for *Englands* sake"
that they came to sojourn in the American wilderness.[24] With
a new, less drastically lost world before them and a new un-
matched vision within, these staunch and able, diligent and determined men had reason to be confident. They had been
called by God to be a "speciall people" and perform a special
work.[25] They were dedicated to a divinely sponsored mission.
They were the avant-garde of international Puritan Christianity.[26]

Having placed God's dealings with man at the center of
human existence, the Puritans traced those dealings from creation to their own time, specifying the changing covenantal
relations between God and man that defined the epochs of
human history. God had disclosed to man the character of the
struggle, defining human history, between the children of light
and the children of darkness. And He had revealed to man,

---

print Series No. 13 (San Francisco, California State Library, 1940),
p. 17.

24. [Edward Johnson] *A History of New-England* (London, 1654),
p. 27.

25. Peter Bulkeley, *The Gospel-Covenant* (London, 1646), p. 15.

26. My treatment of the Bay Colony owes most to the work of Perry
Miller, particularly *Errand into the Wilderness* (Cambridge, Mass.,
Harvard University Press, 1956); and *The New England Mind: From
Colony to Province* (Cambridge, Mass., Harvard University Press,
1953). I am also indebted to Edmund S. Morgan, *Visible Saints: The
History of a Puritan Idea* (New York, New York University Press,
1963); Samuel Eliot Morison, *Builders of the Bay Colony* (Boston,
Houghton Mifflin, 1930); and Boorstin, *The Americans,* pp. 3–31.

preeminently in the Christ event, the character of His ordering
and redeeming activity. Beyond such general dispensations,
however, God had informed the Puritans that He was acting
especially through them.[27]

The Puritans' understanding of human history was forever
altered by this piece of information. They had, of course, to see
their own time as a brief moment in a large drama. But they
saw their moment as one of penultimate climax and viewed
their role as grandly heroic. Their understanding of themselves
accordingly acquired a histrionic bias: they saw themselves
as actors in a prolonged morality play. Their mission represented to them nothing less than a point at which "great
[human] enterprise" and divine Providence intersected in a
special way.[28] Their errand was theirs both "by a mutuall
consent" and "through a speciall overruleing providence."[29]
Both a human project and a divine design lay behind the
Puritan migration, informing the effort of "many skilfull builders" to confederate together in establishing a holy common-
wealth in a wilderness.[30]

The Puritan design was less detailed (and therefore more
flexible) than the Georgian. But the Puritan errand was more
specific (and therefore less vague) in informing purpose. The
Puritans were bound to a dual task. They wanted to build a
perfect—a whole and harmonious—society. And they wanted,

27. See Bulkeley, pp. 382–83; and Samuel Danforth, *A Briefe
Recognition of New-Englands Errand into the Wilderness* (Cambridge,
Mass., 1671). See also Miller, *Errand into the Wilderness*, pp. 1–15.

28. Johnson, p. 28. Cf. Thomas Shepard, *A Treatise of Liturgies*
(London, 1653), p. 3.

29. John Winthrop, "A Modell of Christian Charity," *Winthrop
Papers* (6 vols. to date, Boston, Massachusetts Historical Society,
1929–   ), 2, 293. See Feidelson, *Symbolism and American Literature*,
pp. 77–89; and Miller, *The New England Mind: From Colony to
Province*, pp. 27–39.

30. Bulkeley, p. 14.

like the Georgians, though with far greater intensity of need, to make their society "serve as a model community."[31]

Far from being "wild Opinionists, swarmed into a remote wildernes to finde elbow-roome for . . . phanatick Doctrines and practises," the Puritans were deliberate builders.[32] They came to the New World "to seeke out a place of Cohabitation and Consorteshipp" where they might establish "a due forme of Government both ciuill and ecclesiasticall." In prosecution of the "work and the end" at which they aimed, they were "knit together . . . as one man."[33] Together they would "rebuild the most glorious Edifice of Mount *Sion* in a Wildernesse."[34] As defined by Jonathan Mitchel, the Puritans' "DESIGN" was to erect *"Christ's Kingdom* in whole Societies." Under the providential guidance of God, Edward Johnson said, they would "create a new Heaven, and a new Earth in, new Churches, and a new Common-wealth together."[35]

The Puritans of New England required more of themselves, however, than the building of a new and perfect commonwealth. Having built it, they must make it a transforming model. If they were truly to become "a speciall" and "an onely people," they must make their new society a model for transforming their old country.[36] They had left the land of their birth because it had become "filled with the fury of malignant adversaries"; but they had left so that through them God could

31. Clarence L. Ver Steeg, Introduction, *A True and Historical Narrative of the Colony of Georgia* [1740], by Pat. Tailfer and others with Comments by the Earl of Egmont (Athens, University of Georgia Press, 1960), p. ix. See "Thomas Shepard's Election Sermon, in 1638," *New England Historical and Genealogical Register, 24* (1870), 361–66.

32. Nathaniel Ward, *The Simple Cobler of Aggawam in America* (London, 1647), p. 2.

33. Winthrop, "A Modell of Christian Charity," pp. 293–94.

34. Johnson, p. 26.

35. Jonathan Mitchel, *The Great End and Interest of New-England* [1662] in *Elijah's Mantle* (Boston, 1722), p. 3. Johnson, p. 3.

36. Bulkeley, p. 15.

"create . . . a New England" to renew the old. What they did they did for England's sake, that mere "human policy" might be overthrown and God's truth be restored to its proper place.[37] Only by laboring "in a speciall manner . . . to shine forth in holinesse above other people" could they be true to their pledge to God and one another; only thus could they fulfill, before "heaven and earth, Angels and men," their assigned role. They were to walk their designated way that not only England but "the Nations of the world . . . may be constrained to say of us, only this people is wise, an holy and blessed people."[38] From a "far remote, and vast Wildernesse," New England would show forth the way of the Lord God to all men.[39]

New England's dual design differed from Georgia's not only in being grander and more informing but also in the quality of the dedication with which it was entertained. The Puritans were doubly bound, in covenant with man by mutual consent and with God by His having brought them "over [a] 900 league Ocean at his pleasure" to place them in a new world. The relationship thus sealed, as every Puritan knew, was sacred.[40] The terms accordingly were absolute If the Puritans were faithful in their great work, God greatly would exalt them. But if they failed, betraying their pledge, they would stand "a perjured people."[41] Furthermore, without their strong sense of direction, they would become "monstrous and deformed"; they would be left "desolate and forsaken," a byword for a people "vile" and "despicable."[42]

37. Johnson, pp. 1, 28. Note: Johnson's actual phrase is "humane policy"; I have deleted the *e* in the text to insure clarity.

38. Bulkeley, pp. 382–83.

39. Johnson, p. 26.

40. Ibid., p. 3.

41. Winthrop, "A Modell of Christian Charity," p. 294. Note: Winthrop's actual phrase is "a periured people"; I have substituted a *j* for the *i* to insure clarity.

42. William Hubbard, *The Happiness of a People* (Boston, 1676), p. 10; cf. p. 12. Bulkeley, pp. 15, 383.

If we shall but be as dedicated members of the same dedicated body, said Winthrop, in words that shaped as well as mirrored the Puritan sensibility, then "men shall say of succeeding plantacions: the lord make it like that of New England: for wee must Consider that wee shall be as a Citty vpon a Hill, the eies of all people are vppon vs; soe that if we shall deale falsely with our god in this worke wee haue vndertaken . . . wee shall be made a story and a by-word through the world . . . [and] shall surely perishe out of the good Land."[43] Like the Israelites of old, the Puritans had accepted from God a commisson that defined the special purpose of their society. If they were to be instruments of their Lord, actors for their God, they must faithfully play their role even when, as in 1647, it had become offensive to English Puritans.[44]

The decision to give up speaking the true word of God in England thus represented, at least to the Puritan mind, neither surrender nor retreat, but new strategy. Men like William Laud (1573–1645) had worked conscientiously and successfully not only to defeat the Puritans' assault upon the English establishment but also to frustrate Puritan efforts at infiltration. Whereupon the Puritans left England determined that in the American wilderness they would build a model through which their struggle might yet be won. By giving to England, then to the world, a blueprint by which men of faith and principle could relate belief in a holy, omnipotent God to existence in a sinful, limited world, by becoming instruments for disclosing to man the difference between life in confused disorder and life in holy commonwealths, they yet would win the battle and shape a new era of peace.[45]

43. Winthrop, "A Modell of Christian Charity," pp. 294–95.
44. On the controversy of 1647, see Miller, *The New England Mind: From Colony to Province,* pp. 121–22; Edmund S. Morgan, *The Puritan Dilemma: The Story of John Winthrop,* Library of American Biography (Boston, Little, Brown, 1958), pp. 199–203; and Morison, pp. 244–68.
45. See Johnson, pp. 1–3; John Davenport, *A Sermon Preach'd at the Election . . . 1669* (Boston, 1670); and Cotton Mather, *Magnalia Christi*

New England Puritans continued to preach and print. But
the magnum opus they projected from the outset was to con-
sist neither of tracts nor of sermons—nor even of a systematic
tome on right doctrine, correct polity, and righteous conduct.
The great work of New England, her gift to the world, would
be a model community designed, established, and maintained
by model men. Puritans were, by deliberate choice, servants of
order and opponents of "confused Chaos"—the children, William Hubbard said, of a "God of peace, of Order, and not of
Confusion." What they most feared was loss of that ordering
purpose without which they would become "monstrous and
deformed."[46] For as long as they remained Puritan, they
echoed Winthrop's words: we must be, Peter Bulkeley said in
1651, "as a City set upon an hill."[47]

Despite the qualifications their theology seemed to impose,
the Puritans believed, first, that they could build a new and
whole community in the American wilderness, and second, that
they could persuade the world to accept that community as a
model. They feared neither the separating sea nor the wondrous
wilderness nor the persistent historical process. For they believed that God had brought them to New England in order,
with and through them, to reveal to all men a clear, straight
path into an era of order and truth and beauty. By offering
man freedom at once charged and ordered, the Puritan experiment would free man from the confused aftermath of the
Reformation and, in the same moment, would speak to the
deep longings the Puritans saw at work in the Reformation
itself. The effort, under God, to build the city whose terraces

---

Americana; or, The Ecclesiastical History of New-England [1702] (2
vols. Hartford, 1853–55), *1,* 25–38.

46. Hubbard, pp. 8, 10.

47. Bulkeley, p. 383. Cf. Samuel Willard, *The Character of a
Good Ruler* (Boston, 1694), p. 14; and Joseph Belcher, *The Singular
Happiness* (Boston, 1701), pp. 27–35.

were "the colour of stars" corresponded to the Puritan notion of what constituted meaningful action.[48]

48. I have borrowed a phrase here from Ezra Pound's description of his celestial city, *Cantos* ([New York] New Directions [1948]), "Canto LXXIV." Cf. Johnson, pp. 24–28. Despite the implications of their doctrine of man, the Puritans anticipated what Karl Barth, in *From Rousseau to Ritschl,* trans. Brian Cozens (London, SCM Press, 1959), pp. 14–19, has called "absolute man"—man who believes himself "almost capable of anything." Compare John E. Smith regarding America as quoted above, n. 2, Chap. 1; and Imlac's assertion in Samuel Johnson, *Rasselas* [1759], *The Works of Samuel Johnson* (9 vols. Oxford, 1825), *1,* 230, that "Few things are impossible to diligence and skill." See also below, n. 17, Chap. 9.

3 The Origins of Interpretation: The Puritan Jeremiad as a Literary Form

Still warble, dying swan! still tell the tale,
The enchanting tale, the tale of pleasing woe.

John Keats, "To Byron"

Long after the finest hours of the Puritan experiment, Americans continued to echo the rhetoric of design: they invoked the "wise and glorious purposes" for which men had been "placed" in the New World; they praised the "new order" America had created "to teach old nations"; and they celebrated the "blessings" she was destined to "shed . . . round the world."[1] In fact, however, life in both New England and Georgia proved confusing. Before the end of the seventeenth century the Puritans were forced to redefine their errand and revise their experiment; and within twenty years of its launching the Georgia project had gone so badly that its authors and trustees were forced to sur-

1. Cyrus L. Dunham, Speech, April 6, 1852, 32d Congress, 1st Session, *Congressional Globe*, Appendix, p. 410; and William Gilpin, *The Mission of the North American People, Geographical, Social, and Political* (Philadelphia, 1874), p. 130, as quoted in Henry Nash Smith, *Virgin Land: The American West as Symbol and Myth* [1950] (New York, Vintage, 1957), pp. 198, 40. See James Dana, *Two Discourses* (New Haven, 1801), p. 49; and Timothy Dwight, "Greenfield Hill: A Poem" [1794], especially these lines: "All hail, thou western world! by heaven design'd / Th' example bright, to renovate mankind." See, too, the fine discussion of America's language of dedication in Frederick Merk, *Manifest Destiny and Mission in American History* (New York, Knopf, 1963), p. 261.

render their colony to the crown. Developments in both places forced men to acknowledge that the products of their actions failed to meet the specifications of their designs. By midcentury the builders of Massachusetts knew that they had met with considerable success—that they had established a strong plantation. Yet they found in apparent success what the Georgians found in obvious failure: that they had missed their grand self-designation.

Soon after the fate of the Georgia enterprise became apparent, men began to tell its story. The most interesting of the Georgia stories is the so-called "Tailfer Book"—*A True and Historical Narrative of the Colony of Georgia* (1740), by Patrick Tailfer, David Douglass, and Hugh Anderson, with comments by the Earl of Egmont. The work is deliberately satirical. As spokesmen for "the few surviving Remains of the Colony of *Georgia*," as members of a small group that managed to escape back "to a LAND OF LIBERTY," the authors offer their narrative as "a true and impartial account" of Georgia "from its first settlement, to its present period." Their sole purpose is to recount and explain the "shipwreck" met by the "Plan" of the "Projectors" of that "unhappy colony."[2]

In prosperous Massachusetts, where failure took subtler, more disturbing form, and where loyalty precluded satire, spokesmen for the community followed a less direct path to a more thoroughly interpretive genre. By 1650 the Puritan model had been established in Massachusetts. The "foundation," Peter Bulkeley asserted in 1651, has been "laid, by many skilfull builders." What accordingly was required of later Puritans was that they hold fast, keeping "the foundation . . . the same."[3]

---

2. Pat. Tailfer and others, with Comments by the Earl of Egmont, *A True and Historical Narrative of the Colony of Georgia* [1740], ed. Clarence L. Ver Steeg (Athens, University of Georgia Press, 1960), pp. 3, 7, 8. See also Moses Coit Tyler, *History of American Literature,* pp. 504–08.

3. Bulkeley, *The Gospel-Covenant,* p. 14.

As defined by William Stoughton in 1668, "the solemn work" of the children and grandchildren was "not to lay a new Foundation, but to continue and strengthen, and beautifie, and build upon that which hath been laid."[4]

The work of caretaking and maintaining proved, of course, less heroic and more domestic than the work of designing and constructing a grand model. It also proved more confining and confusing. For New England the decisive event in the middle seventeenth century was England's official refusal to attend the New England model—her official decision to go her profligate way, whoring after toleration, ignoring the model city built specifically for her redemption. Then, to make bad matters almost unbearable, piety in the promised wilderness began to wane. "O," Stoughton said, Election Day, April 1668, "what a sad *Metamorphosis* hath there of later years passed upon us in these Churches and Plantations." "O *New-England,*" he continued, "thy God did expect better things from thee and thy Children."[5]

By smashing the New England dream of being a city upon a hill, England made the Puritan voice, in an unsought, unsettling sense, a voice crying alone in a wilderness. The already tame and domestic task of maintaining the celestial city became provincial as well. It was not as an isolated colony, nor as a tarnished model in a "far remote, and vast Wildernesse," that New England could hope to fulfill her high self-designation.[6] As the century progressed, bringing "Ruine upon Ruine, Destruction upon Destruction"—as it became increasingly apparent that both the Puritan design and the Puritan understanding of "Divine Expectations" were being "frus-

4. Stoughton, *New-Englands True Interest,* p. 16.

5. Ibid., pp. 19–20. See John Higginson, *The Cause of God and His People in New-England* [1663] in *Elijah's Mantle* (Boston, 1722), pp. 6–9; and Cotton Mather, *Magnalia Christi Americana, 1,* 25–38.

6. Johnson, *A History of New-England,* p. 26.

trated"—the whole New England enterprise became problematical.[7] Too much had failed to go according to plan.
The sons and grandsons of the builders continued to celebrate
the beauty of their fathers' vision—a vision of such *"Divine
Original* and *Native Beauty"* that it "would dazzle the Eyes of
Angels, daunt the Hearts of Devils, ravish and chain fast the
Affections of all the Saints"; and they continued to praise the
dedication of their fathers' action—the trials they had passed
through, the tribulations they had overcome. But they did so
in knowledge that men and events on both sides of the Atlantic
were saying no to the Puritan design.[8]

It was not merely that the second and third generations
found it a sad fate "to be styled *Children that are corrupters."*[9]
It was also that they were compelled to wonder whether New
England were doomed to stand, not "as a Citie upon an hill,
[but] . . . desolate and forsaken."[10] Again and again they were
forced to ask whether what they represented, what they had
become, meant that their fathers had come "flying from the
depravations of Europe, to the American Strand" only to fail
and fall short.[11] Finding themselves in a changing world
curiously in conspiracy against the original Puritan aim, later
Puritans were forced, again and again, to seek some way to
reshape their heritage and redefine what they were about.

The steady purpose and free enthusiasm of the builders depended upon unrepeatable experience, and it died when they
died. "The first generation," Stoughton said, "have been
ripened time after time . . . But we who rise up to tread out the

7. Stoughton, pp. 16–17. For a characteristic use of the term *design,*
see Johnson, pp. 24–25; and Increase Mather, *The Day of Trouble Is
Near* (Boston, 1674), p. 22.
    8. Higginson, p. 7.
    9. Stoughton, p. 21. Cf. Plutarch in *Morals:* "It is indeed a desirable
thing to be well descended, but the glories belong to our ancestors."
    10. Bulkeley, p. 15.
    11. Cotton Mather, *1,* 25.

footsteps of them that are gone before us, alas! what are we?" The second and third generation Puritans wanted to fulfill their caretaking assignment. But that assignment was theirs by accident of birth, not by decision to voyage, and they were in fact ill suited to it. They wanted to be about heroic tasks of their own, and that meant, within the historical context in which they found themselves, giving up being a model for England and becoming a strong and prosperous society. If their still young society could not be made the revealing, transforming model their fathers had said it must be, if New England could not renew the old, perhaps she could be significant simply as a thriving, dedicated land.[12]

The initial difficulty the second and third generation Puritans faced in seeking out their own heroic course was a matter of loyalty. They could never bring themselves simply to ignore the task their fathers had bequeathed them; nor could they ever admit that in fact they were not keeping the foundations the same. But the subtler, potentially more divisive difficulty they faced derived from the very character of their fathers' experience. By teaching that "the Successes and Events of [human] Undertakings and Affairs are not determined" by man's intent, that man's effort may be frustrated and disappointed despite "the greatest Sufficiency" and the highest resolve, their fathers' experience questioned the wisdom of all heroic activity.[13]

It was through strangely turned interpretation of their

12. Stoughton, p. 21. Cf. William Burnham, *God's Providence in Placing Men* (New London, 1722), p. 33. See Miller, *Errand into the Wilderness* and *The New England Mind: From Colony to Province* (above, n. 19, Chap. 2). In "Democracy and Its Issues," *Lectures and Miscellanies* (New York, 1852), p. 2, Henry James, Sr., states that democracy "is born of denial." New England's denial of Old England began early, but it was to a considerable degree a response to being rejected as a model.

13. See Urian Oakes, *The Soveraign Efficacy of Divine Providence* (Boston, 1682), p. 5 and passim.

fathers' design that the Puritans sought first to remain loyal sons without remaining captive to their inherited task and second to master their problematical heritage. In tracing the course of their fathers' action—in telling their fathers' story—they sought not only to revise the logic of their own situation but also to redefine the fate of their fathers' design. They wanted to save their fathers as well as themselves from an inadequate fate. Interpretation became for them a way of taming "a time and season of eminent trial."[14] Through it they attempted to master failure—to deliver themselves from an inadequate fate; through it they attempted to salvage one of the failed "Designs of men" and thereby move beyond human "Defeat and Disappointment."[15]

The "jeremiad" was the form Puritan interpretation took. On designated fast-days New Englanders congregated to repent that they had erred and strayed. Neither the theory—that sin was linked with judgment, judgment with repentance, repentance with forgiveness, forgiveness with hope, and hope with reform—nor the practice of public lamentation represented Puritan improvisation. But the role such lamentation played in New England was special because the covenant the Puritans had made with God was special. Unlike the covenant of grace (with which it was, of course, not coextensive), their communal covenant had to do not with eternal salvation of the elect of God but with a pledge to perform a mission within the world. Faithful performance of this mission would lead to victory, and victory would be rewarded on earth, not in heaven: God specifically would bless New England, giving her peace and prosperity within, influence and praise without. Concomitantly, however, betrayal of the agreement would be met not with eternal fire but with present visitations of God's wrath

14. Stoughton, p. 17.
15. Oakes, pp. 15, 13. I have omitted italics in the phrases taken from Oakes. See Shepard, *A Treatise of Liturgies,* p. 3; and Cotton Mather, *1,* 27–28.

—with plagues and droughts, wars and rumors of wars, with scorn and laughter, derision and infamy.[16]

The jeremiad became, increasingly after 1650 and especially after 1660, the characteristic utterance of the Puritans. Again and again, as Perry Miller has shown, they told and retold the story of "God's Controversy with New-England."[17] The original intention of the jeremiad was to inspire reform. After cataloging calamities—droughts and plagues and savage raids —Puritan spokesmen label them tokens of God's displeasure with His people's failure faithfully to run their errand. Various "sad affliction[s]"—"epidemical sickness" and "Pekoat furies" —function within jeremiads as signs of providential chastisement of a recalcitrant and inconstant people.[18] Having been reminded that only "the singular pity and mercies" of their God can shield them from deserved annihilation, suffering them to live, the people are called to repent and reform.[19]

In its classic form, as defined by Perry Miller, the jeremiad was rooted in immediate difficulties. In July 1646, John Winthrop noted that great harm had been visited on grain crops

16. The essence of Puritan lamentation is nicely set forth in [Increase Mather] *Necessity of Reformation* (Boston, 1679). Cf. Bulkeley, pp. 382–83. See also W. D. Love, *The Fast and Thanksgiving Days of New England* (Boston, 1895), and Miller, *The New England Mind: From Colony to Province*. Miller's brilliant work on the jeremiad is the point of departure for all subsequent study of the form, including in particular my own.

17. See Miller, *The New England Mind: From Colony to Province*, p. 30. Michael Wigglesworth's poem "God's Controversy with New-England," written in 1662, was first published in *Proceedings of the Massachusetts Historical Society, 12* (1871–73), 83–93; and has been reprinted in Perry Miller and Thomas H. Johnson, eds., *The Puritans: A Sourcebook of Their Writings* (rev. ed. 2 vols. New York, Harper & Row, 1963), 2, 611–16.

18. Winthrop, *Journal: History of New England, 2*, 286, 326. Thomas Shepard, *Autobiography*, ed. Allyn B. Forbes, *Publications of the Colonial Society of Massachusetts, 27* (1927–30), 387.

19. Shepard, *A Treatise of Liturgies*, p. 8.

by an invasion of caterpillars. "In divers places," he said, churches observed a day of humiliation, whereupon "presently after the caterpillars" disappeared.[20] Later Puritans continued to link "tokens of God's displeasure" with their having become "a people so unworthy, so sinfull, that by murmurings of many, unfaithfulnesse in promises, oppressions, and other evils" they had "dishonoured [God's] Majesty, expos[ing] his worke here to much scandall and obloquie." Year after year "election" sermons reminded the folk that they had "cause for ever to bee ashamed," and cause also to call upon God "rather [to] correct us in mercy, then [sic] cast us off in displeasure, and scatter us in this Wildernesse."[21]

The Puritans tended, however, increasingly to blur the rationale of the jeremiad. More specifically, in a distinctly anthropocentric turn they began to treat consciousness of failure as the chief visitation of God's wrath. The burden of sensed defeat and faithlessness gradually displaced "Pekoat furies" as a token of punishment for defeat and faithlessness. Distinctions between human acts of betrayal, divine judgment of betrayal, and human consciousness of both betrayal and judgment lost their sharpness. The Puritans continued of course to be disturbed by acts that rendered their city a defective model and by calamities that disclosed divine displeasure. But what most distressed them was knowledge that, despite careful and ostensibly successful building, they and their fathers had fallen short. At times, as a result, they appear most to lament the necessity of lamentation. But they were moved by more than longing to have that cup pass from them. They needed new assurance, yet were compelled—because their design had failed—to seek it surreptitiously.[22]

There was accordingly, coincident with the generalizing and

20. Winthrop, *Journal: History of New England*, 2, 277.

21. Shepard, *A Treatise of Liturgies*, p. 8.

22. Shepard, *Autobiography*, p. 387. See Miller, *The New England Mind: From Colony to Province*, pp. 19–39.

blurring of the logic of the jeremiad, a tendency to use it to relativize God's judgment. Early Puritans assumed that they must either keep and fulfill their commission or become not a dimmer beacon on a lower hill but a byword for infamous failure. Later Puritans found themselves in a situation defined by the curious intermingling of three elements: the crumbling of their design, the waning of their piety, and the waxing of their prosperity. And in an effort to overcome the incongruity of obvious prosperity amid felt declension, they not only defined consciousness of failure as punishment for failure; they also decided that to fail in a designation sublime was after all to fail with a difference. If the Puritans would but continue to gaze from their present peak to the serene summit of their ancestors' desire, and if they would but contemn their failure, New England still could be truly new. In lamenting their sad decline, New Englanders subtly thanked their God and notified the world that they yet were not as other men, that they, despite all, were a chosen people dedicated to perfection. Our churches are not perfect, Cotton Mather admitted, but they "are very like unto those that were in the first ages of Christianity," which even Quakers and Roman Catholics knew better than lightly to criticize. We have failed, Mather also acknowledged, but we "Nevertheless . . . have given great examples of the methods and measures wherein an Evangelical Reformation is to be prosecuted."[23]

The Puritans thus used careful dissection rather to minimize than to stress the importance of their failings. By emphasizing the heights from which they had fallen, they underscored the height at which they yet stood. But this strange logic did not alone suffice. The Puritans also used the jeremiad to move completely beyond caretaking and correction. They continued, to be sure, to lament their failure. And they sought to avoid as

23. Cotton Mather, 1, 27, 26. See Thomas Buckingham, *Moses and Aaron* (New London, 1729), p. 4.

well as repent "sins against the purpose and Covenant" of their
community; they felt, after all, no desire to adorn the Puritan
edifice with "hay and stubble, in stead of gold and precious
stones." But what they most needed—and what they finally
found in the jeremiad—was a way of skirting the requirement
that they persevere in what they called the "old way" of New
England.[24]

That the caretaking generations had been left to make their
way with "a fixed unalterable" design through an era char-
acterized by drastic change and seemingly dedicated to under-
mining their design—that they, in the name of all they held
dear and holy, were required to remain loyal to a design that
had failed—proved more than curious and perplexing. It constituted the most troublesome problem the second and third
generations had to confront.[25] And though they tried to avoid
the implications of their failure, those implications became the
elements of their characteristic nightmare. Why had the God
who had sent His chosen few into a wilderness to build a model
society, through them to give to the world a model for ordered
and meaningful society, so soon permitted England to intensify
her flirtation with social and religious pluralism? Why should
New England be forced to suffer the knowledge that nothing
had made her more anachronistic within the world she wanted
to save, that nothing did more to chafe her relationship with
that world, than her efforts—efforts prescribed by her covenant
with her Lord God—to stem the tide of toleration? Why had
her God bound her to a design so unalterable that it defined all
adjustment and accommodation as betrayal? And why had her
God sent her into a land that demanded and rewarded preoccupation, not with building and maintaining a model city
and living model lives, but with hard work and close trading?
The Puritans knew, of course, that trial, temptation, and un-

24. Bulkeley, p. 14.
25. Stoughton, p. 29.

certainty were the appointed lot of man: that it was not given man to know *"what* Afflictions shall come upon him" or what shall be "the Time of his Death"; that he was called to "follow the Lord, as it were blind-fold[ed]." But the wilderness they knew, placed against an English backdrop, seemed to confront them not with trial but with insoluble dilemma: with choice between the disloyalty of compromise and revision and the failure of scorn and irrelevance.[26]

Puritan orthodoxy possessed, it should be noted, one direct solution to the dilemma of the caretaking generations—that of radically applying to the pursuits of the first generation the wisdom set forth in Urian Oakes' sermon of 1677. Puritans knew, almost by right of birth, that mere men were never able "infallibly" to determine the issue of their plans and activities; that God alone governed time and ordered history, and that God's ways were to man inscrutable. "God is the Lord of Time, and Orderer, and Governour of all Contingences," Oakes insisted, including the "Time and Chance that further or hinder the Designs of men." Men accordingly should labor, Oakes continued, "to be prepared and provided for Disappointments," for "Changes and Chances," for "Occurrents and Emergencies that may blast" their "Undertakings"; for only with sound preparation could they hope in the face of "such Frustrations" to keep "Faith and Prayer . . . a going" and to avoid either flying "out against God" or fainting and sinking "in Discouragements."[27]

Radical application of this "good Counsel to men of projecting Heads" would have permitted explanation of the failure of the Puritan design, which would in turn have justified revising or abandoning it. Indeed, such a step would have undone even the need of using the jeremiad to generalize and relativize

26. Increase Mather, *A Discourse concerning the Uncertainty of the Times of Men* (Boston, 1697), pp. 9–11, 20–21. Italics omitted.

27. Oakes, pp. 15, 37. Italics omitted. Cf. John Webb, *The Government of Christ Considered and Applied* (Boston, 1738), pp. 7, 11–12.

judgment. But Puritans were no less the children of their
fathers than of their God: they were no more capable of asserting that their fathers had misread God's commission than they
were capable of flying out against the God who had placed them
in their trying land. They used Oakes' good counsel to explain
their own false starts. But in their effort to move beyond their
appointed tasks and yet remain loyal to their fathers, they extended in two ways their already revised jeremiad.[28]

On one side they used it to substitute tribute for action. They
made humiliation a form of homage, lamentation a mode of
loyalty. By decrying their failure, by contemning their disloyalty, they defined themselves as a dedicated people. Preach-
ing, hearing, and reading jeremiads became tests of loyalty
and acts of heroism. The ingenuity and eloquence the clergy
could muster in detailing declension, the openness and re-
morse the people could summon in accepting judgment—these
were strange tests of fortitude, courage, and devotion. But to
the Puritans they were altogether necessary. For it was only by
substituting formal repentance for active reform and loyal discourse for loyal action that the Puritans managed in good con-
science slowly to move beyond caretaking and enter their
changing world.[29]

On the other side, however, they made the jeremiad a work
of celebration. In it they not only confronted their "great and
dangerous *Declensions";* they also celebrated, and in celebrating reclaimed, the great work of their fathers. Had the
second and third generations been concerned solely with their
own freedom, had they been less loyal sons, they should have
felt no further need of the jeremiad. But because they wanted
also to free their fathers' design from disappointment and defeat, they made their works of complex lamentation works of

28. Ibid., p. 37.
29. See Miller, *The New England Mind: From Colony to Province,*
pp. 19–39 and passim.

praise and celebration.[30] In 1648 Thomas Shepard called "all the Godly wise" to the task of celebratory interpretation: "let us . . . consider and look back," he said, "upon the season of this great enterprise." In 1669, John Davenport, one of the last survivors of the first generation, extended the recitative jeremiad. But the form belonged to the second and third generations, who used it to recorder the entire New England experience.[31]

By recalling "the Considerable Matters, that produced and attended the First Settlement of Colonies," by telling of the "more exemplary" among "the *Actors*" in the settlement story, and by relating "Memorable Occurrences, and amazing Judgments and Mercies," the makers of the jeremiads established a standard and defined the genius of dedicated action. Quoting Virgil's *Aeneid*, Cotton Mather stressed the importance of understanding what drove men eminent in piety to endure so many calamities and to undertake so many hardships. The explanation he offered was dedication to the Puritan design. The *"Actions"* that "signalized" Puritan settlement and construction were authored by men so dedicated that they withstood "temptatlous," overcame "Disturbances," and confuted "enemies"; their "Methods" and their dedication together enabled them to weather "out each horrible tempest."[32]

For latter-day Puritans, however, dedicated action took a

30. Thomas Prince, *The People of New-England* (Boston, 1730), p. 36. See F. O. Matthiessen, *American Renaissance: Art and Expression in the Age of Emerson and Whitman* (New York, Oxford University Press, 1941), p. 629. Matthiessen quotes Thomas Mann, "Freud and the Future," wherein Mann states that life in myth is "life, so to speak, in quotation," that myth "is a kind of celebration, in that it is a making present of the past," and that in myth—in "the performance by a celebrant of a prescribed procedure"—the celebration of life "becomes a religious act."

31. Shepard, *A Treatise of Liturgies,* p. 3. See Davenport, *A Sermon Preach'd at the Election . . . 1669,* p. 15.

32. Cotton Mather, *1, 25.*

different form. Deprived of the tasks of radical social and theological construction, they turned to construction of another sort. They reconstructed "the Beginning" of the "remarkable" work of their fathers.[33] They defined "the End and Design" that had inspired and informed that work.[34] And they recounted and praised those of their fathers' *"Actions"* that seemed to them "of a more eminent importance."[35] In short, they substituted the dedicated action of telling and retelling their inherited story for the dedicated action of pursuing their inherited task. Through their lamenting-recounting-celebrating jeremiads, they hoped to "preserve and secure the interest of Religion in the Churches of . . . New-England."[36] But beyond renewing life at home, they sought to complete their fathers' "Great Design." They saw in their jeremiads analogues and extensions of the grand action from which they had derived. Having redefined action, and having moved to new unity by tracing grand action, the makers of jeremiads were able to proffer their works not as mere lament but rather as a mode of constructive activity, a form of creative endeavor.[37]

The jeremiad accordingly became not simply a way of reviving "religion" in New England, but more strangely a way of spreading "abroad in the world, some small Memorials" of the New England story.[38] The Puritan interpreters thus would salvage a design that had failed. Beyond "Defeat and Disappointment," beyond the death of a dream, they reconstructed the story of New England.[39] Whether that story would *"live* any where else or no,"* at least it would *"live"* in and through

33. Prince, p. 22.
34. Jonathan Mitchel, *Nehemiah on the Wall in Troublesom Times* (Cambridge, Mass., 1671), p. 27.
35. Cotton Mather, *1*, 25.
36. Ibid., p. 26.
37. Prince, p. 26. See Cotton Mather, *1*, 25–28.
38. Cotton Mather, *1*, 26.
39. Oakes, p. 13.

interpretations of her "History."[40] By this indirection the Puritans were able to approximate the perfection they had missed. In 1730, a century after the inauguration of the Great Migration, Thomas Prince composed a sermon in which all things are duly ordered: New England is "a Countrey" of "Religion, good Order, Liberty, Learning and flourishing Towns and Churches"; wherefore it possesses "a destinguishing Name in the World" and reflects "singular Honour to the Persons and Principles of it's [sic] original Setlers" and the "very grievous Trials . . . Hardship and Affliction" they endured. Echoing biblical passages of promise that had all along provided the model of Puritan hope, Prince envisaged and recorded perfection achieved only in vision and record.

> And now the WILDERNESS and the solitary Place is Glad for them: The Desert rejoices and blossoms as a Rose . . . the Glory of LEBANON is given to it, the Excellency of CARMEL and SHARON; they see the Glory of the LORD and the Excellency of our GOD. The Waters of the Divine Influence break out in the Wilderness, and the Streams in the Desert: The parched Ground becomes a Pool; and the thirsty Land, Springs of Water: In the Habitations of Dragons where they lay, there grows up the Grass; and an High Way now is there, which is call'd the *Way of Holiness,* over which the Unclean do not pass, and the Wayfaring Men do not err therein.[41]

Despite the "great and dangerous *Declensions"* of "transcendently guilty" men, both the Puritans' original design and the action to which it led are preserved and completed in the story that the jeremiads tell.[42] Through poetic rendering, the work of the Puritan builders is redeemed: the wayfaring men within

40. Cotton Mather, *1,* 27.
41. Prince, pp. 24, 28. Italics omitted. In this passage Prince is echoing mainly the prophet Isaiah.
42. Prince, p. 36.

no longer err; those without now see the glory of the Lord; within the New England Way has become and without it is acknowledged as the Way of Holiness. And further, should "the Plantation . . . soon after this, *come to nothing,*" as another interpreter put it, its story nonetheless would survive in the lamentation and celebration of its telling.[43]

The jeremiad thus became, to borrow from Wallace Stevens, a "poem that took the place of a mountain," an interpretation that embodied a failed design and so preserved and, in one sense, realized and perfected it. Through the jeremiad second and third generation Puritans "recomposed" their heritage. Through it they were able to "discover, at last, the view toward which they had edged," and to find, at last, "A place to go in [their] own direction." With it they became "complete in an unexplained completion," and were able to accept their "unique and solitary home."[44]

That the jeremiad became imaginative interpretation does not mean, of course, that any jeremiad is a literary masterpiece. None is. In their own way, however, the latter-day Puritans were true, though very imperfect and partial, poets: they followed, if not to the bottom, at least into the darkness of their night, there to order words of themselves and of their origins, there to seek a basis of renewal; in their tales of pleasing woe, they sang, as best they could, "of human unsuccess / In a rapture of distress."[45] Their characteristic decision was, to be sure, rather to skirt than fully to explore the

43. Cotton Mather, *1,* 27.
44. Wallace Stevens, "The Poem That Took the Place of a Mountain," *Collected Poems* (New York, Knopf, 1964), p. 512. Cf. what Stevens calls, in "The Well Dressed Man with a Beard" (p. 247), the yes that follows the final no.
45. Auden, "In Memory of W. B. Yeats," pp. 141–43. Cf. Yeats, *The King's Threshold* [1904], *The Collected Plays of W. B. Yeats* (London, Macmillan, 1952), p. 114, where Seanchan, a poet, says: "And I would have all know that when all falls / In ruin, poetry

incongruity, first between the intent of the design and the result of the actions of their fathers, and second between the purposes to which they had been dedicated as children and the causes to which they were giving themselves as men. But in their jeremiads they acknowledge and, in their most interesting moments, attempt even to master these incongruities: they attempt, that is, to reconcile, by proclaiming them one, the intent and the achievement of their fathers, and they attempt, while going about other business, to remain loyal to the purposes to which their fathers had dedicated them.

---

calls out in joy, / Being the scattering hand, the bursting pod, / The victim's joy among the holy flame, / God's laughter at the shattering of the world."

Part Two: Design, Interpretation, and the Drama of Self-Portraiture

The life of every man is a diary in which he means to write one story, and writes another. . . .

J. M. Barrie, The Little Minister

4 Anticipations of an Autobiographical Form: Edwards' *Personal Narrative* and Franklin's *Autobiography*

> *And in such indexes, although small pricks*
> *To their subsequent volumes, there is seen*
> *The baby figure of the giant mass*
> *Of things to come. . . .*
>
> William Shakespeare, Troilus and
> Cressida

Accidents of history moved New England Puritans, before the close of the seventeenth century, to interpretation of the problematic fate of their collective design. During the eighteenth century accidents of personal experience moved Jonathan Edwards and Benjamin Franklin toward appropriation of the interpreted design for autobiographical purposes. Edwards and Franklin of course gave to the stories of their lives shapes suggested by their apprehension of the experiences that had moved them to the autobiographical act. But a part of their experience was the shared heritage, however differently they related to it, of New England Puritanism and its literary traditions. Autobiography, to be sure, was not one of the dominant traditions in Puritan New England. The Puritans of the New World produced no autobiography as fine as *Grace Abounding* (1666), nor any literary figure as distinguished as that "poor servant" of God, John Bunyan. Far more than private drama, they stressed the story of their shared design.

But they nonetheless took individual struggle seriously enough
to honor it with a considerable and even a diverse body of
"personal literature."[1]

Unlike the Puritan journal, which characteristically centers,
as does John Winthrop's, on an individual's relation to predominantly public events, the Puritan diary characteristically
focuses, as does Samuel Sewall's, on personal events treated
informally. In the diary of the prodigiously self-conscious
Cotton Mather, to be sure, it is at least possible that private
examination became public performance, but Puritan diaries
tend to be random and relatively private.[2] More, however, than
either journals or diaries, biographies disclose the Puritans'
overriding concern. From John Norton's *Abel Being Dead Yet
Speaketh* (1658), a life of John Cotton, down to and including
the many lives recounted in Mather's *Magnalia Christi Americana* (1702), Puritans produced biographies in impressive
numbers. By 1718 Cotton Mather alone, according to his son's
count, had published "lives of no less than *one hundred and
fourteen Men,* and more than *twenty* Women," and thereafter
published "Accounts and Characters of many more."[3] Central
to understanding all of them is the term *exemplary.* "Our New-
England shall tell and boast of her WINTHROP," Mather
writes—of all his exemplary "virtues," not only his Christian
"excellencies" but also his *"heroical"* action in prosecuting
New England's "noble design."[4]

Even in autobiographies, where the specter of vanity muted
celebration, the exemplary urge is controlling. Thomas Shep-

1. See Kenneth B. Murdock, *Literature and Theology in Colonial
New England* (Cambridge, Mass., Harvard University Press, 1949),
Chap. 4.
2. Puritan diaries sometimes circulated among friends.
3. Samuel Mather, *Life of Cotton Mather* [1729], as quoted in
Kenneth B. Murdock, Introduction, *Selections from Cotton Mather*
[1926], American Authors Series (New York, Hafner, 1960), p. xxxiv.
4. Cotton Mather, *Magnalia Christi Americana, 1,* 118–19.

ard's *Autobiography* makes peace with the communal consciousness of New England Puritanism by linking God's call-
ing of him into the fellowship of grace to God's delivering him
"out of Egipt" into a new land. Both the exodus from England
and the great and difficult work of establishing New England
are stressed. But in keeping with the Puritans' incurable preoccupation with the fate of their children, on whose perse-
verance so much depended, Shepard addresses his work to his
"deare son." The writing has been undertaken, we come to
understand, to insure that not even the father's death shall
separate the son from the father's story. Through the father,
the son will "learne to know and loue the great and most high
god: the god of his father." Following Augustine's noble example, Shepard makes his work a story of spiritual struggle.
Its climactic moment comes when God calls Shepard into "the
fellowship of his grace." What precedes that call—Shepard's
consorting with "loose and lewd company" and his floundering
in "shame and confusion"—is prefatory; and what issues
directly from it—Shepard's fear before the "terrour of gods
wrath" and his struggle with "the vanity of the woorld"—is
stressed and yet is almost incidental. The act of grace, the gift
that redeems and orders the whole of Shepard's life, overcoming sin and leading beyond terror to faith, is the true center
of his story: it makes his life a meaningful story, a story worth
telling; and it introduces into it an ordering principle that makes
coherent relation possible.[5]

Behind the exemplary lives (biographical and autobiographical) that Puritans recounted lay the conversion narrative. In their original purity, New England churches limited

5. Shepard, *Autobiography*, pp. 393 (cf. 375), 352, 360–62. As
Allen Tate has noted ("Emily Dickinson," *The Man of Letters in the
Modern World: Selected Essays, 1928–1955* [New York, Meridian,
1955], p. 213), the New England heritage had, despite its limitations,
"an immense, incalculable value for literature: it dramatized the human
soul."

membership to "visible saints." Other men were expected and
even required to attend services. But membership was open
only to men and women who, through prescribed procedure including narration of spiritual growth as well as profession of
faith and acceptance of the church covenant, had demonstrated
as nearly as other saintly men could discern that they were
members of God's elect. This procedure met the requirements
of the Puritans' defined purpose—that, namely, of building a
veritably perfect society in a radically imperfect world. For it
not only protected the purity of the churches; it also insured
that the society would remain under the direction of men dedicated to the Puritan design.[6]

An individual's witness to such dedication culminated in his
narration of his spiritual autobiography. Following preliminary
steps, a candidate adjudged to warrant serious consideration
"was called upon to demonstrate the work of God in his soul,"
which meant, with infrequent exceptions, that "he was expected to make a narration, perhaps fifteen minutes in length,
of the way in which God's saving grace [had come] to him." He
was expected, moreover, to follow a pattern so formalized "as
to give the . . . appearance of a stereotype."[7] The tradition of
such narration remained predominantly oral, a final safe-
guard against flagging dedication. But it nevertheless established, as a New England habit, interpretation of the spiritual
vicissitudes of an individual's life and of the workings of God's
plan for the individual's redemption.

Whether or not he wrote it strictly for "private Advantage,"
Jonathan Edwards patterned his *Personal Narrative* on the
public formula of his ancestors. In 1723 Edwards had been
troubled by his failure to experience "conversion in those par-

6. See Morgan, *Visible Saints*, pp. 64–112; and Perry Miller,
Orthodoxy in Massachusetts, 1630–1650 (Cambridge, Mass., Harvard
University Press, 1933), Chap. 6.

7. Morgan, *Visible Saints*, pp. 89, 91.

ticular steps, wherein the people of New England, and anciently the Dissenters of Old England, used to experience it."[8] Yet by the time of the writing of his *Narrative,* which was completed no earlier than January 1739, Edwards found precisely the pattern Edmund S. Morgan has identified as that of the Puritan fathers: Edwards moves from "feeble and false" awakenings; through periods of prideful obedience, "backsliding," and "fitful harkenings to the word"; to realization that he is helpless and that Christ is "his only hope"; and finally, amidst faith and doubt, to a growing yet never perfect sense of "assurance."[9]

Far from being the public account of a candidate seeking admission to a church (the usual context for such narration), however, Edwards' *Narrative* not only remained private throughout his life but was separated by several years from both the events on which it concentrates and the time of his entrance into the church. The experiences it recounts are recollected from the vantage point of mature faith; they are, in a radical sense, interpreted experiences.

The Puritans' traditional interpretive pattern served Edwards well; it enabled him to reclaim (one might almost say discover) his experience. And he in turn served it well; he salvaged it from the obscurity with which time was shrouding it. By exploiting and extending, with genuine poetic instinct, the convention he appropriated, however, Edwards altered the Puritan pattern of spiritual autobiography. His *Narrative* remains aggressively orthodox; there is no theological compromise. But its divergence from the traditional pattern alters its aesthetic quality by changing its tone and mood and broadening its focus. In keeping with tradition, Edwards centers his *Narrative* on "the gracious design" by which God has led him to

8. Sereno E. Dwight, ed., *Works of President Edwards: With a Memoir of His Life* (10 vols. New York, 1829–30), *1,* 93.
9. Morgan, *Visible Saints,* p. 91.

salvation.[10] But in addition to tracing God's salvific design, he interprets an impotent design of his own. Edwards' *Narrative* combines interpretation of his planned effort to be religious with interpretation of God's gracious design for judging that effort and surpassing even Edwards' greatest expectations.

Edwards begins his *Narrative* with a straightforward account of the events leading to the true awakening that is the source of his "new sense of things."[11] From the outset it is clear that only the final, true awakening has made Edwards' life significant: "I had a variety of concerns and exercises about my soul from my childhood; but had two more remarkable seasons of awakening before I met with that change by which I was brought to those new dispositions, and that new sense of things that I have since had." The first of Edwards' brief seasons is presented as the rather innocent affair of a young boy, and is treated gently. Edwards deplores the "self-righteous pleasure" that he, in retrospect, is able to discern both in his boyish concern "about the things of religion" and in his satisfaction with being "abundant in duties." But in context the spontaneity of the early episode somewhat counteracts its speciousness: "it was my delight to abound in religious duties. . . . My affections seemed to be lively and easily moved, and I seemed to be in my element when I engaged in religious duties" (pp. 24–25).

In the "delight" imbuing it, the first season of awakening differs sharply from the second. Whereas the first had coincided

10. See Perry Miller, ed., Jonathan Edwards, *Images or Shadows of Divine Things* (New Haven, Yale University Press, 1948), p. 54.

11. Jonathan Edwards, *Personal Narrative,* in Samuel Hopkins, *The Life and Character of . . . Jonathan Edwards* (Northampton, 1804), p. 24. All page references in the text of this section of this chapter are to this edition of the *Personal Narrative*. For a discussion of this text of the *Personal Narrative,* see Daniel B. Shea, Jr., "The Art and Instruction of Jonathan Edwards's *Personal Narrative,*" *American Literature, 37* (1965), 18, n. 6.

with "a time of remarkable awakening" in Edwards' father's congregation and had been explored by a boy who believed it would last, the second was inspired by terror and cultivated by a man who had learned from experience how quickly such seasons could fade. Following a time when "it pleased God . . . to seize" him with pleurisy and shake him "over the pit of hell," and following "great and violent inward struggles" and "repeated resolutions" and "vows to God," the second awakening appears to the older Edwards to have made the younger Edwards a dedicated, single-minded man.[12] Moved not by the "affection and delight" that had accompanied his youthful exuberance but by a stern and calculated, even a desperate assault upon the religious, Edwards was indeed brought not only "to seek salvation in a manner" he had never before known, but to make that search the ordering principle of his life. By living according to a religious formula, he would attain salvation: "I made seeking my salvation the main business of my life" (pp. 24–26).

It is the spirit of calculated and careful enterprise that sets Edwards' second season of awakening in sharp contrast to his young, exuberant absorption. Because salvation here has become the telos of a designing mind, the process of seeking salvation has become rigorously programmed and the process of living has become rigorously planned. Salvation—and therefore the life dedicated to it—has become a matter of precise horizontal organization and planned vertical expansion.

The peculiar irony permeating Edwards' autobiographical

12. See Shea, p. 19, where he discusses Edwards' *Narrative* as "governed by the purposes that informed most of his work during the period of the Great Awakening"; first his concern to reject the broadened church-way of Solomon Stoddard; and second his effort, by examining the morphology of conversion, to distinguish "between those affections that are rational and scriptural . . . and those that are founded in whimsical conceits, strong impressions on the imagination, and vehement emotions on the animal spirits."

sketch derives from the fate of his enterprise unto salvation. Although wholly unsuccessful and even positively damning, his old "concerns" for the state of his soul and his careful "exercises" in pursuit of its redemption are peculiarly relevant. Empty, perverted, and corrupting, they nonetheless bespeak a need that is finally fulfilled. Within the *Personal Narrative,* the gift of grace is an enabling gift. Given God's act of redefinition, Edwards is able to make meaning of the whole of his experience. Through self-examination and self-interpretation, he moves to unity both within himself—among his needs and longings, his plans and exercises—and between himself—between everything he has been and done—and God's redemptive activity. The whole of his life—including his foolish days of intoxication and his barren days of organized religious enterprise, including each of his selves, the selves of intoxication, calculation, and interpretation—takes shape within the *Personal Narrative* as a single, crowded yet coherently patterned moment meaningfully related to the whole of God's redemptive activity.[13] In retrospect he sees that the "wonderful alteration" wrought by grace has conjoined spontaneous delight and considered commitment, inspiring "not only . . . conviction, but a *delightful* conviction" of "the justice and reasonableness" of divine sovereignty (pp. 24, 26–27). Edwards accordingly depicts his "sense of the glory of the Divine Being" as having moved him beyond intoxication, first to "a calm, sweet abstraction of [the] soul from all the concerns of this world," and then to "a kind of vision, or fixed ideas and imaginations," not only of solitary communion with Christ but of being "wrapt and swallowed up in [the] God" in whom "majesty and meekness [are] joined together." Finally, pure lyricism is the result: Edwards sees himself as having come "to sing, or chant . . . [his] medi-

13. See Robert F. Sayre, *The Examined Self: Benjamin Franklin, Henry Adams, Henry James* (Princeton, Princeton University Press, 1964), pp. 34–39.

tations; to speak [his] thoughts in soliloquies . . . with a singing voice" (pp. 27–29).

Later, to be sure, Edwards pictures himself discovering "the
bottomless, infinite depths" of his own corruption and acquiring
a more appropriately extreme sense of humility and "exceeding
dependence" upon God (p. 41). But the *Personal Narrative* is
in its own way a divine comedy. For in Edwards' world God
undoes man's plans only then to lead man to a paradise beyond
man's capacity to desire and envisage. Edwards interprets both
his dreams and his enterprises, delineating aspects variously
foolish and corrupt, and he traces defeats, both simple and
tortured. But the tone of his work is defined by celebration of
the glorious way in which the yearnings that led him to his
futile plan have been consummated, through the "wonderful
alteration" wrought by God's "gracious design," not in mere
"conviction" but in *"delightful* conviction" (pp. 26–27). The
Narrative is but a sketch, yet it is not properly speaking a fragment; for it places the whole of Edwards' life—its moments of
barren intoxication, futile calculation, and empty self-assertion
—within a finally radiant context; it renders renewal of what
before was not simply without form and meaning but was corrupting and self-defeating.

The *Autobiography* of Benjamin Franklin, a successful
nation's most successful success story, was a deliberate act.
Having emerged from "Poverty and Obscurity . . . to a State of
Affluence and some Degree of Reputation in the World,"
Franklin supposed that others might find "the conducing
Means" he had employed "fit to be imitated." He hoped, to
be sure, also to recapture his life and endow it with permanence:
"the next Thing most like living one's Life over again," he
says, "seems to be a *Recollection* of that Life; and to make
that Recollection as durable as possible . . . [by] putting it
down in Writing." But in composing his memoirs, as in so much

else, Franklin subordinated private need to public service. In the section addressed to his son and in those addressed to a broader public, he entertains by sketching his rise and instructs by presenting himself as a model.[14]

The most striking single feature of Franklin's memoirs is his plan for moral perfection. Structurally, the episode is central and shaping. It does for Franklin what knowledge of divine election did for Edwards: it gives him a way of ordering his life. The portions of the work that precede it are prefatory: they stand as an inquiry into the origins of the author and his project. Following this interpreted derivation and the carefully, uncharacteristically detailed treatment of the plan itself, the work becomes a history of various attempts at implementation —various plans and subprojects through which Franklin endeavored fully to realize his plan "for regulating" his "future Conduct in Life" (p. 106).

In first mentioning his plan for perfection, Franklin refers to the record, in his Journal of a Voyage, 1726, of "the *Plan* . . . formed at Sea" for shaping his future life (p. 106). Only "the preamble and heads" of the plan survive, but in the preamble Franklin gives a special twist to an analogy he liked.

> Those who write of the art of poetry teach us that if we would write what may be worth the reading, we ought always, before we begin, to form a regular plan and design of our piece: otherwise, we shall be in danger of incongruity. I am apt to think it is the same as to life. I have never fixed a regular design in life; by which means it has been a confused variety of different scenes. I am now entering upon a new one: let me, therefore, make some resolutions, and form some scheme of action, that,

14. Benjamin Franklin, *Autobiography,* ed. Leonard W. Labaree and others (New Haven, Yale University Press, 1964), pp. 43–44. All page references in the text of this section of this chapter are to this edition of the *Autobiography.* See Sayre, pp. 12–33.

henceforth, I may live in all respects like a rational creature.[15]

The project for moral perfection is, within the *Autobiography,*
the form Franklin's design takes; it represents his determination
to live, as a rational and social creature, a life shaped by "a
regular plan and design."

Given the basic thrust of Franklin's story celebrating success, it is easy to overlook the perils he encounters in the "confused variety of different scenes" that precede and follow his
move from Boston to Philadelphia. From those perils he learns
not only his need of a plan for a rational life but also the elements necessary to it. The first serious conflict between Franklin and his world occurs when, as a boy of twelve, he is taught
what is "good, just, and prudent in the Conduct of Life" (p.
55). In an effort to thwart the boy's longing for the sea, the
father indentures him for nine years to an older brother. For
the next five years, in the first phrase of his serious initiation,
Franklin remains in Boston, where he combines hard work and
a solitary, bookish life with the writing of immature poetry.

The Boston years of the *Autobiography* show Franklin
gathering impressions, running risks, and learning a trade.
While his father is trying to save him both from going to sea
and from becoming a poet, his brother is teaching him how
easily men abuse arbitrary authority, and the good leaders of
Boston are teaching him how organized society disciplines
the unruly and disruptive. But Franklin already is becoming
Franklin's own best instructor. He devises a plan—of controlled imitation—for improving his *"Manner* in Writing,"
and he adopts the Socratic method of dispute. The young
Franklin's motives are significant. He is convinced that skill in
writing will prove an important asset; and he finds the guise
of the humble doubter both safe and effective. In these en

15. Leonard W. Labaree and others, eds., *The Papers of Benjamin
Franklin* (7 vols. to date, New Haven, Yale University Press, 1959–   ),
1, 99–100.

deavors, he is seeking consciously to become "very artful and expert" in dealing with life (pp. 61, 64–65).

Early in the *Autobiography,* Franklin thus defines life in terms of the complex art of being safe and effective in the performance of a self-appointed role or roles. Having already learned the importance of being able to play various roles and to communicate with skill, he is prepared when the situation suggests it not only to "put on" the mask of "the humble Enquirer and Doubter" (p. 64) but also to create the persona of Silence Dogood—that is, to contrive, in the name of safe and effective mediation between private sensibility and public arena, variously to disguise his true identity. On this basis, Franklin is sufficiently prepared to cut short his apprenticeship. When chance opens the way to successful flight, he makes his move. "I took upon me," he says, "to assert my Freedom" (p. 70).

In leaving the old and entering the new, without family or friends, unsponsored and free, Franklin begins a new phase of initiation, years of confused and uncertain experimentation. No scene in the *Autobiography* is more fully dramatized than the young Franklin's entrance into the strange streets of Philadelphia. By being "the more particular" in his description of the journey and especially of the "first Entry," Franklin consciously, in a characteristically histrionic mode, seeks to contrast his "unlikely Beginnings"—as a runaway boy, poorly dressed, fatigued, hungry, financially destitute, friendless, and homeless—"with the Figure [he had] since made there" (p. 75).

The move to the second and final phase of Franklin's initiation, the three years following his assertion of his freedom, entails a shift in the character of his contest with his world. The Franklin who emerges during these years is not so much precocious as prematurely old: his "Inclinations for the Sea" (like his urge to be "a Poet") have "by this time worne out" (p. 71; see p. 60), and his resistance to parental prudence and social establishment soon subsides. The departure from Boston is only in part a bold move of youth to freedom; it also reflects the remarkable extent to which the young Franklin has learned the importance of being "prudent in the Conduct of Life" (see p. 55): "I was the rather inclin'd to leave Boston, when I reflected that I had already made myself a little obnoxious to the governing Party; and . . . might if I stay'd soon bring myself into Scrapes; and farther that my indiscrete Disputations about Religion began to make me pointed at with Horror by good People as an Infidel or Atheist" (p. 71).

Although at this point Franklin already has gone far toward mastering the art of life, he has not yet, as the ensuing action of the *Autobiography* shows, learned sufficiently that the game can be perilous, that disciplined consistency and patience play vital roles in the outcome, and that the social context defines the character of the game elsewhere than in Boston. The tensions that emerge to replace the conflicts of Franklin's youth correspond to these gaps in his education, to these necessary lessons still unlearned.

Minor triumphs, secured by ingenuity, cleverness, industry, and especially a generally winning way and a remarkable capacity for showmanship, are juxtaposed to encounters that are often disillusioning and at times genuinely trying. In the first years of his independence, the young Franklin falls financial victim to his two closest companions—first to John Collins in Philadelphia and then to James Ralph in London. And between these experiences Franklin is left stranded in London by a man who had voluntarily become his sponsor. Having journeyed from Philadelphia to London, under the direction of Sir William Keith, governor of Pennsylvania, Franklin learns that he has been duped. Keith, Franklin concludes, simply "had acquired" the "Habit" of "playing . . . pitiful Tricks" on the unsuspecting, and thus intentionally had imposed "grossly on a poor ignorant Boy" (p. 95).

It is after his stay in London, during the journey back to Philadelphia, that Franklin devises "a regular plan and de-

sign" for the purpose of "regulating [his] future Conduct in
Life." By conceiving and pursuing a "scheme of action," he
will avoid the "danger of incongruity"; he will live not "a
confused variety of different scenes," but "in all respects like
a rational creature." Patiently and prudently, with close attention to method, he sets out first to attain the social respectability
necessary to the figure he intends to make in Philadelphia, second to achieve the financial independence he deems prerequisite
to freedom, and third "to acquire the *Habitude* of all . . .
Virtues" he considers essential to happiness (pp. 106, 150).

Franklin's plan makes his life radically social. Whereas men
in Edwards' world are called to worship God in service and
adoration, men in Franklin's world are called to serve society.
Because it presupposes the priority of society, because it implies a drastically social existence, Franklin's plan leads him
beyond quest for social influence, financial independence, and
the acquisition of virtue to a lifetime of service. For Franklin
the answer to what constituted meaningful action was promoting "useful Projects" (p. 204) and pursuing "beneficent Design[s]" (p. 199).

Within the *Autobiography*, Franklin promotes many projects. But his most inclusive design is his plan to write a book
on the "ART *of Virtue*," a book that will act as a guide for
"the Society of the *Free and Easy*." Having persuaded others
of "the Utility and Excellency" of his way of planning and
living his life, he will form and lead an international "united
Party for Virtue," a kind of elite avant-garde for enlightened
rationalism. "But it so happened," Franklin notes, "that my
Intention of writing and publishing this [work] was never
fulfilled"—and that the *"great and extensive Project"* (of organizing "the Society of the *Free and Easy"*) related to it, a
project that would have required "the whole Man to execute,"
also "remain'd unfinish'd" (pp. 157–58, 161–63).

Thus, despite Franklin's claim in reference to his Journal of
a Voyage, 1726, that he had "pretty faithfully adhered" to

his basic plan "quite thro' to old Age" (p. 106), what the
Autobiography tells is a rather complexly patterned story—
the story of a man who adheres to what he takes to be rational
only to find himself forced to sacrifice his grandest undertakings. After Franklin has voluntarily sacrificed the possibility
of pursuing an essentially private life to the business of living
a radically social, public life of promoting useful projects, he
is forced, by "necessary close Attention to private Business" in
his early years and thereafter to "public Business," repeatedly
to postpone and finally to leave unfinished the most extensive
and inclusive of his projects (p. 158; cf. p. 161).

What Franklin learned in the protracted process of writing
his *Autobiography,* which was begun August 1771 and was
left unfinished at the time of his death, April 17, 1790, was that
he could no longer hope to realize his great dual plan of writing
his "ART *of Virtue"* and establishing a society dedicated to
practicing and propagating it. But what he discovered during
that protracted process was that he could make his *Autobiography* serve not merely as a way of presenting himself as
a model and of reliving his "Life" but also as a way of redeeming his plan. For in it he could write of how his overarching
purpose had been conceived and born, of how life had fulfilled
it in part but also had worn and changed some, and shrouded
and buried other, of its features. Writing his life thus became
Franklin's way of dispatching his younger self anew into the
world that had undreamed his dream.

Life, we are told, has forced him to postpone his great
"Enterprize" until he no longer possesses "Strength or Activity left sufficient" to begin it. Yet in his narrative he can
proclaim "that it was a practicable Scheme," that it "might
have been very useful," that he has not been "discourag'd by
the seeming Magnitude of the Undertaking," that indeed he has
"always thought . . . one Man of tolerable Abilities may work
great Changes, and accomplish great Affairs . . . if he first forms
a good Plan, and, cutting off all . . . that would divert his At-

tention, makes the Execution of that same Plan his sole Study and Business" (p. 163). In thus recovering and endowing his younger self and his failed plan with new life, dispatching them again into the world, Franklin propagates the great "enlightened" faith of the Western *Aufklärung*—faith in the efficacy of the plans and actions of "absolute man."[16] But what is more, he makes his unfinished memoirs a surrogate for his grandest scheme: it was to the propagation of a united party dedicated to his Art of Virtue that Franklin came gradually to dedicate his *Autobiography*. By tracing the derivation, sketching the character, and recording the fate of his *"great and extensive Project,"* he would deliver it from obscurity, would give it new life.[17]

The younger Franklin, who is both in and of the world of the *Autobiography,* accepts life as a full "dramatic Piece" and responds with a serious performance: he lives the public, social life; he practices the virtues society honors, cultivates the talents society rewards, and accepts at face value the success society bestows. The older observing, interpreting Franklin— particularly in his treatment of his own greatest project—displays more tentative commitment and entertains a more complex possibility: that, in mastering life in its social form, in learning to play life's game by life's rules, he has become servant to a master that in the end pays with specious coin.[18] Be-

16. Barth, *From Rousseau to Ritschl,* pp. 14–19.

17. Aware that men were given to constructing "pretty systems" which they then found themselves "obliged to destroy" (Letter to Peter Collinson, August 1747, in Carl Van Doren, ed., *Benjamin Franklin's Autobiographical Writings* [New York, Viking, 1945], p. 51), Franklin remained a true experimentalist even in his faith in absolute man.

18. See Letter to George Whitefield, July 1756, in Albert H. Smyth, ed., *The Writings of Benjamin Franklin* (10 vols. New York, Macmillan, 1905–07), *3,* 339. In the best definition of the most striking feature of Franklin's character, Carl Becker has stated that "Nature alone met [Franklin] on equal terms, with a disinterestedness matching his own"

cause in it he was able to conjoin the total involvement of the participant with the tentative commitment of the observer, because in it he was able to give full play to both his characteristic roles—as projecting man of action and as disinterested, observing man of interpretation—Franklin was able to make his *Autobiography,* despite its entangled composition, his classic.[19] Left without a God to redeem his failed efforts, he found in interpretation not only a way of making a model of his life and thereby redeeming his lost project, but a way also of fully relating the two roles his apprehension of life taught him to be essential. Later, in a substantially different context, Henry David Thoreau was to learn from Ralph Waldo Emerson to call the perfect blending of something very close to these same two roles the "poetic life"; and later still Thoreau was to attempt through deliberate experiment not only to explore these roles but more perfectly to reconcile and unify them.

(Dictionary of American Biography, 6 [1931], 597). What needs to be added, as I have tried to indicate, is that Franklin was able to find matching disinterestedness in his disinterested self, that he found it throughout his life in observing himself, and that in his later years his older self found and rendered it by recalling and recording the life of his earlier self.

19. For discussions of problems of the composition and text of the *Autobiography,* see Max Farrand, Introduction, *Benjamin Franklin's Memoirs: Parallel Text Edition* (Berkeley, University of California Press, 1949), or an earlier edition of the same essay in *Huntington Library Bulletin, 10* (1936), 49–78; and Leonard W. Labaree, Introduction, *Autobiography,* pp. 22–40.

5 Extension of the Form: Thoreau's *Walden*

> *For, feeling has to him imparted power*
> *That through the growing faculties of sense*
> *Doth like an agent of the one great Mind*
> *Create, creator and receiver both,*
> *Working but in alliance with the works*
> *Which it beholds. Such, verily, is the first*
> *Poetic spirit of our human life,*
> *By uniform control of after years,*
> *In most, abated or suppressed; in some,*
> *Through every change of growth and of decay,*
> *Pre-eminent till death.*
>
> William Wordsworth, The Prelude

In 1841, at about the time Thoreau began in his journal to plan the Walden excursion, Emerson fashioned in his journal one of the clearest formulations of a nineteenth-century version of the problem with which Franklin had grappled, a problem to which Thoreau addressed the whole of his life. "There are two directions in which souls move," Emerson said. One is "entranced waiting, the worship of Ideas: the other is activity . . . the following of that practical talent which we have, in the belief that what is so natural, easy, and pleasant to us and desirable to others will surely lead us out safely: in this direction lies usefulness, comfort, society . . . The other is solitary, grand. . . . We have no one example of the [unified] poetic life realized."[1] Believing his world "a fit theatre" in which to act "any part," and knowing that neither Edwards' nor Franklin's answer—"Neither the New Testament nor Poor Richard"— spoke to his "condition," Thoreau sought to live the unified life in which all activity and all utterance would be spontaneously poetic.[2]

Thoreau's effort to live this unified life was troubled, on one level, by tension between his urge simply to "live" and his desire to "utter" his "poem."[3] The art form closest to Thoreau's Emersonian aesthetic was the open, ostensibly formless journal in which the relation between living and uttering, between symbolic activity and imaginative utterance, was close. The journal proved inadequate, however, to Thoreau's needs. Repeatedly he went beyond it to write lyric poetry and poetic essays. And in that move he encountered a deeper difficulty: his poetic activity became rather deliberate program than spontaneous response and his poetic statements rather deliberate performance than fortuitous uttering.[4]

In his essay "Walking" (1862), Thoreau confronts his characteristic situation. Walking is for him, in its purest form, open-

1. Edward W. Emerson and W. E. Forbes, eds., *Journals of Ralph Waldo Emerson* (10 vols. Boston and New York, Houghton Mifflin, 1909–14), *6, 80.*

2. *The Writings of Henry David Thoreau* (Walden Edition, 20 vols. Boston, Houghton Mifflin, 1906), *7, 129; 8, 164.* See *9, 41–42, 99; 14, 7–8; 17, 227.* Hereafter cited as *Writings.*

3. See ibid., *1, 365;* cf. *7, 157, 275.* In both *A Week on the Concord and Merrimack Rivers* and "A Plea for John Brown" *(Writings, 1, 407; 4, 436),* Thoreau quotes the following lines: "Unless above himself he can / Erect himself, how poor a thing is man!" In these passages Thoreau is quoting Samuel Daniel (see *Writings, 1, 427).* The lines derive from Seneca, however, and may also be found in Wordsworth. See E. de Selincourt and H. Darbshire, eds., *The Poetical Works of William Wordsworth* (5 vols. Oxford, Clarendon Press, 1940–47), *5,* 119.

4. See Feidelson, *Symbolism and American Literature,* pp. 135–50, 300–11.

ended voyaging, unprogrammed going forth. It is free of ulterior motive and independent of preconceived end. Unfolding organically, as a process of sheer discovery, "sauntering" is sacramental: the outward, visible activity is at one with an inward, invisible unfolding. In Thoreau's essay, however, the world of Concord is a fallen world, and the "art of Walking" is a dying art. With the land in "the hands of the Infidels," any effort to live the natural, poetic life must be self-conscious; what should be unprogrammed going forth perforce becomes deliberate "crusade." Every true walker, in addition to being a voyager, must be a knight "of a new, or rather an old, order," the "ancient and honorable" order of Walkers, who are of "chivalric and heroic spirit" and who see themselves as constituting "a sort of fourth estate, outside of Church and State and People."[5]

By deriving "saunter" from the journey of those who went out meandering *"à la Sainte Terre,"* Thoreau is able to make the poetic walk a heroic crusade. But in the process he acknowledges incongruity between ideal and actual poetic activity. In contrast to pure process and pristine symbolic activity, even more drastically than sacramental activity, the concept of the journey *"à la Sainte Terre"* implies a teleologically oriented endeavor. Far from being engaged simply in savoring fortuitous visionary moments and disparate symbolic acts, the saunterer who moves toward "the boundary of Elysium," anticipating a "Holy Land" in which "the sun shall shine" within and without man, "warm and serene and golden," is engaged in a planned movement toward a defined end.[6]

What "Walking" shows is that, given his desire both to live and to write his poem, Thoreau needed to find a way of making again spontaneous the life and art that his fallen world forced him to make deliberate. What *Walden* shows is how he at-

5. *Writings, 5,* 205–06. Compare *7,* 253, on sauntering as "a great art."
6. Ibid., pp. 205, 247–48.

tempted to do this by subjecting a carefully designed and conducted (a deliberate) experiment to extravagant (spontaneous) interpretation.

Thoreau begins *Walden* with a disarmingly simple explanation of its origin; the "bulk" of the book, we are told, was written during the two years and two months of Thoreau's sojourn, from July 4, 1845, to September 6, 1847, on the shore of Walden Pond. We now know, however, primarily as a result of the scholarship of J. Lyndon Shanley, that the making of *Walden* was complex as well as protracted. It began, to be sure, as a straightforward account of Thoreau's months at the pond; but by 1854 the poet's donnée had forced him to shape and reshape his narrative until the experience of more than two years compressed into a single seasonal cycle and until, in passing through seven versions, the work nearly doubled in length. As Shanley has noted, "the journals made it clear that Thoreau added to *Walden* between 1847 and 1854, and especially after 1850, [but] only the manuscript could reveal to how great an extent *Walden* is the result of a gradual re-creation of his experience rather than simply a recounting . . . And, further, only the manuscript could show the way in which Thoreau reshaped his material as the image of what he wanted to make became clearer."[7]

The manuscript and journal show, however, that more was at work in the making of *Walden* than the urgings of happy experience aesthetically re-created and reshaped to match its author's vision. *Walden* constitutes Thoreau's final confrontation with the fate of a carefully planned experiment. In stressing, early in *Walden,* that he had attempted to live and build "deliberately," Thoreau is anticipating his defense, late in *Walden,* of *"extra-vagant"* expression. Thoreau prepared for radical interpretation by engaging in deliberate, ritualistic ac-

7. J. Lyndon Shanley, *The Making of Walden* (Chicago, University of Chicago Press, 1957), p. 5.

tion: he viewed carefully planned activity as a prelude to subsequent endeavor, by speaking *"without* bounds," to recapture lost spontaneity.[8]

Beginning in 1841, first the open and then the planned aspects of Thoreau's experiment took shape in his journal. I want only, Thoreau wrote in April, to "build my lodge on the southern slope of some hill, and take there the life the gods send me. Will it not be employment enough to accept gratefully all that is yielded me between sun and sun?"[9] By December, through dialogue with self and friends, Thoreau had chosen a definite site, had shifted to the more commodious metaphor of the seasons, and had defined both his motive and his projected employment. "I want to go soon and live away by the pond, where I shall hear only the wind whispering among the reeds. It will be success if I shall have left myself behind. But my friends ask what I will do when I get there. Will it not be employment enough to watch the progress of the seasons?"[10]

By the time—in 1845—of his removal to Walden Pond, Thoreau's design was dual. He "went to the woods" in order to engage in a great "experiment of living": he wanted to learn how "earnestly [to] live [life] from beginning to end"; he wanted "to live deliberately" (pp. 56, 100–01). But he also went to the woods to prepare himself for the work of interpretation and disclosure. He wanted, he continues, "to drive life into a corner, and reduce it to its lowest terms, and, if it proved to be mean, why then to get the whole and genuine meanness of it, and publish its meanness to the world; or if it were sublime, to know it by experience, and be able to give a true account of it in my next excursion" (p. 101).

Before he went to the woods, Thoreau knew—he had

8. *Writings,* 2, 100, 357. All page references in the text of this chapter refer to this volume of the *Writings,* in which *Walden* is contained.

9. Ibid., 7, 244.

10. Ibid., p. 299.

learned primarily from the Concord and Merrimack river voyage—that the logic of his spirit made every excursion a prelude to publication and every publication a form of excursion. Not only by renewing him but also by giving him his poetic donnée, his physical excursion into nature prepared him for his literary excursion into society. By building a house and constructing a life designed to foster, reveal, and give form to the "vital heat" within him, Thoreau would make discovery of life preparation for poetic utterance; he would begin in his journal the making of his poem about his effort to live poetically.

At least as Thoreau finally saw it, the Walden experience—his most carefully planned and enacted venture—required interpretation in an extravagant mode. In the "Conclusion," which was a late addition, Thoreau expresses concern, not lest his interpreting imagination distort his experience, but lest his "expression may not be *extra-vagant* enough" to meet his need of speaking *"without* bounds" (p. 357). Thoreau knew that plans could crumble, that designs could abort. "The youth," he once wrote, "gets together his materials to build a bridge to the moon, or perchance a palace or a temple on the earth, and at length the middle-aged man concludes to build a wood-shed with them."[11] But Thoreau also knew that poetic "imagination" could make meaning of "isolated and unexplained facts," that it could "restore" and bring to completion "the ruins of [man's] temples."[12] Given such knowledge, he was prepared to risk deliberate building of his own.

In part personal journal, in part polemical essay against society, and in part poetic interpretation of life in the woods, *Walden* is a peculiar literary work. It combines, in form, sub-

11. Ibid., *10,* 227.
12. Ibid., *7,* 165. Given such power, poetry became for Thoreau a kind of "miracle"; see *Writings, 1,* 350.

stance, tone, and mood, the immediacy of a journal with the brief remove of early reshaping and the redefining view of detached recollection. Thoreau was able harmoniously to combine these disparate forms only by making his work radically autobiographical.[13] The immediate focus of the work shifts—from the dual motive of the plan behind the experiment to the action of the poet within the woods, from his forays into the village to the village's invasions of the woods, from the poet's immediate recording of given episodes to his imaginative re-creation of his entire experience. But the work's controlling focus is the self and life of the poet. Because the poet's life in the woods is so various and beautiful as to be at one with his poetic endeavor per se, the poet is able to make interpretation of that experience definition of the poetic self planning and executing it. Exploration and interpretation of the pond and the woods necessitate exploration and interpretation of "new continents and worlds" opening up "within" the poet (p. 353). The foray into the corporeal world of shared experience is simultaneously a penetration of the incorporeal world of the self.[14]

The first major development in *Walden* defines and explores the poet's planned life of the woods. Thoreau's revision of Benjamin Franklin, his redefinition of economy, centers on the building of his extravagantly simple hut. The architectural structure of the hut is a function of the motive behind the Walden experiment as a whole. It reflects Thoreau's basic design. On one side it opens to the world; on the other it is a "porch at the entrance of a burrow" (p. 49). As is appropriate to shelter for one living beside a pond in the woods, the hut is a good port to put out from as well as "a good foundation" to

13. *Walden* is obviously not an autobiography, but it constitutes Thoreau's effort to give "a simple and sincere account of his own life" *(Writings, 2,* 4; cf. *7,* 269–70).

14. See Wallace Stevens, "Effects of Analogy," *The Necessary Angel,* p. 118.

build on (p. 23). It is, in short, the work of a designing mind—an artifact built to free man from enslavement to convention and entombment in the fallen village: "if one designs to construct a dwelling-house," Thoreau writes, "it behooves him to exercise a little Yankee shrewdness, lest after all he find himself in a workhouse, a labyrinth without a clue, a museum, an almshouse, a prison, or a splendid mausoleum instead" (p. 31). The peculiar beauty of Thoreau's hut derives in part from the care its maker takes to make it a dwelling-house. But it derives also from the spirit of the activity itself. Such building is proper endeavor. The "pleasure of construction," and especially the "simple and natural" act of building one's own house, gives "expression [to] man's struggle to free [and renew] himself" (pp. 51, 41). For such making is not simply but poetically natural. "There is some of the same fitness in a man's building his own house that there is in a bird's building its own nest. Who knows but if men constructed their dwellings with their own hands . . . the poetic faculty would be universally developed, as birds universally sing when they are so engaged" (p. 50)? Thoreau's deliberate building—whether in framing his hut-like "superstructure" with boards ritualistically placed "on the grass" in straightening and purifying sun (pp. 48–49); or in constructing his cellar by breaking ground and burrowing into the earth; or in making *Walden,* which had to be built word by word—is all of a piece. The poet's various plans and actions are analogous in intent and result; each constitutes one moment in his effort to live the poetic life.

Having built his hut, made his cellar, and begun preparation for utterance, Thoreau begins, in the second chapter, to generalize the poetic motive present in his acts of construction: his effort "to build . . . deliberately" his small cabin takes its place as one phase of his effort "to live deliberately." In his generalization, moreover, he composes, not "an ode to dejection," but a eulogy to life in the woods (pp. 50, 100–01, 94). Acting in faith that the "universe constantly and obediently answers to

our conceptions" and that "The poet or the artist never yet
had so fair and noble a design but some of his posterity at least
could accomplish it" (p. 108; see p. 104), the poet dedicates
himself to the labor of thought and the work of penetration.
Having found "pasture enough for [his] imagination" in a place
"forever new and unprofaned" (pp. 97–98), he seeks to "mine
and burrow" his way to the axis of existence (p. 109; see pp.
108–09).[15]

In the remaining phases of the first movement of *Walden* (in
the chapters on "Books," "Sounds," "Solitude," "Visitors,"
and "The Bean-Field"), Thoreau continues to trace and explore his implementation of his plan. He relates his present life
to the past—to books which are "the treasured wealth of the
world" (p. 114); to the future—in which he anticipates the
emergence of "noble villages of men" (p. 122); and to eternity
—for it is "in dealing with truth" (in true exploration of his
"nature and destiny") that man is "immortal, and need fear no
change nor accident" (p. 110). Then, with context of action
broadened, Thoreau finds in the past the beginnings of his own
interpretive endeavor. "I had this advantage, at least," he
writes, "that my life itself was become my amusement" (my
"society" and my "theatre") and that it "never ceased to be
novel. It was a drama of many scenes and without an end"
(p. 125). Watching himself as he walks "along the stony shore
of the pond" (p. 143), studying the stillnesses and sounds,
measuring the solitude and relatedness of his new "mode of
living" (p. 78), the poet becomes "suddenly sensible" of an
"infinite and unaccountable . . . atmosphere sustaining" his
life (p. 146).

Interpretation of his own experiment accordingly becomes
for the poet freeing rather than limiting. Enabled to be "beside
[himself] in a sane sense," he is able to commence making of his
own life and experience "a kind of fiction, a work of the imag-

15. See *Writings, 8,* 155.

ination only." Because he is "not wholly involved in Nature,"
he writes, because he is able to "be either the driftwood in the
stream, or Indra in the sky looking down on it," he is able to
know himself "as a . . . scene, so to speak, of thoughts and
affections." "However intense my experience," he writes, "I
am conscious of the presence and criticism of a part of me,
which, as it were, is not a part of me, but spectator, sharing no
experience, but taking note of it" (pp. 149–50).

Implementation and interpretation meet and merge in the
ritual of the bean-field. Anticipated by varied allusions (see
pp. 11, 60–61, 111, 123, 161), the chapter's first line stresses
the culminative status of the bean-field: *"Meanwhile* my beans
. . . were impatient to be hoed" (p. 171; italics added; cf.
pp. 111, 123, 278, 283). Like the small labor of building the
hut, the "steady . . . small Herculean labor" of the bean rows
is labor par excellence. It unites poet and renewing soil. Performed without either ulterior motive or full understanding,
as "a rare amusement," in a field that is "one of the oldest
scenes stamped on [the poet's] memory," the act of cultivation becomes an act of love, a mode of discovery, an "inexhaustible entertainment" (pp. 171, 179, 172, 176).

The bean-field can be so multifarious a scene only because
in it the deliberate and the spontaneous, the good and the wild,
mingle. Neither brutalized by savage elements nor perverted
by empty conventions, the bean-field becomes a meeting place
of the distinctively human and the wholly natural (see pp.
233–34). "Mine was, as it were, the connecting link between
wild and cultivated fields; as some states are civilized, and
others half-civilized, and others savage or barbarous, so my
field was, though not in a bad sense, a half-cultivated field"
(p. 174). It is only through careful cultivation that the poet is
able "to know beans" (p. 178). But it is only through his
extravagant interpretation, only by his making spontaneous
poetry of deliberate activity, that the act of knowing beans
becomes a thousand things. We see the poet as he stoops to

dabble "like a plastic artist in the dewy and crumbling sand";
we see him when he discovers, among "other natural stones,"
remnants and ashes of "unchronicled nations"; but we also
see him as he extends his ritualistic activity until it knows no
terminus ad quem, until it embraces everything and becomes
inexhaustible. Finally, the poet says, "It was no longer beans
that I hoed, nor I that hoed beans" (pp. 173, 175).

In "The Bean-Field," *Walden's* first major thematic movement—the implementation of the poet's planned expedition
into the woods—culminates in the union of concerted activity
and interpretive imagination. Renewed by his labor, the poet
becomes a "true husbandman"; in consort with the bean-field,
he is fruitful. Because he has largely realized his original purpose, he is freed "from anxiety" and is filled "with a calm trust
in the future" (pp. 184, 177).

In the summary introduction to the next chapter, "The
Village," the first major thematic movement of *Walden* gives
way to the second, in which the character of the poet's self-
planned life of the woods is set in contrast to the "civilized life"
of the village. Having earlier introduced the village's way as a
"fool's life" of "quiet desperation" (pp. 3, 6, 8), Thoreau now
explores it in four chapters—"The Village," "The Ponds,"
"Baker Farm," and "Higher Laws." Only after "hoeing, or
perhaps reading or writing," and only after he has bathed in
the pond, is the poet prepared again to enter the village (p.
185). But having been renewed, he can tolerate and even as-
similate experience of the village. Just as he has walked in the
woods to see and hear birds, so now he saunters through the
village to see and hear men. Because he has been renewed,
however, he is an offense to the village. He has made it, in
relation to himself, a "desperate party." Throughout the first
movement of *Walden,* tension between the vital life of the
woods (the scene of poignant sounds and communing solitude,
the habitat of breathing inhabitants and renewing ways) and the
stultifying life of the village (the scene of noisy machines and

tired voices, the dwelling place of crowds of isolated, gasping, enslaved men who exploit nature in order to feed their lust for power and possession) is a persistent, though subdued, theme. Raised, in the eighth chapter, to the level of open conflict—"I was seized and put into jail"—that theme becomes dominant (p. 190).

With tension between the life of the woods and the way of the village dominant and defining, a second dialectic gives pattern to the action of *Walden*. When the poet enters the village, the sound and sight of birds and squirrels give way to the presence of men and boys; "instead of the wind among the pines," the poet hears "the carts rattle" (p. 185). Then, in the opening lines of the next chapter, "The Ponds," Thoreau reverses the movement. Having "had a surfeit of human society and gossip," the poet rambles beyond his dwelling place "westward" to lands whose wildness cannot be domesticated, whose fruit cannot "be transported" without loss of its "ambrosial" essence (p. 192). And there he finds ponds which, though they can be violated, cannot be possessed. Walden, pure, serene, sublime, is "a perfect forest mirror" (p. 209). Lying "between the earth and the heavens," it "partakes of the color of both." Though deep, it is "transparent" (pp. 196–97). In contrast, Flint's Pond, which has been violated and profaned by an "unclean and stupid farmer," is "impure." With "crooked" fingers a "grasping" man has "ruthlessly laid bare" the pond's shores, deflowering its beauty and purity. Though he "never *saw* it . . . never bathed in it . . . never loved it . . . never protected it," the violator of the pond has presumed "to give his name to it" (pp. 216–17). Flint's Pond thus stands, in contrast to Walden and White Pond, as one pole in the dialectical action of the second movement of *Walden*.

Walden and White Pond remain pure; as their names suggest, they are "crystals on the surface of the earth, Lakes of Light" (p. 221). But like Flint's Pond, "Baker Farm" has been corrupted. It is the dwelling of one of society's outcasts—one of those who take "life bravely, after their fashion, face to face, giving it tooth and nail," but who, because they lack the "skill to split its massive columns with any fine entering wedge, and rout it in detail," are doomed to failure (p. 229). Set in contrast to pine groves, which stand "like temples, or like fleets at sea," and in contrast to rare trees, which stand like pagodas and shrines to be visited in both "summer and winter" (pp. 223–24), the Field family of Baker Farm has been reduced to the endless, futile toil of " 'bogging' for a neighboring farmer" (p. 227).

Leaving the Fields' roof "after the rain" (p. 229), the poet realizes anew that he must go forth to "fish and hunt far and wide day by day" in order to grow "wild" according to his nature (p. 230). "As I came home through the woods," he writes, "I caught a glimpse of a woodchuck . . . and felt a strange thrill of savage delight, and was strongly tempted to seize and devour him raw; not that I was hungry then, except for that wildness which he represented." Ironically, however, the poet's renewed hunger for the wild renews awareness that he must move beyond it. *Walden's* wildest scenes lead to "reverence" for the "spiritual" as well as the "savage." Having learned to "love the wild not less than the good," the poet moves on to "Higher Laws" (p. 232).

Coming from a life unnatural, barren, perverted, the poet has been forced, both in his first removal and in his subsequent return to Walden, deliberately to seek out what should be his freely.[16] Nature functions in *Walden,* however, not simply to fulfill but rather, through her own "greater scheme," to redefine the poet's experiment.[17] In the loon episode, where the loon intently plays its own "pretty game"—pitting itself against the poet, working with a plan of its own "quickly" and deliberately to lead him "to the widest part of the pond" (pp.

16. See W. B. Yeats, "The Lake Isle of Innisfree," *Collected Poems* (New York, Macmillan, 1956), p. 39.

17. *Writings, 7,* 136; *1,* 12. See *7,* 326–27, 344, 363.

259–60)—Thoreau mirrors the way nature works intently, in the first two movements of *Walden,* to lead him to fulfillment beyond his own great expectations. The loon episode in "Brute Neighbors"—the first chapter of the third and final movement of *Walden*—functions, in short, as a kind of synecdoche for the work's first two movements. But in Thoreau's effort to anticipate the loon's point of emergence from the pond and imitate its powers of penetrating the pond's depths, this episode introduces the thematic core of the final movement. In six successive chapters—"Brute Neighbors," "House-Warming," "Former Inhabitants; and Winter Visitors," "Winter Animals," "The Pond in Winter," and "Spring"—Thoreau celebrates the poetic imagination that makes possible his interpretation of his design and nature's greater scheme.

In "The Pond in Winter" and in "Spring," Thoreau rounds off his celebration of the penetrating and renewing power of the poetic imagination. Following the example of the loon, who "had time and ability to visit the bottom of the pond in its deepest part" (p. 260; see p. 328), the poet penetrates "the liquid and trembling surface of the pond" (p. 312). Having already looked down "into the quiet parlor of the fishes," where "a perennial waveless serenity reigns" (p. 313), the poet goes on to plumb and measure the depths of the pond.

> As I was desirous to recover the long lost bottom of Walden Pond, I surveyed it carefully, before the ice broke up, early in '46, with compass and chain and sounding line. There have been many stories told about the bottom . . . [But] Walden has a reasonably tight bottom at a not unreasonable, though at an unusual, depth. I fathomed it easily . . . The greatest depth was exactly one hundred and two feet . . . This is a remarkable depth for so small an area; yet not an inch of it can be spared by the imagination . . . I am thankful that this pond was made deep and pure for a symbol. (pp. 315–16)

Enabled to "determine the shape" and to "calculate the varia-
tion" (p. 318) of the pond's depths, the poet is trebly enriched.
He can map and chart Walden; he can use "this experience" to
make a "plan" of other ponds; and he can, by analogy, penetrate and explore man's own "depth and concealed bottom"
(pp. 319–21).

With the coming of "Spring"—which "is like the creation
of Cosmos out of Chaos and the realization of the Golden Age"
(p. 346; cf. pp. 268–69)—the third movement of *Walden*
attains a still finer height. "The brooks sing carols and glees to
the spring" (p. 342); "the grass-blade, like a long green ribbon,
streams from the sod . . . lifting its spear" with "fresh life"—
"the symbol of perpetual youth"; and the pond slowly comes
alive, from trembling surface to slumbering depths, until,
"sparkling in the sun" (pp. 343–44), it again contains and
nourishes and mirrors life. Like pond, leaf, and brook, the poet
exudes life. Seeing a "very slight and graceful hawk," the poet
rises with him; combining "nobleness and poetry," playing
"with proud reliance in the fields of air," he becomes sublime
in his "lofty tumbling." Having penetrated and measured the
pond in the winter, he blends, in spring, with the "tenant of
the air" who yet is "related to the earth" (pp. 348–49). As
from the sky the poet beholds the pond, a ribbon glistening in
the sun.

In his epilogue, "Conclusion," Thoreau extends the unity
of the thematic strands that make *Walden* what it is. The poet's
plan and the life to which it led, the quietly desperate village
that made necessary the planned return to the wild so that the
good might be recovered, and nature's commodious scheme
for leading the poet to higher reaches—each is recalled, each
has its place within the "Conclusion." But the correspondence
between the work of nature and the work of the poetic imagination is dominant. Just as the renewing encounter with the wild
led the poet beyond nature qua nature, so also does poetic
interpretation of the motive, plan, and character of the entire

Walden experience lead beyond that experience, first to discovery of "whole new continents and worlds within" (p. 353), and then beyond "an invisible boundary" to discovery of art (see p. 356). Deliberately simple, spontaneously extravagant nature coupled with deliberately simple, spontaneously extravagant planning and deliberately simple, spontaneously extravagant interpretation have, in consort, made possible discovery *"without* bounds"—"success unexpected in common hours" (pp. 357, 356).[18]

Such success—success unintended in the poet's design, success discovered under the auspices of nature and through the powers of poetic imagination—is the object of praise in *Walden.* The poet celebrates his experiment because it has lent itself to the imaginative interpretation that has redeemed it from time, making it "wonderful" (p. 360). In writing of the artist of the city of Kouroo, "who was disposed to strive after perfection"—disposed, that is, to strive to make a work into which vitiating "time [did] not enter" (p. 359)—Thoreau celebrates redeeming art. Here too he praises "humanity rather than" himself (see p. 55); he celebrates man's victory, through art, over human destiny. What Thoreau discovered in the making of *Walden* was that he, like "the astonished artist" of Kouroo, had achieved more than he had in the beginning dared to dream (p. 360). By subjecting his effort to achieve wholeness at Walden to poetic interpretation, he not only saved his designed dwelling from becoming "a splendid mausoleum" (p. 31); he made "a world with full and fair proportions" (p. 360), and thus vindicated "man's struggle to free himself" from failure (p. 41), man's struggle to conceive and construct a world fecund and charged yet shaped and ordered.

In 1838, a little more than ten years before Thoreau concluded his Walden experiment, Henry Brooks Adams was born

18. On exaggeration as a means of translating experience into "poetry" and therefore into "truth," see *Writings, 7,* 411–12.

into a family that, like Franklin and far more than Thoreau, stressed social, political life. In the public arena, the Adamses found the proper scene for working out their plans and experiments. In the course of following his inherited plan, Henry Adams met with what he finally came to regard as failure. In 1907 he published privately a work, *The Education of Henry Adams,* in which he seeks, like Thoreau in *Walden,* "to free himself" from the consequences of failure. In the *Education* Henry Adams seeks to invest with "the dignity of tragedy" the life in which he has "missed the dignity of [high] office."[19] At the same time, however, he seeks to find in the poetic life of investing unexpected failure with meaning a kind of success that he has never expected, intended, or foreseen. Which is to say that, if the *Education* does not, like *Walden,* exactly move beyond tragic failure to comic success, it at least interlaces the two. In the process of that interlacing, moreover, Adams finds in his experience, in his meetings with failure and success, what Thoreau barely looked for in his experience: namely, as we shall see, a kind of paradigm of the story of America, and beyond America, of the Western world, perhaps even of mankind.

19. See Alfred Kazin, *On Native Grounds: An Interpretation of Modern American Prose Literature* (New York, Reynal and Hitchcock, 1942), p. 21.

6 Apotheosis of the Form: Henry Adams' *Education*

> *The day shall come, that great avenging day,*
> *When Troy's proud glories in the dust shall lay,*
> *When Priam's powers and Priam's self shall fall,*
> *And one prodigious ruin swallow all.*
>
> > Homer, The Iliad (in Pope's translation)
>
> *it is great*
> *To do that thing that ends all other deeds,*
> *Which shackles accidents and bolts up change.*
>
> > William Shakespeare, Anthony and Cleopatra

The Education of Henry Adams represents Henry Adams' effort, with a labor of the imagination, to offset the destructive work of "wasteful Time";[1] it is his effort to render his self, his heritage, and the complexly troubled relation between them inviolable. The *Education* grew, moreover, out of deliberate appropriation of autobiography as a literary form. The work's proper subtitle is, to be sure, "A Study in Twentieth-Century Multiplicity," not "An Autobiography," but as early as January 1883 the urge to tell his story had established itself in Adams'

---

1. William Shakespeare, Sonnet 15, ll. 11–14.

consciousness. "I am clear," he wrote John Hay, "that you should write autobiography. I mean to do mine."[2] Moreover, to Adams autobiography meant not a loose memoir but a distinct art form with distinct problems and possibilities. In the Preface of 1907, he places his work in a tradition defined by Rousseau and Franklin. Later, in his Editor's Preface, he compares his work with *The Confessions of St. Augustine,* which he had praised, in a letter of February 1908 to William James, as a work shaped by a definite "idea of literary form." Augustine, as Adams saw him, was preeminent as an artist in autobiography because he had a "notion of writing a story with an end and object, not for the sake of the object, but for the form, like a romance."[3] In short, like its companion piece, *Mont-Saint-Michel and Chartres,* which is an extended piece of praise to a "method" that had inspired art of "singular unity," the *Education* is a monument to Adams' devotion to "form."[4] The one Adams toward whom all other Adamses in the *Education* muddle and grope is the artist as "weary Titan of Unity" —the artist as one cognizant that man's problem, "From cradle to grave," is the peculiarly and preeminently human problem "of running order through chaos, direction through space, discipline through freedom; unity through multiplicity."[5]

2. Letter to John Hay, January 1883, in Worthington C. Ford, ed., *Letters of Henry Adams, 1858–1918* (2 vols. Boston and New York, Houghton Mifflin, 1930–38), *1,* 347. On the problem of the *Education* as autobiography, see Ernest Samuels, *The Young Henry Adams* (Cambridge, Mass., Harvard University Press, 1948), p. ix.

3. Letter to William James, February 1908, Ford, *Letters, 2,* 490. See Sayre, *The Examined Self,* pp. 7–10; and J. C. Levenson, *The Mind and Art of Henry Adams* (Boston, Houghton Mifflin, 1957), p. 306.

4. Henry Adams, *Mont-Saint-Michel and Chartres* [1904] (Boston and New York, Houghton Mifflin, 1913), pp. 382–83. This work is hereafter cited as *Chartres.*

5. Henry Adams, *The Education of Henry Adams* [1907] (Boston and New York, Houghton Mifflin, 1918), pp. 455, 12. All page references in the text of this chapter are to this work.

There is more behind the *Education,* however, than appreciation of the devotion of the Middle Ages to "organic unity
both in . . . thought and in . . . building."[6] Haunted by what he
took to be a widening gap between available fact and acceptable
truth, the Adams of the *Education* is seeking poetically to use
facts in order aesthetically to overcome tension between truth
and fact. Late in the *Education,* in the tone that made Brooks
Adams suspect Henry of never being "quite frank with himself
or with others,"[7] Adams remarks that no historian who "values
his honesty" can at all afford concern for truth; the historian
who "cares for his truths," Adams asserts, "is certain to falsify
his facts" (p. 457). Aware that the men of his day were called
to live between the reigns of different forms of ordered meaning, in what was theologically an interim and politically an
interregnum, Adams sought to explore the problems and possibilities thus created. What did it mean to live in an era in
which concern for fact as available and accepted datum had to
be kept apart from concern for truth as ordered and acceptable
meaning? For us, Adams says in *Chartres,* "the poetry is history, and the facts are false." In terms of the tension thus
established between truth as meaning and facts as data, the
Education is concerned with truth, not with fact, with poetry,
not with history. To borrow again from its companion volume,
"the world" of the *Education* is "not a schoolroom or a pulpit,
but a stage."[8]

In part because it is more a stage than a schoolroom or
pulpit, and in part because it is both an autobiography and a
companion volume to *Mont-Saint-Michel and Chartres,* the
Education is fabulously complex. In its early stages it unfolds

6. *Chartres,* p. 380.
7. Brooks Adams, "The Heritage of Henry Adams," introduction to
Henry Adams, *The Degradation of the Democratic Dogma* (New York,
Macmillan, 1919), p. 1.
8. *Chartres,* pp. 226, 108.

as the story of a boy strangely born under the shadow and consecrated to the service of a distinct family heritage: "Had he been born in Jerusalem under the shadow of the Temple and circumcised in the Synagogue by his uncle the high priest, under the name of Israel Cohen, he would scarcely have been more distinctly branded" (p. 3). What complicates the *Education,* however, even more than Adams' sense of his finely textured heritage, is the distance he pushes his story beyond the personal.

The vision that defined the Adams heritage derived, at least in its most impressive form, not from the first Henry, who arrived in Massachusetts in 1636, but from the later Henry's great-grandfather and the family's first President. Writing from Paris during the Revolution, John Adams defined for his family his sacred duty: "I could fill volumes with descriptions of temples and palaces, paintings [and] sculptures . . . but I could not do this without neglecting my duty. The science of government it is my duty to study, more than all other sciences; the arts of legislation and administration and negotiation ought to take place of, indeed to exclude, in a manner, all other arts."[9] The Adams men sought, it should be stressed, to be commodious. But they were essentially men of action. Having allotted certain room for the life of the mind, they gave themselves to political concerns: they approached life, as Adams remarks in the *Education,* as something to be reformed. They understood themselves to be makers of history.

Having acknowledged the political bias of the Adams family, however, John Adams went on to define the Adams notion of the American experiment. "I must study politics and war," he continued, "that my sons may have liberty to study mathematics and philosophy," and that "their children" may be free

9. Letter to Abigail Adams, 1780, in Charles F. Adams, ed., *Familiar Letters of John Adams and His Wife Abigail Adams* (New York, 1875), p. 381.

"to study painting, poetry, music, architecture."[10] As the generations passed, however, the Adamses did not move from politics to philosophy to art. Personal inclination, inbred and encouraged, as well as social developments, led them to retrace John Adams' pattern of dedication rather than follow the specifications of his vision.[11] It was in the fourth rather than the third generation, and it was only after the revised version of John Adams' vision had been completely disrupted, that an Adams—Henry Adams—was able, by moving from politics to philosophy to art, and by giving himself to the task of filling "volumes with descriptions of temples and palaces," to realize the original Adams vision. In the meantime, the Adamses remained distinctly political. "There are two things," the young Henry wrote to his brother Charles Francis, in 1858, "that seem to be at the bottom of our constitutions; one is a continual tendency towards politics; the other is family pride." John Quincy no less than John, and Charles Francis no less than John Quincy, gave priority to the science of government and the art of politics. And neither Henry nor the younger Charles Francis doubted that "the family bent" was political genius.[12]

At its most specific, the Adams heritage means to the Henry of the *Education* that he must become President. In the *Education* John Quincy stands simply as "the President"—and concomitantly, as at once the epitome of the Adams type and as

---

10. Ibid. Cf. Turner, *The Frontier in American History,* pp. 261–63, for a related formulation in a very different context by a very different man.

11. See Levenson, pp. 5–8.

12. Henry Adams, Letters to Charles Francis Adams, Jr., November 1858 and November 1867, Ford, *Letters, 1,* 5, 136. Note in the first of these letters Adams' clear sense that he is to find his triumph in "what never entered into [his] calculations; Art." Note too that this notion derives from Adams' first deep encounter with accidental education.

America's "only picture of a full grown statesman."[13] What is required of Henry as an Adams is that he become within his context what John Quincy had been in his.

Two early episodes in the *Education*, one at the ancestral home in Quincy and one at the White House in Washington, make clear what is expected of an Adams as an Adams. The Irish gardener, we are told in the first chapter, "once said to the child: 'You'll be thinkin' you'll be President too!' " To the young Adams—a boy accustomed "to sit behind a President grandfather, and to read over his head the tablet in memory of a President great-grandfather, who had 'pledged his life, his fortune, and his sacred honor' " to the political dream of his country—what is new in the gardener's casual remark is not the idea of being President, not the idea that what "had been would continue to be," that a live tradition "would outlast one Adams more." On the contrary, what made the episode so new that the boy "never forgot it" was "that there should be a doubt of his being President" (pp. 15–16). When Henry is taken for the first time to see the White House and to meet President Taylor, the boy's sensation of his ascendancy again is stressed. The interpreting Adams can find in himself as boy "no sense of strangeness" on meeting the President, nor any basis for such sensation. "The President was friendly," the White House familiar. Confronted with a place where "all [his] family had lived," and where, "barring the eight years of Andrew Jackson's reign, [they] had been more or less at home . . . ever since it was built," the boy knows neither awe nor estrangement: he "half thought he owned it, and took for granted that he should some day live in it" (p. 46).

The complexity of Adams' fate, as it is depicted within the *Education,* is a function of his becoming, in relation to his

13. Charles Francis Adams, Sr., Letter to Charles Francis Adams, Jr., November 1861, in Worthington C. Ford, ed., *A Cycle of Adams Letters, 1861–1865* (2 vols. Boston and New York, Houghton Mifflin, 1920), *1,* 67.

inherited designation, a variant. From one point of view Adams, when he stands starkly as an Adams, is forever a failure. More precisely, he is forever a failed statesman. Even before we have followed the working out of the Adams design, we know that Henry "never got to the point of playing the game at all" (p. 4). We know that the older Henry is not at all what the small boy assumed that he would be and intended that he should become; for we know that he is writing as an imaginative, interpreting autobiographer and not, like John Adams as he appears in the *Education,* as a great statesman and President collecting his papers and compiling his memoirs.

Although perhaps less drastic than the *Education* suggests, Henry Adams' case, even in a context dominated by the decline of his family's fortune, was in fact extreme. In a line of four generations and among four brothers, he stood alone in never having completed preparation in the law and never having held public office.[14] It w   the quality of his commitment to looking on, however, that   most to make Adams a variant of the family type. A   oent was in fact intellectual and artistic. Despite his activistic heritage   me gradually to subordinate and finally to sacrifice statesmanship to his work as teacher, historian, journalist, and n   and then to his culminating endeavor as imaginative autobiographer. The *Education* accordingly stands in part as the story of failure to attain a high designation. Its hero is, on one side, a failed statesman. But the *Education* is also the story of how its strange hero remained a true Adams by becoming the interpreter and orderer of his failure: how the failed-statesman-turned-poet learned not only to reflect, in the tone of his telling, the character of his curious failure and the paradox of victory beyond defeat, but also fully to explore and discover the significance of his own experience.

Adams' personal story is, in its own way, complexly pat-

14. See Levenson, pp. 4, 6.

terned. But the *Education* takes us far beyond the personal, and in so doing becomes even more complex. The scene shifts from Quincy and Boston to Mount Vernon and Washington, from the White House to Harvard College, from Massachusetts to Berlin and Rome, from Washington to London; it carries us around the globe, takes us back to the Middle Ages, and leads us finally to a cosmic theory; and, as the action shifts and expands, images begin to swarm and problems to bristle. The critical issue, put bluntly, is that of unity. How can a single work move freely from family heritage to national scene, from politics and history to science and religion, from life to art, from the story of a self to a theory of history, coherently within the framework of autobiography?

What is vital is definition of the way Adams makes history a source of complexity in his personal story. The *Education* is essentially the story of Adams' relation to an inherited design that he failed to realize in life yet managed to redeem through an interpretive narrative. As such, the *Education* is a study of ironical failure and paradoxical success. In moving from formal student to apprentice statesman, from journalist-reformer to historian, from philosopher to artist, however, Adams fulfills and even surpasses Tocqueville's prediction that America would become the subject of American poetry.[15] By linking American history to modern Western developments, thus making American history a peculiarly "modern instance," and by linking the reversal of the political fortunes of the Adams family to the transformation of the American nation, thus making the Adams story a peculiarly American case, Adams manages to interlace the destiny of his inherited design and of himself as its inheritor with the course of both American and modern history. He wants somehow to establish a relation—he wants somehow to suggest an analogy— first between his story and America's story, and then between

15. Tocqueville, *Democracy in America,* 2, 78–79.

these stories and man's history. The Adams who sits on the steps of Santa Maria d'Aracoeli in Rome contemplating the ruins of two civilizations is also the Adams who lies on Wenlock Edge meditating the disruption of the kingdom of Siluria, the decline of the Middle Ages, and the possible disintegration of the modern world, just as he is the Adams who ponders the political decline of the Adams family and the political transformation of the American nation. What is more, the final, interpreting Adams insists that each of the problems thus contemplated and meditated and pondered is at last the same problem—the problem, namely, of whether man's effort, through action, to build acording to the specifications of his needs and visions, according to "the beautiful circuit and subterfuge of [his] thought and [his] desire,"[16] must always end in ruins; and, concomitantly, of whether it is possible for man, through thought, to give significant and meaningful answer to this most human of problems.

Conscious, like Whitman's poet-hero, of having descended from "parents born here from parents the same, and their parents the same,"[17] the hero of the *Education* places himself within the context of a live tradition: he sees himself as having become, by age ten, the "priest and politician" of his family's "plan" (pp. 22, 88). But Adams discovers the universal through the particular. As Henry Brooks Adams—as one born "Under the shadow of Boston State House" and "christened . . . after the tenets of Boston Unitarianism"—the feels himself "distinctly branded" (p. 3); but as "HENRICUS ADAMS / ADAE FILIUS ET EVAE" (p. 368)—as one confident that what "had lasted since Adam would outlast one Adams more" (p. 16)—Adams also sees himself as a fit and proper representative of the modern predicament. His problem, as he pictures it, is not

16. Blackmur, ed., *The Art of the Novel,* pp. 31–32.
17. Walt Whitman, "Song of Myself," l. 7 of the final version of the poem, in *Leaves of Grass,* ed. Harold W. Blodgett and Sculley Bradley (New York, New York University Press, 1965), p. 29.

his only—nor his fate. He finds in his experience meaning that is deeply without being simply personal. The connections and relations he is able to establish begin with himself and his origins, with each of the selves, active and contemplative, that he has been and become. But they end nowhere. Adams' story is inexhaustible because it reaches out to touch America's story, and Rome's and Christianity's. What is specifically Adamsesque is peculiarly American and archetypally human.

Since the purpose of all Adamsesque education is to learn humanely "to control power" (p. 36), what is vital to an Adams is that he learn to respond to his natural and historical environment with certain intelligence—that is, "with vigor and economy" and control, "not at haphazard, but by choice" (p. 314). An Adams, as a type, is an inveterate reformer. The structure of the Adams design defines the poles of the Adams world. On one side, the Adams family holds fast to the ancestral home at Quincy, to the distinctly humane and familial, and yet, as Henry elsewhere suggested, gravitates toward the White House in Washington, toward the distinctly political and national.[18] It is because "for numberless generations" the Adams family has "viewed the world chiefly as a thing to be reformed" that the "unchanged" duty of each Adams is political. Henry Adams takes "education politically" because the design that defines his heritage is based on "the law" or "the principle of resistance"—because it has been devised for statesmen, dedicated to public service, and therefore founded on subordination of writing and scholarship, indeed of all observing-interpreting endeavors, to active political life (pp. 7, 43, 7, 21).

In contrast, the ideal represented by Henry's Brooks side— by his middle name and his Boston and winter side—is simple,

18. See Adams, Letter to Charles Milnes Gaskell, November 1877, Ford, *Letters of Henry Adams, 1*, 302.

full acceptance by man of himself as a creature of nature and history. From this perspective the vital lesson is of course very different: man must learn successfully to adapt himself to his context. Survival and, even more, success require that man content himself with being a product of forces that transcend and control him, that he accept himself as a product of forces, biological and physiological, economic and political, to which, though he cannot shape and control them, he can attune himself. Although he is as "kind and benevolent" as the Adams grandfather, the Brooks grandfather represents those eighteenth-century tendencies Adams renders as having become dominant in the interim nineteenth century (pp. 10–11). The Brooks plea is a plea for survival and success. The Brookses speak in the name of forces that reward adaptation but oppose resistance, foredooming every effort through reform specifically to shape the world according to man's vision. As an Adams, "as a child of Quincy," Henry not only is "not a true Bostonian" (p. 19); he also is incapable of caring "for nineteenth-century style" (p. 11). "Time and experience" work gradually to encourage "gentler judgment" of the Brooks world; but even when he was "only ten years old, his face was already fixed, and his heart was stone, against State Street" (p. 25).

The whole of Adams' world enforces one lesson—the reliability of his heritage. His inherited ideas and values will "be alone respected" because they are "alone respectable." The "problem of life" accordingly is as simple as it is classic: "moral law" provides "a sure guide" to politics, and social perfection is "also sure" because man, by virtue of the beneficence of his ends and the magnitude of his power, can be trusted to work "for Good." In all such instruction, however, the boy's world conspires "to deceive and betray" him (p. 33). Adams' fate thus is sealed. On one side, he cannot relinquish his heritage; he is incapable of renouncing "his ancestral prejudices, his abstract ideals, his semi-clerical training, and the rest, in order to perform an expiatory pilgrimage to State Street, and ask for the fatted calf of his grandfather Brooks and a clerkship in the Suffolk Bank" (p. 22). But on the other side, he finds himself forced to live in a world increasingly dominated by the Brooks law of adaptation. The rails from distant cities, the steamers from foreign lands, and "the telegraphic messages" announcing the nominations of Clay and Polk "suddenly cut" Adams off from his "eighteenth-century, troglodytic" world (p. 5).

The *Education,* as a personal story, is the story of an Adamsesque boy forced to work out his fate in a Brooksean world. The action of Henry's father establishes a pattern that links Henry's fate to other fates. The effort of the elder Charles Francis to preserve the Adams heritage, first by insisting that leaders be "statesmen, not politicians" (p. 32; cf. p. 112), and second by insisting that men sacrifice wealth and material success to concern for intelligent action guided by humane principles, that they subordinate expediency to the implementation of moral principles, reflects the father's grappling with a problem that the son later makes his own. In the father's support of the Free Soil Party, the character, relevance, and fate of the Adams vision is at stake. The year of that support, the year 1848, was decisive for the "boy's road through life . . . for twenty years to come" (p. 25)—it "violently affected his character" (p. 29)—precisely because it reestablished a pattern of struggle, a "law" or "principle of resistance" (pp. 7, 21).

Throughout the *Education,* Adams' problem—of learning to be loyal to his family's mission and yet fully accept "the stamp that belonged to [his] time" (p. 26)—follows the lines set by his father. The threat to which the Free Soil Party constitutes a response leads in the *Education* to the threat posed by "contradictions." When Mr. Adams takes him to Mount Vernon, the young Adams experiences for the first time a rough, unfinished road. To the boy the "moral of this Virginia road" is easily learned: "Slavery was wicked, and slavery was the cause of this road's badness." But what lies altogether beyond the boy's understanding is how Mount Vernon could stand "at the end of the road," how George Washington could be the "product of the crime." In response to such "contradictions," in answer to the inexplicable and imponderable, the young Adams can only "repeat what he [is] told—that George Washington stood alone." But the interpreting Adams, in contrast, sees Mount Vernon in a context that makes the issue acute. Whereas all "other points shifted their bearings," taking on "varied lights" and assuming "new relations," Washington's home remained dependably fixed: it "always remained where it was, with no practicable road to reach it; and yet, when he got there, Mount Vernon was only Quincy in a Southern setting" (pp. 47–48). As a human ideal of a humanely ordered world, Mount Vernon is to the South as Quincy is to State Street: in the *Education,* as in James' *The Wings of the Dove,* the ideal—of charged and fecund multiplicity within ordered and directed unity—stands somehow before man "like a temple without an avenue."[19]

From Quincy and Mount Vernon the circle of the incongruous widens. Both at Harvard College and in Germany planned efforts to make Adams a statesman, to make him an orderer of the world he must meet, are foiled. Far from preparing him for statesmanship, Harvard, at least as seen in retrospect, tends slowly to turn his "violent political bias" (p. 60). And in Europe "the curious and perplexing result of the total failure of German education [is] that the student's only clear gain" has nothing to do with Civil Law, but rather is "accidental, unintended, unforeseen" (p. 80).

It is in Rome, however, that the first phase of Adams' education culminates. For it is there that he loses "his simple-minded faith" in the efficacy of human "intentions" (p. 83). To the young man who arrives in Rome in 1859, still "seeking education in a serious spirit" and still "taking for granted . . . that nature tended" to a meaningful "end," the ancient city repre-

19. Henry James, *The Wings of the Dove* [1902], *The Novels and Tales of Henry James* (26 vols. New York, Scribner, 1907–17), *19,* 59.

sents "altogether the most violent vice in the world" (p. 89).
Far from answering the need that has brought him to Rome,
far from providing education for a life of statesmanship, the
ruins of Rome can only leave him unfit "for every sort of useful activity." Beyond the power of any "young Bostonian" by
vent of "reason or common sense" to anticipate, Rome piles
up "conundrum after conundrum in his educational path,"
multiplying things "unconnected . . . that he had got to con-
nect" and things "insoluble" that had "to be somehow solved"
(p. 90).

No more "a beetle to be dissected and dropped" than a bad
novel to be read and discarded, Rome, in retrospect, as the
interpreting Adams sees it, yields itself neither to the penetrating power of "cheap imagination" nor to the ordering power
of "cheaper politics" (pp. 90–91, 93). All problematical issues
lead to its political and religious ruins, which teach neither
meaning nor even sequence but only the futility of all human
endeavor.

> Rome was actual; it was England; it was going to be
> America. Rome could not be fitted into an orderly,
> middle-class, Bostonian, systematic scheme of evolution.
> No law of progress applied to it. Not even time-sequences
> —the last refuge of helpless historians—had value for it.
> The Forum no more led to the Vatican than the Vatican
> to the Forum. Rienzi, Garibaldi, Tiberius Gracchus,
> Aurelian might be mixed up in any relation of time, along
> with a thousand more, and never lead to a sequence. The
> great word Evolution had not yet, in 1860, made a new
> religion of history, but the old religion had preached the
> same doctrine for a thousand years without finding in the
> entire history of Rome anything but flat contradiction.
> (p. 91)

The tension between Rome's ruins and man's needs makes
universal a problem that has been personal and familial and

that is going, with the Civil War, to become national. Though "bitterly denied" by "priests and evolutionists," tension and incongruity—tension between the finite "doings of man" and the infinite forces at work to raze them and incongruity between what man has endeavored with "the most excellent intentions" to do and what he has done—are the primary features of the world of the *Education* (pp. 91, 90, 84). If "no one"—if neither "priest [nor] politician"—can "honestly read in the [religious and political] ruins of Rome any other certain lesson than that they were evidence of the just judgments of an outraged God" or of the just triumph of inhuman forces "against all the doings of man," then man must reconcile himself to living in a world in which he can never hope to see his will prevail (p. 90).

Faced with deep and wide resistance—confronted with a world in which every experience and fact, including his own aesthetic and intellectual bent, has "conspired to ruin his sound scheme of life, and to make him a vagrant as well as pauper" (p. 93)—Adams moves toward the interpretive role. Confronted with Gibbon's question ("the eternal question:—Why!"), he takes it to himself: "No one ever had answered the question to the satisfaction of any one else; yet every one who had either head or heart, felt that sooner or later he must make up his mind what answer to accept. Substitute the word America for the word Rome, and the question became personal" (p. 92). In short, if the "bewildering complex of ideas, experiments, ambitions, energies" represented by the ruins of Rome remain meaningless, then "the Western world" is "pointless and fragmentary" and Adams' ruined "scheme of life" is representative. In entertaining the possibility that Rome finally means "nothing," Adams accordingly faces the possibility that human existence—personal, national, universal—is unrelieved "nightmare" (pp. 93, 83).

As history becomes increasingly "tortured," as the widening circle of the problematic moves out to encompass both politics ("the ruins of the Capitol" of Rome) and religion (the "stupendous failure of Christianity"), the problem of interpretation, the problem of finding meaning in man's impotence, can only become increasingly "fascinating" and "vital" (pp. 472, 91). As seen by the interpreting Adams, the young Adams is drawn by the image of Gibbon—who, as he sat "in the Church" "musing . . . on the ruins of the Capitol," had conceived "the idea of writing the Decline and Fall of the city" (p. 91). But in Adams' world man's failure to build eternal edifices is matched by his failure to comprehend that failure—his failure, through interpretation, to harness tension, master contradiction, and overcome incongruity. Indeed, it is only when the range of "unsolved" "mystery"—the circle of the problematic—widens to encompass not only design and action but interpretation as well that Adams becomes fully engaged. As he goes again and again "to sit at sunset on the steps of the Church of Santa Maria di Ara Coeli," he sees not only ruins but failed interpretation; he sees that "not an inch had been gained by Gibbon—or all the historians since—towards explaining the Fall" (p. 91).

Following the culminating chapter on "Rome" and the first decisive sessions on the steps of the Church where he ponders "the chief monuments of [the] failure" of the "two great experiments of Western civilization," Adams returns to America to find "Treason" rapidly wrecking a third experiment (pp. 91, 98). In Rome everything has "conspired to ruin his sound scheme of life" (p. 93). In Quincy he sees "an unknown energy" playfully disrupting "his generation," dispossessing his family, and transforming his nation. No one, Adams writes, had "planned"—no one had "wanted . . . or expected or intended" —the Civil War (p. 98). Coming inexplicably out of efforts to achieve harmony and live in peace, the war disrupts domestic concord, muddles foreign relations, and stifles the growth of a people dedicated to a democratic dream.

The second phase of Adams' apprenticeship as a statesman

is defined, despite growing preoccupation with the question of Rome, by his plunge into the "lurid atmosphere of politics" (p. 98). During the years of civil crisis, however, Adams is only partially caught up in helping his father serve the Adams mission of making history. Because he cannot quiet his need to uncover meaning in the history he sees unfolding in Washington, he is doubly employed, as his father's private secretary and, in secret, as a "newspaper correspondent." Seeing only "cross-purpose," he finds Washington "a dismal school" for one seeking lessons in meaningful order (pp. 106, 100, 108): "no one could teach; all were as ignorant as himself; . . . all were trying to learn and were more bent on asking than on answering questions. The mass of ignorance in Washington was lighted by no ray of knowledge. Society, from top to bottom, broke down" (p. 106).

Following his father abroad, in service to a broken society and in conscious imitation of his father and grandfather before him, Adams learns again that the makers of history have no prescience of the courses they are following. The widened horizon brings "endless waves of confusion," not new understanding (p. 115; see p. 113). The lessons of "Diplomacy" and "Political Morality" serve to muddle, not to clarify (pp. 110, 145). "The true issue"—the significance of man's "intent"—resists solution, promoting "sheer chaos" (pp. 151, 153). The men whom Adams sees making history are no less ignorant—they are no less the "victims of blindness"—than the "young and insignificant" men who watch and study them (p. 154).

Standing for once in a moment of great crisis "at the centre of action, with his hands actually touching the lever of power" (p. 210), Adams finds that intelligent and directed action, action informed and controlled by coherent vision, is impossible. Later, through interpretation, he finds that what he had accepted as understanding also had been confused. Even in retrospect the interpreting mind finds only past failure: it sees only the fact of error in its earlier understanding, not new pattern. What is available to sight signifies nothing save its own impenetrability: "All the world had been at cross-purposes, had misunderstood themselves and the situation, had followed wrong paths, drawn wrong conclusions. . . . One would have done better to draw no conclusions at all. One's diplomatic education was a long mistake" (pp. 161–62). Even with works of art, works of his own hands, man's understanding is not reliable. Dealers and curators, critics and artists alike consistently fail to concur in the information—pertaining to value and meaning, and even to authorship and date—that they give Adams.

Central throughout the second phase of Adams' apprenticeship as a statesman, the search for new certainty reaches its climax in the chapter on "Darwinism." During the dark, lingering winter of 1867–68, "Darwin was convulsing society" with a "safe, conservative, practical" "substitute for religion"—that is, with "ideas" that "seemed to lead . . . to some great generalization which would finish one's clamor to be educated" (pp. 224–25). "Steady, uniform, unbroken evolution" met man's need for "Unity and Uniformity," assuring him of large meaning and order. Yet, in Housman's Shropshire, "on the Wenlock Edge of time," when Adams comes "to look south along the Edge to the abode of [man's] earliest ancestor and nearest relative," when he comes to ponder the meaning of "the ganoid fish, whose name, according to Professor Huxley, was *Pteraspis,* a cousin of the sturgeon, and whose kingdom, according to Sir Roderick Murchison, was called Siluria" (pp. 226, 229), he finds that, on Wenlock as in Rome, with the natural order as with the historical world, imponderability is the given.

> Ponder over it as he might, Adams could see nothing in the theory of Sir Charles but pure inference, precisely like the inference of Paley. . . . He could detect no more evolution in life since the *Pteraspis* than he could detect it in

architecture since the Abbey. All he could prove was
change. . . .

All this seemed trivial to the true Darwinian, and to Sir
Charles it was mere defect in the geological record. . . .
[But Adams] could prove only Evolution that did not
evolve; Uniformity that was not uniform; and Selection
that did not select. To [others] . . . it was a form of religious hope; a promise of ultimate perfection. Adams
wished no better; he warmly sympathized in the object;
but when he came to ask himself what he truly thought,
he felt that he had no Faith. (pp. 230–31)

The discussion of "Darwinism" finally leads Adams from the
dead kingdom of Siluria and the ruined Abbey of Wenlock
back to Rome, the ultimate scene of inquiry into the problematic. "In February, 1868, he was back in Rome" to sit
"once more on the steps of Ara Coeli, as had become with him
almost a superstition." Still tragic and solemn and haunted,
Rome is haunting as well: "The long ten years . . . had changed
nothing for him there. He knew no more in 1868 than in 1858.
He had learned nothing whatever that made Rome more intelligible to him, or made life easier to handle" (pp. 235–36).

In England, even before Darwin's prodigious entrance into
the story, Adams had foreseen a changed and changing
America in a world moving "beyond connection with the past."
And he had anticipated in himself the need to overcome his
disjointed life and "to spin a new web in some new place with
a new attachment." With the course pursued by his father no
longer open to him, as a "literary survivor" of a wrecked political plan, only one profession—"the press"—"seemed possible" to him. Perhaps from this "inferior pulpit" he still could
make sense of the Adams heritage of resistance and reform;
and perhaps in seeking to salvage his own heritage and to work
out his own fate, he could help America to salvage her in-

heritance and realize and understand her destiny (pp. 209–11; see pp. 237, 240–45).

Thus begins the third—the independent—phase of Adams' education as a statesman. He becomes a "young reformer." Soon, however, he finds himself in a world that continues increasingly to give itself to the Brooksean way—a world in which "the State Department had ceased to be the centre . . . and the Treasury had taken its place," and in which reform is rapidly becoming obsolete. For a time, to be sure, Adams finds himself "more at home than he ever had been before, or was ever to be again." Seeing that "the whole government . . . was alive with them," he feels "as though he and his friends [own the] administration" (pp. 245, 247, 249). But the advent of Grant—whom Adams and "four-fifths of the American people" had appointed to "the task of bringing the Government back to regular practices, and of restoring moral and mechanical order"—cuts "short the life which Adams had laid out for himself in the future." Although "Grant's intention had been one of reform," his action smashes Adams' plan (pp. 260, 262, 263). "To the end of his life, [Adams] wondered at the suddenness of the revolution which . . . changed his intended future into an absurdity so laughable as to make him ashamed of it. . . . He had made another total misconception of life—another inconceivable false start. Yet, unlikely as it seemed, he had missed his motive narrowly, and his intention had been more than sound" (p. 262).

The social, political "Chaos" met by the "young reformer" and "man of action" (pp. 245, 284–85) is matched by the chaos he promptly meets in the natural order. "The last lesson" —"sum and term of education"—comes when Adams confronts the struggle between evanescent life and eternal death. In Italy he finds his sister "as gay and brilliant in the terrors of lockjaw as she had been in the careless fun of 1859" (p. 287). As he watches her muscles grow rigid while her mind remains bright, as he watches her endure ten days' torture only to die in convulsions, Adams can feel only the impossibility of man's contest with nature.[20]

> The first serious consciousness of Nature's gesture—her attitude towards life—took form then as a phantasm, a nightmare, an insanity of force. For the first time, the stage-scenery of the senses collapsed; the human mind felt itself stripped naked, vibrating in a void of shapeless energies, with resistless mass, colliding, crushing, wasting, and destroying what these same energies had created and labored from eternity to perfect. (p. 288)

As if to match nature's "chaos of anarchic and purposeless forces," society and history become "fantastic"—"a vision of pantomime"—and then give way to the "catastrophe," the "full chaos" of war in Europe (pp. 288–90).

Having failed as a young reformer, as "a man of action," to order man's present, Adams returns to the problem of the past. In an effort to make sense of the "tangled skein" of man's story, he becomes a professional historian (pp. 285, 302). Because none of his "many experiments" in teaching and interpreting history "wholly" succeeds (p. 304), however, he comes to feel that full success is impossible. The problem of the past, the question of Rome, remains. History will not yield its secret core to man's probing; whatever full, final meaning its surface of facts may shroud remains hid from man's gross eyes. To the end it presents itself as in "essence incoherent and immoral"; and to the end it has "either to be taught as such—or falsified" (p. 301). Adams finds that he must teach either historical facts that are inhuman or human truths that are unhistorical.

Adams' "Failure" as a writer and teacher of history completes his move from an activistic to an intellectual posture. In shifting from various efforts actively to serve the Adams mis-

---

20. See Adams' Letters to Charles Milnes Gaskell, July 1870, Ford, *Letters of Henry Adams, 1,* 188–91.

sion and follow the Adams pattern, Henry Adams moves, not toward the Brooks way of simple accommodation, though adjustment is involved, but rather to a radical redefinition of the Adams heritage. Life, Adams writes, echoing the apocalyptic vision in Revelation, "had been cut in halves, and the old half had passed away" (pp. 299, 317). What Adams promptly commences to seek and move toward is harmony and unity in which all that is worn will somehow be made new and all that is at war, within and among men, and between man and his world, will somehow be lifted into new harmony. In short, he moves toward resolution and vision that are aesthetic, not political; the new heaven and earth are the promise, not of life, but of art. Having bypassed twenty active years, of which he says simply that he "performed" his duties and settled "his account with society" (pp. 315–16), Adams concerns himself with perfection of understanding. The effort directly to order life is left to Clarence King and John Hay. While King seeks to tame the natural order—to chart its past and uncover its secrets, to organize surveys and "induce Congress to adopt" programs designed to increase man's control over the natural world (p. 312)—and while Hay seeks to order history—to tame the chaos of the political world and bind the members of the world community with treaties—Adams becomes a philosopher and then a philosophical artist. Though still an Adams in the most basic of all senses, though still a weary titan of unity and order, Adams must now specifically grapple with the question of Rome, with the problem encountered on the steps of Aracoeli.

Adams' effort to run order through chaos, to bring harmony to tension, rhythm to contradiction, and form to incongruity, leads, first, to his philosophy of history, and second, to his decision, by writing the *Education,* to make his search for order an imaginative quest.

When Adams begins his story "Twenty Years After," he, Clarence King, and John Hay already have become "in-

separable" (pp. 314, 321); and already they have begun con-
certedly to serve and to increase the thin, disorganized ranks
of the orderers (see p. 315). Throughout the second movement
of the *Education,* this triumvirate is central. What Adams says
apropos of King clearly applies as well to Hay. What is shared
among the three is not only "a certain parallelism of life, a
community of thought, [and] a rivalry of aim"; they also face
"the same problems" and have "the same obstacles to overcome" (p. 312).

The three friends' search for order is an odyssey that leads
"further and further into a wilderness where twilight is short
and the shadows are dense" (p. 395). It is altered first by the
disappearance of King. The story of King is the story of man's
preoccupation with the scene and context of his habitation.
What is at stake is man's ability, through science, deliberately
to control nature. As a mortal man engaged with the immortal
chaos of nature, however, King is born to die. Like James'
Milly Theale, he is blessed with inexhaustible resources for life
and an illimitable desire to live, yet he carries within him the
seeds of impending disaster.

On one side, King is distinctly romantic. He is an explorer
and adventurer par excellence; he persistently follows "the
ambitious course" in pursuit of "great success" (p. 328). Yet
his method is distinctly scientific. As one dedicated to the
"scientific scheme" (p. 347), he is deliberate and patient: King
"moulded and directed his life logically, scientifically, as Adams
thought American life should be directed. He had given himself education all of a piece, yet broad" (p. 312). What awaits
King, however, is not the "prize" (p. 313)—the success—
such a deliberate approach should bring; despite "fitness un-
rivalled," he is doomed to early "wreckage," not only of his
"fortunes" in the economic "convulsion of 1893," but of his
life as well (p. 346). The " 'best and brightest man of his generation,' " Hay writes to Adams " 'with talents immeasurably
beyond any of his contemporaries; with industry that has often

sickened me to witness it; with everything in his favor but blind luck; hounded by disaster from his cradle, with none of the joy of life to which he was entitled, dying at last, with nameless suffering, alone and uncared-for, in a California tavern. *Ça vous amuse, la vie?'* " (p. 416; see p. 346). Like Adams' sister, King struggles not only to endure but to remain brilliant and charming to the end; in the face of a fate at once personal and universal, he maintains "the old King manner," coupling "grace and tenderness," until he and his "foe have done their struggle" (p. 416). But he finally is destroyed by the forces that made him and worked to perfect him, the victim of that chaos that is the final law of nature.

The story of John Hay, of man's search for social and political, national and international, order, is the story of mortal man's struggle to master immortal history. It is the story of fleeting victory—of evanescent order won by Hay's dedicated effort and paid for with his life. Because he is a "serious statesman," Hay is able to move beyond despair—beyond his sense that man's labor to order life is useless—to see anew that life is "gay" as well as "horrid" and to feel anew that man must enter the struggle even "at cost of life." Hay senses "the artistic" aspects "of his own work" (pp. 365, 394, 392). But as a man of action he lives in and through man's struggle for meaningful order, giving himself, not for gain or profit, and not to illusion of final victory, but because the struggle itself is peculiarly human.

Hay's success must of course be ambiguous. As he approaches "the summit of his career," he necessarily sees "himself on the edge of wreck"; as the struggle grows "in proportions," he feels his strength decline "every day." Hay's "great triumph" is not a treaty or conference or military stroke; it is so uncertain that it must remain "invisible" (pp. 436, 465). Even Adams, "who had set his heart on seeing Hay [triumphantly] close his career," is able to do no more than "urge that vanity for vanity, the crown of peacemaker [is] worth the cross of martyrdom": that man must wage his struggle for peace even when "the cross [is] full in sight, while the crown [remains] still uncertain" (p. 502).

Like King's doomed combat with nature, Hay's ambiguous struggle with history, his final martyrdom to the cause of order, is enriched by its context—that is, by Adams' defining struggle to order his thought and compose an aesthetically coherent image of his life. Confronted with a context curiously in conspiracy "to block his intended path in life," left with "no office" and with no invitation "to fill one," Adams enters upon the "exceedingly solitary" yet grandly inclusive way for which his "Accidental education" has prepared him (pp. 332, 322, 331, 83).

To the new Adams, Aracoeli tends "more and more to draw all the threads of thought to a centre"; each of his varied journeys and each of his questions leads back "to its steps" (p. 367). On his voyages around the earth and into the past, as well as on his pilgrimages back to Rome, Adams is grappling with the problematic; his forays represent searches for "proof of sequence and intelligence in the affairs of man," some "sense of possible purpose" in human history (p. 363).

In interpreting his move "across the darkening prairie of education" (p. 396), Adams interrelates his effort to achieve intellectual consonance with his effort to render aesthetic resolution. The intellectual effort, however, is logically and dramatically prior to the aesthetic. Adams' "new sense of history" (p. 355)—together with the theory to which it leads—provides the culminating step in his drive for intellectual resolution. The purpose of the theory is to define a direction in history. Adams' concern is not with facts but with a truth like the truth of poetry. The "tired student" of the problems that long have "tortured history" cannot give up. "As long as he [can] whisper" he must go on as he has begun, continuing the struggle. Because " the standard formulas" have failed, he must "invent" one of "his own." Upon the task thus defined, Adams "must begin at once." It is a search, not for "absolute truth," which all the ruins and failures of history proclaim man incapable of conceiving, but for coherent vision shaped "after his own needs" (pp. 472–73).

> Among indefinite possible orbits, one sought the orbit which would best satisfy the observed movement of the runaway star Groombridge, 1838, commonly called Henry Adams. As term of a nineteenth-century education, one sought a common factor for certain definite historical fractions. Any schoolboy could work out the problem if he were given the right to state it in his own terms.
>
> Therefore . . . [Adams] sat down as though he were again a boy at school to shape after his own needs the values of a Dynamic Theory of History. (pp. 472–73)

Adams' theory participates in the most fashionable tendency of his time—the tendency, sponsored by the "great word Evolution," to make "a new religion of history" (p. 91); and it couples understanding of the natural world with interpretation of the historical process. But the formula is what it is precisely because, invented to fill the void created by failed formulas, it is shaped to meet man's needs. In short, it is a monument to man's refusal simply to adapt himself to a nonhuman world. In it, in keeping with "the law" or "the principle of resistance" (pp. 7, 21), man refuses to accept the specious success of mere survival; he insists upon achieving order through transformation of a world not made for him. Adams thus refuses to cease invention without having fashioned a formula, but he also acknowledges that "Unity is vision" (p. 398)—that " 'Order and reason, beauty and benevolence, are characteristics and conceptions . . . solely associated with the mind of man' " (p. 450)—that "Chaos [is] the law of nature" and "Order . . . the dream of man" (p. 451).

Like the efforts of King and Hay, Adams' intellectual effort is limited. For, though it is not paid for with Adams' life, it does not increase man's control over life. Nor does it endure. Because it must always be subject to the shifting angle of man's vision of a changing world, intellectual formulation too is evanescent. On this count, Aquinas, like Rome, is actual: he is Newton; he is going to be Darwin and Marx. In short, like King's expeditions and Hay's treaties, Adams' formula is doomed inevitably to become a relic and ruin of the past. Like all who attempt to move toward the civilized, Adams meets "scandalous failure" in the very moment of his "complete success" (see p. 477; cf. p. 472).

In recognition that his formula is an invention of himself for himself, Adams must add that he finally cares "no more" for "his dynamic theory of history . . . than for the kinetic theory of gas" (p. 501).[21] Like the "true" lies of Joseph Conrad's

21. On Adams as an historian, see Levenson, pp. 135, 367–76; and W. H. Jordy, *Henry Adams: Scientific Historian* (New Haven, Yale University Press, 1952), passim and esp. pp. 220–88. Adams' theoretical statements should be read, it seems to me, with attention to the complex irony that informs them. Adams was capable for instance of referring to "The Rule of Phase Applied to History" as "a mere intellectual plaything . . . not meant to be taken too seriously" (Letter to Brooks Adams, February 1909, quoted in Ford, *Letters of Henry Adams, 2,* 515, n. 1); and of saying that his "A Letter to American Teachers of History" was "a mere bit of amusement . . . a joke, which nobody will know enough to understand" (Letter to Brooks Adams, January 1910. ibid., *2,* 533). Adams' longing for final—"scientific"—understanding of history was real and enduring, but he formulated his own "scientific" theories rather to honor man's need for such understanding than in belief that they represented it. In 1909 he wrote Brooks Adams giving him permission to do as he would with "The Rule of Phase Applied to History"; to "my point of view," he added, it is "only a sort of jigsaw puzzle, put together in order to see whether the pieces could be made to fit. Too well I knew the inadequacy of the public mind . . . The fools begin [sic] at once to discuss whether the theory was true" (Henry Adams, Letter to Brooks Adams, February 1909, in Harold D. Cater, ed., *Henry Adams and His Friends: A Collection of His Unpublished Letters* [Boston, Houghton Mifflin, 1947], p. 639).

characters, Adams' intellectual formula is a heroic act in an ironic mode. His invention affirms human affirmation. When made in full knowledge that man's formulas are his own invention, the act of affirming formulation is supremely an act of life. Adams' man finally is moved by needs that no enervating recognition of the bleakness of man's fate can extinguish. Knowing that all specifically human visions of meaning are "illusions" (to use Conrad's word) or invented "formula[s]," mere "convenient fiction[s]" (to use two of Adams' own), Adams nonetheless defines man's final wisdom as recognition that the illusions are "necessary": that the formulas are "infinitely precious," the fictions man's highest "achievement"; that in the end they are, all ironically, man's "only truth."[22]

In response to life Adams accordingly shapes his own convenient and fitting fiction, which he must entertain in the proper spirit and render with the proper tone. At this point skepticism and faith merge. Because he can find no value and meaning outside himself, because he can look back to no revelation, nor forward to any realization of an absolute, Adams must accept his world as the natural habitat of none of the values that it is human to create and humane to try to live. Man's "convenient fiction[s]" thus represent a heroic response to the chaos that surrounds him, engulfing his efforts at order.

For King the scientist and Hay the statesman, as well as for

22. Robert Penn Warren, Introduction, Joseph Conrad, *Nostromo* [1904] (New York, Random House, 1951), pp. xxii–iv. Henry Adams, Letter to Charles Francis Adams, Jr., May 1863, Ford, *A Cycle of Adams Letters, 1,* 278. Despite knowledge that failure was probable, that man "should cease" in his effort to find meaning was not, for Adams, "within the range of experience" (*The Degradation of the Democratic Dogma,* p. 126). For the context within which Adams understood himself to be at work, see the works cited above, Chap. 1, n. 20; and for notions related to Adams' conception of the proper response to that context, see Stevens as cited above, Chap. 3, n. 44; Yeats as quoted above, Chap. 3, n. 45; and Kermode as quoted below, Chap. 9, n. 22.

Adams the philosopher, it is chaos that is real, chaos that
sooner or later cannot not be known. Yet each of these men
moves, and must move, beyond knowledge of chaos to make
"All [his] life" a struggle for impossible order and unity (p.
398). Only in such struggle, only in affirmation, are Adams'
men supremely human. Given the complexly ironic aspects of
Adams' vision, however, the supreme instance of man's effort
to give order and meaning to "something that defie[s] meaning" (p. 499) must necessarily be not a rational theory but a
work of the imagination. The climax of the *Education* comes
not when Adams invents his intellectual formula, his theory of
history, but when he sets for "himself . . . the task" of writing
Mont-Saint-Michel and Chartres and *The Education of Henry
Adams* as companion volumes from which he could "project
his lines forward and backward indefinitely," defining himself
and his world in infinite context (p. 435). The *Education,* in a
word, represents Adams' final effort not only to assure that he
has not "sat all [his] life on the steps of Ara Coeli" merely to
accept "assassination" as "forever . . . the last word of Progress" (pp. 471–72), but also to assure "that the family work of
a hundred and fifty years" will not fall into the abyss of final
failure but will be lifted "into the grand perspective of true
empire-building" (p. 363).

Despite the overwhelming presence of nature, which is seen
in the *Education* as having always "hurried and hustled" man
without ever consulting his "convenience" (p. 493), and despite
the overpowering presence of history, which is seen in the
Education as the leveler of man's planned efforts to build an
eternal city of man, new vision is made possible. When Adams
returns to New York for the last time, he sees a radically new
world. It is, to be sure, "unlike anything man had ever seen—
and like nothing he had ever" intended or "much cared to see";
but to Adams' new vision, it is also "striking" and "wonderful"
(p. 499).

Within the *Education,* it is from John LaFarge that Adams

learns to replace or complement the way of the "American mind," the way of direct assertion or denial of "something that it takes for a fact," with the way of art (p. 369). As the one "alternative" to arithmetic and statistics (p. 351), art is concerned with the logic and truth of the imagination. From LaFarge, Adams learns to carry "different shades of contradiction in his mind," and, rather than " 'reason too much,' " to seek "a tone—a shade—a *nuance*" (p. 370). It is preeminently in its poetic, imaginative mode that the human mind itself becomes for Adams "the subtlest of all known forces" (p. 476). Just as man responds to existence—to being caught up in the flux and movement of his natural and historical environment —by seeking actively to impose specifically human and humane order, thereby to make life of mere existence; and just as the human mind responds to inchoate existence and to partially ordered life by seeking to "invent" a formula that will permit man "to fit" the "pieces" of the "puzzle" into meaningful pattern; so does the aesthetic imagination creatively respond to all man's ordering efforts, seeking to make art of them, seeking, that is, by ordering all man's ordering efforts, to turn failure into triumph.[23]

Even more than his invented formula (which might conceivably lead to a plan of action), the *Education* is limited because it does not directly further Adams' mastery of actual life. But unlike his philosophical theories, it is, as a work of art, neither tentative nor evanescent, but absolute. It constitutes his supreme no to chaos and disorder. For in it he declines simply to accept himself as having appeared "suddenly and inexplicably out of some unknown and unimaginable void"; in it he refuses simply to pass his life in the physical chaos of nature and history and in "the mental chaos of sleep," quietly to wait until he awakes, following years of "growing astonishment,"

23. See Adams as quoted above, n. 21, and cf. the *Education*, pp. 50, 156–57, 469, 472–73.

to find himself "looking blankly into the void of death" (p. 460). In it he insists, to the contrary, on charged and consummated vision. Having acknowledged the actuality of chaos, he accordingly must become a "fabulist" who celebrates his struggle "to escape the chaos which cage[s]" him (p. 460). For only as such a fabulist can he celebrate that struggle in each of its realms—in nature and history—and under each of its aspects—under the eye that seeks to discern order and the will that seeks to impose it, under the apprehending mind that seeks to invent formulas, and under the imagination that seeks to fashion images of man and his failed efforts.

Because the *Education* is the story of a man whose "accidental education" prepares him for the act of telling it, it is finally the story of its story. Throughout his autobiography, Adams' imagination behaves "like a young pearl oyster, secreting its universe to suit its conditions until it [has] built up a shell of *nacre* that embodie[s] all its notions of the perfect." Adams thus celebrates his own image of perfection: for him it is "true" and beautiful because it is he that has "made it." Adams' imaginative construct comes to be what it is and to embody the triumph it embodies only at great cost and sacrifice and only within its limited realm. But it may "justly" be called "a work of art"; for, as an effort at supreme order and as a labor of inclusive affirmation, it constitutes its maker's ultimate act of life, his final adherence to "the principle of resistance" (pp. 83, 458, 21).

Part Three: Design, Interpretation, and the Art of Fiction

> *Historical sense and poetic sense should not, in the end, be contradictory, for if poetry is the little myth we make, history is the big myth we live, and in our living, constantly remake.*
>
> Robert Penn Warren, Foreword,
> Brother to Dragons

7 Definition of a Fictional Form: Hawthorne's *The Blithedale Romance*

Illustrious acts high raptures do infuse,
And every conqueror creates a muse.

Edmund Waller, "A Panegyric
to my Lord Protector"

Nathaniel Hawthorne made his literary life a search for "a neutral territory . . . where the Actual and the Imaginary may meet, and each imbue itself with the nature of the other."[1] He respected what he called the "solid and substantial" actuality of the material world: the common-sense reality that men, as Henry James later put it, "cannot possibly *not* know, sooner or later, in one way or another." But he was also drawn to the internal, incorporeal world of thought and imagination: to "the beautiful circuit and subterfuge," to borrow again from James, "of our thought and our desire."[2]

Hawthorne's search for "a neutral territory," for "an available" area "between fiction and reality," was protracted, complex, and only occasionally successful; finding proper subjects

1. "The Custom-House, Introductory to *The Scarlet Letter*," *The Centenary Edition of the Works of Nathaniel Hawthorne,* ed. William Charvat and others (3 vols. to date, Columbus, Ohio State University Press, 1962–), *1,* 36. See Feidelson, *Symbolism and American Literature,* pp. 6–16; and *"The Scarlet Letter,"* p. 32.

2. Hawthorne, Letter to James T. Fields, quoted in Newton Arvin, *Hawthorne* [1929] (New York, Russell and Russell, 1961), p. 207; and Blackmur, ed., *The Art of the Novel,* pp. 31–32.

for his romances proved difficult.[3] As we see in "The Custom-House, Introductory to *The Scarlet Letter*," however, one situation of two elements—first a problematic given, a scene or event or cipher that presents itself as a riddle or mystery, and second a man of "thought and imagination," a man whose habit of mind and disposition to life move him to interpretation of things problematic—persistently suggested itself to Hawthorne. When the strange persona of the Custom-House "essay" sees that the "rag of scarlet cloth" is a "capital letter A" and that it had clearly been "intended . . . as an ornamental article of dress," but that "how it was to be worn, or what rank, honor, and dignity, in by-past times, were signified by it" are problematical, he immediately seizes upon it as "a riddle" that is "most worthy of interpretation."[4]

Of the several possible varieties of riddles and mysteries, those turning on problems of intention play a particularly prominent role in Hawthorne's fictions. Irony of intent is the dominant feature of his story of two lovers whose "plan" is twisted by "seeming accidents" until they are led to build not the house they had envisaged but "a marble tomb"; and it is central as well in his stories of Endicott's campaigns, Rappaccini's "experiment," and Aylmer's "plan."[5] To Hawthorne, however, such irony represented more than a compositional resource; it informed his understanding of artistic endeavor. He was fascinated by the predicament of an artist who, in the process of composing his story, finds himself so completely out of control that his tale "shapes itself against his intentions."[6] And he was convinced that in his effort to move from original

3. Preface, *The Blithedale Romance*, Charvat and others, *Works*, *3*, 2.

4. "The Custom-House," Charvat and others, *Works*, *1*, 37, 31; cf. *1*, 26.

5. *American Note-Books*, in *The Complete Works of Nathaniel Hawthorne*, ed. George P. Lathrop (Riverside Edition, 12 vols. Boston, 1887), *9*, 37–38. Cf. Hawthorne's story "The Lily's Quest."

6. Ibid., p. 28.

conception to achieved artifact, "an artist or a poet" was "sure to fall short" of his "first idea." Indeed it was because an artist was certain to fail that he was certain to produce a work fit to stand as an epitome of "human work." By virtue of the traces it would retain of a "half obliterated design," it would suggest not a lesser but a "greater mystery and beauty."[7]

At Stonehenge in 1856, Hawthorne found what seemed to him "Materially . . . one of the poorest of spectacles." But he also found what fascinated him.

> There never was a ruder thing than Stonehenge made by mortal hands; it is so very rude, that it seems as if Nature and man had worked upon it with one consent, and so it is all the stranger and more impressive from its rudeness. The spectator wonders to see art and contrivance, and a regular and even somewhat intricate plan, beneath all the uncouth simplicity of this arrangement of rough stones; and, certainly, whatever was the intellectual and scientific advancement of the people who built Stonehenge, no succeeding architects will ever have a right to triumph over them; for nobody's work, in after times, is likely to endure till it becomes a mystery who built it, and how, and for what purpose.

It is because Stonehenge—"a few huge, rough stones, very imperfectly squared"—represents mysteries of art and contrivance, plan and arrangement, origin and purpose, that its crudeness presents itself to Hawthorne as (potentially) a thousand things. Although "Materially it is one of the poorest of spectacles," it is well worth seeing because of the infinitely varied "moral considerations suggested by it." Paradoxically, mystery makes the stones meaningful by making a mystery of their meaning.[8]

7. *The English Notebooks by Nathaniel Hawthorne*, ed. Randall Stewart (New York, Modern Language Association, 1941), p. 157.
8. Ibid., p. 360.

Within a world at once haunted and enriched by mystery,
the act of interpretation, and especially the artist's act of
heightened interpretation, became for Hawthorne altogether
necessary. In the interpretive song of the poet "the world
assumed another . . . aspect"; man's days and works, his "half
obliterated design[s]," remained unfinished until "the poet
came to interpret, and so complete" them.[9] To the poet of the
Custom-House, the scarlet letter, that strange "affair of fine
red cloth, much worn and faded," presents itself as a bare
beginning. The "frayed and defaced" traces "of gold em-
broidery" suggest the wonderfully skilled work "of a now forgotten art, not to be recovered even by the process of picking
out the threads"; the fullness of what "had been intended"
by it and what had been done with it accordingly are riddles.
Only through "careful examination," "absorbing contemplation," and imaginative interpretation can the poet hope to
uncover the "deep meaning" of "the mystic symbol."[10]

Unlike *The Scarlet Letter* but like the story of that story—
that is, like the Custom-House "essay"—*The Blithedale Romance* (1852) was written out of the same historical situation
it depicts. Like the poet of the Custom-House, the narrator
of *The Blithedale Romance*, Miles Coverdale, is a poet within
the action he narrates. Structurally the closest analogue to *The
Blithedale Romance*, aside from the Custom-House piece, is a
novel published in 1851—Herman Melville's *Moby-Dick. The
Blithedale Romance* is a stricter—yet simpler and poorer—
working out of the structure explored and, in a sense, violated,
by Melville.

Moby-Dick is obviously a strange work of art—a kind of
literary sport. Basically, to be sure, it is structured by juxta-

9. "The Great Stone Face," Lathrop, *Works, 3,* 432–33; and
Stewart, *English Notebooks,* p. 157.
10. "The Custom-House," Charvat and others, *Works, 1,* 31–32.

position of Ishmael and Ahab; it is one man's story of another man's action and fate: it is Ishmael's "expanded meditation" upon action shaped by Ahab's "fixed purpose."[11] In his "forward dedication," in his determination to strike through the problematic "pasteboard masks," thereby to force encounter with the hidden core (or void) of life, thereby to compel the universe to disclose to him the character of its ultimate design, the "enraged and mighty" Ahab dominates the action of his world.[12] Not only does he replace "the natural, nominal purpose" of the voyage with his own "private purpose"; he also makes his private purpose "our vengeful errand." He is Melville's hero of action. Ishmael, in contrast, is man seeing and interpreting. He responds to Ahab's overpowering purpose—I too "was one of that crew," he says; "my shouts had gone up with the rest."[13] But in contrast to the mindless crew, Ishmael makes the task of interpretation his own. Having gone to sea to find the proper scene for meditation, he defines not only Ahab but all the "inscrutable" creatures of "inscrutable" Ahab's world—that is, Moby Dick, the squid, and the spirit spout and skeleton of the whale—as things provided by the sea for his meditation.[14] He is Melville's hero of sight and voice.

Ishmael is, however, a researcher, editor, and anthologist, as well as interpreter, and by becoming more he at times becomes something less than a thoroughgoing interpreter. If we are to appreciate the "careful disorderliness" that is "the true method" of this story,[15] we must view the simpler form of the

11. Herman Melville, *Moby-Dick*, ed. Charles Feidelson, Jr., The Library of Literature (New York, Bobbs-Merrill, 1964), pp. 183, 227.

12. Ibid., pp. 170, 220, 159.

13. Ibid., pp. 286, 311, 239. Cf. pp. 216, 266.

14. Ibid., pp. 221, 298. Cf. pp. 174, 309–11, 364–66; and Chaps. 36, 41, 42.

15. Ibid., p. 465. See George R. Stewart, "The Two *Moby-Dicks*," *American Literature, 25* (1954), 417–48.

early chapters—where Ishmael is, in a conventional way, a
first-person narrator recounting adventures in which he figures
prominently—as a form appropriate to the relatively stable
and tame world of the shore; and we must view the complexly
mixed form of the later chapters—where Ishmael is only in-
frequently a narrator of action in which he figures prominently
and is rather more frequently a narrative presence who recounts
the action of Ahab and his crew, or a consciousness that creates
scenes and actions, or a scientific researcher who classifies
whales, or a spectator who witnesses dramas and records
monologues within the novel, or a raconteur who retells tales
and redelivers sermons—as a form appropriate to the "watery,"
the "shoreless, indefinite" world of the sea.[16]

   Through Ishmael and Ahab, Melville renders the fullest
possible responses to the problematical world of the sea; and
through them he structures his rendering. On one side there is
Ahab, whose will it is we see in action. He alone makes his
strange aggregation of isolatoes, who at the outset share only
their estrangement from the shore and their intense isolation,
into a dedicated, one might even say consecrated, crew; and
he alone charts the course by which the *Pequod* finally meets
Moby Dick. On the other side there is Ishmael, through whose
consciousness, although it is at times almost refined out of
existence, Ahab's story comes to us. The language and meditation, not the action, of *Moby-Dick* belong to Ishmael.
Ishmael, to be sure, is not without a "design" of his own. The
self-conscious artistry with which he makes himself a Nan-
tucketer and names himself Ishmael enables him, moreover, to
achieve his intention—that of becoming a whaler and voyager.[17] But what in the course of the book he increasingly becomes is the voyager as meditator and interpreter.

   Ishmael's response to Ahab's "fixed purpose" of encounter

16. Ibid., pp. 23, 149.
17. Ibid., p. 90.

parallels his response to the very large oil painting in The
Spouter Inn. In seeking to understand the "meanings" of
Ahab's intention and fate, Ishmael engages not only in "careful
inquiry" and "diligent study," but in "earnest contemplation,
and oft repeated ponderings"; and he does so in an effort to
turn what in itself seemed only "portentous, black [formless]
mass," what in itself only "puzzled and confounded" him, into
something "blue": he seeks, in short, to realize the "indefinite,
half-attained" yet marvelous "sublimity" implicit both in his
own voyage and in Ahab's planned action. In the end, of
course, what we have is "expanded meditation."[18] Ishmael
blends into his interpreting narration several sub-forms—plays
and stories and treatises. Yet even in its expanded form the
narrative belongs to him, for he uses it to salvage both his story
and Ahab's. The salvaging of these stories represents, moreover, his triumph over the indefinite, highly problematical, and,
in the end, devastated world that is given him for contemplation. That triumph is limited: it stops short of the ultimate, religious finality Ahab demands. But within its human, aesthetic
limits, it is fully achieved.

Ishmael possesses to a remarkable degree what Keats called
"Negative Capability." His desire to make meaning of the
puzzling and confounding action that he witnesses never dis-
places his ability to entertain "uncertainties, mysteries, doubts,
without any irritable reaching after fact and reason."[19] He is
blessed with rare interior spaciousness: he is willing "to sail
forbidden seas, and land on barbarous coasts" without chart-
ing or surveying them; and he is able to "be social" with "a
horror."[20] His commodious consciousness buoys him up in the

18. Ibid., pp. 65, 35–36, 183.
19. John Keats, Letter to George and Thomas Keats, December
1817, *The Letters of John Keats*, ed. Maurice B. Forman (3d revised ed.
London and New York, Oxford University Press, 1947), p. 72; italics
omitted.
20. Melville, *Moby-Dick*, p. 30.

destructive sea, permitting him to survive and say. The commodious manner of his making—the way in which he expands his meditation—corresponds to his own spaciousness. The essential inscrutability of life, what Ahab chiefly hates, Ishmael accepts as the primary characteristic of specifically human vision. He survives because he is able to "be social" not only with horror and evil but with the final ambiguity of things: he can accept a "black bubble" as a life-giving force, a coffin as a life buoy.[21]

The only finality Ishmael attains is accordingly the attenuated finality of artistic narration—in the achievement of which he acknowledges his failure to grasp the "ungraspable phantom" he pursues.[22] The knowledge toward which he moves—that the watery part of the world, the shoreless and indefinite world of the sea, is the proper scene for specifically human meditation precisely because it is indefinite and indeterminate, is inscrutable and yields no final answer as to man's fate, is for Ahab sad and inadequate knowledge. Yet it is all that Ishmael knows, and because he is able to make uncertainty and homelessness—permanent exile—a way of life, it is all he needs to know.

Miles Coverdale's negative capability is considerably more limited than Ishmael's. Mystery at once fascinates and horrifies him. On one side he sees it as the source of his vocation. From the outset he is concerned "as to the success of our Blithedale enterprise": he sees the "Knot of Dreamers" as a problem and Hollingsworth and Zenobia and Priscilla "as the indices of a problem" that it is somehow his "business to solve." Although he wants to be equal to this task, Coverdale deeply fears novelty and disorder. He wants "to see a sufficient cause for everything," and when he "can see none," when life

21. Ibid., pp. 221, 30, 724. Italics omitted.
22. Ibid., p. 26.

becomes potentially a destructive element, he becomes evasive. As we shall see, he not only gives way to ill-natured and "irritable reaching after fact and reason"; he also substitutes little mysteries and problems for the big ones that threaten and frighten him.[23] Despite its hazy moments, the story of *The Blithedale Romance* is in outline simple enough.

The action centers on the Blithedale experiment, a utopian endeavor dedicated to bettering mankind by leaving "the rusty iron frame-work of society behind" and constructing a model "Arcadia" in which thought and action—the "yeoman and the scholar"—will be united and in which a new, perfect way of ordering life thereby will be realized (pp. 19, 38, 66). In drawing together not only Coverdale, a minor poet, and Hollingsworth, an ardent reformer, but also the passionate Zenobia and the delicate Priscilla, the story of the Blithedale experiment becomes entangled, however, with a cloudy story centering on Old Moodie, Priscilla, Zenobia, and Westervelt. Coverdale accordingly becomes concerned not only with two stories but with the relationship between them. As the action moves from Boston to Blithedale, from Blithedale to Boston and back again to Blithedale, we see the utopian experiment progress. But we also see Hollingsworth at work to replace the nominal purpose of the of the Blithedale experiment with his own private design. Gradually we learn that Zenobia and Priscilla are half-sisters and that Old Moodie, their father, is determined to keep Priscilla from suffering from his misdeeds. And gradually we learn that Westervelt, a mesmerist, somehow has got and wishes to reinforce influence over Priscilla, and somehow has been linked, in an earlier time, to Zenobia. But through it all—as we see the various characters pursue their own ends until they

23. *The Blithedale Romance,* Charvat and others, *Works, 3,* 6, 14, 69, 75. Note: *The Blithedale Romance* is the third volume of this edition, and all references in the text of this chapter are to this volume.

undermine the utopian experiment, as we see both Zenobia and Priscilla come to love Hollingsworth, and as we follow Zenobia to her suicide—we follow Coverdale's curious narration, his curious effort to bring order to the events he witnesses.

The opening scene of *The Blithedale Romance* introduces thematic and metaphoric patterns that define the novel's basic reality—the reality of the baffling and the mysterious—and represent its basic action—the action of men who seek variously to confute their confusing world. As "the exhibitor" of the Veiled Lady, as the director of "the remarkable performances" of the girl we eventually come to know as Priscilla, the man we eventually come to know as Westervelt moves beyond acceptance of mystery as the essence of reality perversely to make a game of the mysterious. In his "management of his 'subject'" Westervelt seeks, through "skilfully contrived circumstances of stage-effect," to increase and exploit mystery and to control and manipulate man's fascination with it (p. 5). In Old Moodie, who turns out to be the father of Priscilla, we see a different response to confusion. He is neither a professional performer nor a servant of the mysterious. Rather, he wants to redeem his dark past by changing its direction. During the course of the novel, beginning in the first chapter, Old Moodie accordingly pursues a "design" of his own making. In addition, however, he gravitates toward Hollingsworth, whom Coverdale commends to him as a "solid character, and a philanthropist to boot." Yet even before Old Moodie begins to move toward him, Hollingsworth has begun following an independent course of action: in "his strange . . . plan for the reformation of criminals," we see yet another response to disorder and confusion (pp. 7, 36).

The world of *The Blithedale Romance* is shaped in part by such active responses to confusion and disorder. But as Henry James observed, the story's narrator, Miles Coverdale, is "contemplative, observant, analytic." He takes pleasure, "not in doing, but in perceiving"; he is, in a word, "half a poet, half a critic, and all a spectator."[24] What he accordingly needs is a means of penetration and a "mode of accounting" (p. 33). He accepts as his peculiar function the tasks of observing and interpreting: in response to all encounters with the problematic, in response to the muddled and opaque, in response to "enigma[s]" and "riddle[s]" he seeks "to catch . . . by the tail" the "slippery purport" of what he sees (p. 6).

The Blithedale Romance basically focuses, in short, on the juxtaposition of Hollingsworth and the architects of the Blithedale experiment with Coverdale. Like the action-minded planners whom he epitomizes, Hollingsworth acts in naïve faith that planned action will lead to envisaged results. He assumes that action must precede understanding. "Let us not pry farther into her [Priscilla's] secrets," he warns the doers of dreams; if we shall but act, "whatever is desirable for us to know will be melted out of her." However much Hollingsworth may speak of "Providence," the essence of his faith is confidence in his ability to free himself from the past by mastering the present and shaping the future. Prior to the decimation of his faith and his consequent descent into despair, Hollingsworth is not perplexed by mystery; indeed, he is seldom cognizant of it (p. 30).

In his total inability to ignore the mysterious, Coverdale stands alone among the Blithedalers and specifically in contrast to Hollingsworth. Because he is "contemplative, observant, analytic," because he is "half a poet, half a critic, and all a spectator," Coverdale shapes, not life itself, but man's efforts to shape and order his life. He is the interpreter.

> Destiny, it may be—the most skilful of stage-managers—seldom chooses to arrange its scenes, and carry forward its drama, without securing the presence of at least one calm observer. It is his office to give applause, when due, and sometimes an inevitable tear, to detect the final fitness

24. Henry James, *Hawthorne*, p. 129.

of incident to character, and distil, in his long-brooding
thought, the whole morality of the performance. (p. 97)

Coverdale's obvious sentimentality reinforces Hawthorne's
persistent undercutting of his role, suggesting that he will fail
to measure the scenes and define the drama he observes, and
that his notion of the final fitness and whole morality of the
performance will surely be less than adequate. Yet it is through
Coverdale that Hawthorne renders the world of *The Blithedale
Romance.*

Coverdale begins his story by depicting himself as a seeker
of mystery. At the outset he tells us that, on the evening before
his "departure for Blithedale," he went abroad in attendance
to "the wonderful exhibition of the Veiled Lady"—that "now
forgotten celebrity" who once had "come before the public"
under "circumstances of stage-effect" so "skilfully contrived"
that they at once "mystified and illuminated [her] remarkable
performances." Westervelt, "the exhibitor" of the Veiled Lady,
at least as Coverdale sketches him, is something of an artist.
And he is so more in the "romantic" or even "Gothic" than in
the "naturalistic" mode. He "affects the simplicity and openness of scientific experiment," but he employs "all the arts of
mysterious arrangement, of picturesque disposition, and artis-
tically contrasted light and shade." He is concerned not with
presenting the extraordinary under the aspect of the common-
place, but with presenting the ordinary and extraordinary
under the aspect of the inexplicable, and with setting what is
apparently miraculous "in the strongest attitude of opposition
to ordinary facts" (pp. 5–6).

In part Coverdale's interest in such a spectacle must be attributed to his incurable tendency to be "a spectator." Such
an "enigma" as the Veiled Lady's "identity"—"enshrouded"
as it is "within the misty drapery of the veil"—could but excite
Coverdale's curiosity (p. 6). But Hawthorne uses the very
casualness of Coverdale's disclosure of his one act at that per-

formance to suggest the nature of the episode's centrality. The "pretensions" of the Veiled Lady, Coverdale remarks, have little to do with the story of the Blithedale venture "except" that he there "had propounded," for her "prophetic solution, a query as to the success" of the forthcoming venture (p. 6). Coverdale's attendance to the spectacle, both actually—that is, in his past, in preparation for the "Blithedale enterprise"—and imaginatively—in his present, in narration of the Blithedale story—is born of the motive essential to all that he does. Coverdale is the questioning narrator of *The Blithedale Romance* because he was created to concern himself with its fate (p. 6).

Within *The Blithedale Romance* mystery is more than self-perpetuating; it obeys a literary equivalent to the law of geometric progression. Coverdale's various entanglements with the problematic are always in part the work of his insatiable need to sit before the stage of the mysterious. But his entanglements derive finally from his halting obedience to the task for which he was made: interpretation of the meaning of the fate of the Blithedale enterprise. Like the reality it renders, the mode of the novel's rendering is run through with the problematic. The limited, confused, frequently wavering, and at times unreliable Coverdale is not what he is without reason. He is, to be sure, indecisive; and since he is forever turning back, he commits himself here to simple, direct recording and there to full, imaginative reordering. To see in his vacillation an index merely of his own foolishness and failure, however, is to insist upon a simpler alternative than the language and action of the novel permit.[25] Coverdale's unreliability points beyond itself to a confused and confusing reality that seems willfully, and therefore perversely, to lend itself to "a variety of [contradictory] interpretations" (p. 6). His vacillation interacts with—it matches and corresponds to—his muddled and mysterious world.

25. See Frederick C. Crews, "A New Reading of *The Blithedale Romance*," *American Literature*, 29 (1957–58), 147–70.

As early as the third chapter—"A Knot of Dreamers"—
veils have become so prevalent and masks so pervasive that
they threaten to reduce the heroic enterprise to absurd masquerade: "the presence of Zenobia caused our heroic enterprise to show like an illusion, a masquerade, a pastoral, a
counterfeit Arcadia, in which we grown-up men and women
were making a play-day of the years that were given us to live
in" (p. 21). Coverdale tries of course "to analyze" Zenobia's
impact; but he is certain not to meet "with much success," for
his world is without a stable center. On every side it is with
meaning "enshrouded within the misty drapery of the veil" that
he has and must have to do (pp. 21, 6).

Veils and masks, shrouds and disguises swarm throughout
the novel until, indeed, beyond the threat to reduce the heroic
experiment to masquerade, they threaten to turn the masquerade into a nightmare—until, in fine, a "shadow of . . . catastrophe" threatens to revise if not annihilate the vision of the
"Knot of Dreamers." Even apart from her role as the Veiled
Lady, Priscilla moves in a "mist of uncertainty." She is of
course not in the least sinister. She neither cultivates complication nor employs the arts of "contrived circumstances" and
"mysterious arrangement" (pp. 38, 49, 5–6). Whereas Westervelt—her "exhibitor"—disguises himself with a counterfeit
laugh, false teeth, and sham spectacles, whereas it is not at all
certain that his remarkable face is not "removable like a mask,"
Priscilla is a goddess of simplicity. Yet she serves very considerably to muddle and entangle "the Blithedale affair" (pp. 5,
95, 8). She is so extravagantly simple that she comes to possess
the "peculiar excellence" of embodying and representing mystery: it is because an "uninitiated person" cannot "discover"
their apertures, which "to a practised touch" readily open "as
wide as charity or prodigality might wish," that the purses she
makes become "a symbol of [her] own mystery" (p. 35).

The mystery that haunts the world of *The Blithedale Romance* derives from a special version of the familiar tension

between appearance and inner essence: namely, from tension between the realm of the private and subjective and the arena of the public and objective. At the end of the novel's first chapter, we learn that, far from being a true and proper name, Zenobia is merely a "public name"—"a sort of mask" in which another mysterious creature "comes before the world, retaining all the privileges of privacy." Like "the white drapery of the Veiled Lady," Zenobia's name is "a contrivance." Zenobia's mask is, to be sure, "a little more transparent" than Priscilla's veil (p. 8). But if it is not unnecessarily opaque, if it is used, not as Westervelt uses Priscilla's veil, for deliberate disguise and willful multiplication of mystery, but for necessary mediation, it is as a result more rather than less ominous. For the case of Zenobia would then suggest that within *The Blithedale Romance* the private self can enter the public stage only through such mediation, just as the case of Hollingsworth would suggest that private thoughts and desires can enter the public arena only in the form of projects and schemes, plans and designs.

In a world so constructed, Coverdale sees all meaning and significance, whether intended or accidental, and whether deliberately disguised or necessarily masked, as uncertain. Even the "breadth, depth, and spaciousness" of an old-fashioned kitchen hearth poses a problem for him by obscuring the outlines of its burning log, its source of illumination and warmth. He accordingly must either quit his search for understanding or he must reconcile himself to analyzing impressions without hope of "much success" and to pondering "strange" events that fade before he can "make out" what they "meant" (pp. 20–23).

More than either Priscilla or Zenobia, Hollingsworth defines the uncertainties of the strange world in which Coverdale moves. Whereas they suggest and reinforce the problematic and the mysterious per se, Hollingsworth suggests and reinforces those aspects of the problematic and the mysterious closest to the Blithedale experiment. Hollingsworth, as Zenobia finally sees, also plays a role and dons a mask: he self-consciously poses as a dedicated philanthropist—as a man of "inflexible severity of purpose," the selfless architect of a "visionary edifice," the selfless author of a "philanthropic dream." Furthermore, in joining the Blithedale experiment, he makes the role of the Blithedaler a mask. In his faith that man, through planned action, can shape reality, in his demand for perfect order, for achieved perfection, Hollingsworth epitomizes all that stands behind the Blithedale enterprise. Yet, ironically, he is committed to it only in order to further his "strange," private "plan." For him, the role of the Blithedaler is but a temporary public form for his private dream. The whole of his "purposed" devotion he gives to a plan born of "the solitude of his heart and mind" and nourished by "the intensity with which he contemplate[s] his own ideas" (pp. 43, 56, 36).

In Hollingsworth we see most clearly how and why the "quest of a better life," the "scheme for beginning the life of Paradise anew," is troubled through and through. Like Hollingsworth's design, the grand experiment presupposes "the world's improvability" (pp. 10, 9, 20); more specifically, it assumes that man, via planned construction, can rise above "the boundaries of ordinary life"—that man, with calculated purpose, can bend and train anew the "crooked and unmanageable boughs" of life (pp. 18, 13). Despite its heroism and good hope, however, the gallant enterprise is doomed from the outset to become an "exploded scheme." "For, little as we know of our life to come," Coverdale has himself say in the narrative, "we may be very sure . . .that the good we aim at will not be attained. People never do get just the good they seek. If it come at all, it is something else, which they never dreamed of, and did not particularly want" (pp. 9, 75–76).[26]

26. Cf. "Chiefly about War Matters," Lathrop, *Works, 12,* 332; and *Life of Franklin Pierce,* ibid., p. 417. See also Randall Stewart, In-

Early in his "query as to the success of [the] Blithedale enterprise," Coverdale discerns in Hollingsworth—in his "inflexible severity of purpose" and in his "purposed" devotion to his own design—a heightened version of the Blithedale spirit. The Blithedalers' plan is vague. Their venture is the outgrowth more of agreement to discard "the old system" than of consensus "As to what should be substituted" for it (p. 63). Hollingsworth's design, on the other hand, is visionary, intricate, specific.

> His specific object . . . was to obtain funds for the construction of an edifice, with a sort of collegiate endowment. On this foundation, he purposed to devote himself and a few disciples to the reform and mental culture of our criminal brethren. His visionary edifice was Hollingsworth's one castle in the air; it was the material type, in which his philanthropic dream strove to embody itself; and he made the scheme more definite, and caught hold of it the more strongly, and kept his clutch the more pertinaciously, by rendering it visible to the bodily eye. I have seen him, a hundred times, with a pencil and sheet of paper, sketching the façade, the side-view, or the rear of the structure, or planning the internal arrangements . . . I have known him to begin a model of the building with little stones . . . Unlike all other ghosts, his spirit haunted an edifice which, instead of being time-worn, and full of storied love, and joy, and sorrow, had never yet come into existence. (p. 56)

Hollingsworth here, of course, is peculiarly American and modern as well as peculiarly Blithedalean. Born without a usable past, he creates a usable future: deprived of castles on the Rhine, he contemplates visionary edifices. But Hollings-

---

troduction, *The American Notebooks by Nathaniel Hawthorne* (New Haven, Yale University Press, 1932), p. lxxii.

worth's intense contemplation of "his own ideas"—his intense
dedication to that "strange" and "impracticable plan" of which
he alone is author—places him in a relation to the Blithedale
experiment that is not unlike the relation of the Blithedalers to
the community whose "system of society" they have determined
to replace (pp. 36, 13). Hollingsworth is, in fine, the American
as a man of design and action, just as Coverdale is the American as a poet and interpreter.[27] Coverdale's effort to get at
"the whole morality of the performance" accordingly comes
increasingly to concentrate on Hollingsworth, who in turn
comes increasingly to dominate the action of the novel. What
is essential is defining "Hollingsworth's character and purposes" and fathoming the significance of what he "mean[s] to
do" and defining the meaning of what he actually does (pp. 97,
94, 68; cf. pp. 69–70).

From the moment when Old Moodie accosts Coverdale to
the moment when Coverdale accosts Hollingsworth and Priscilla, interruptions trouble the action of *The Blithedale Romance*. Through Old Moodie the past impinges, "accidentally
delay[ing]" Hollingsworth even before he can depart for
the Blithedale farm. Through Westervelt, human perversity
muddles life on the farm as well as in the city. Through a storm,
contrived, it almost seems, for the "especial behoof" of the
adventurers, nature makes the day of inception a dark, cold
day and raises in the night that follows a blizzard that neither
shelter nor fire can offset (pp. 11, 18). Illness turns dream to
nightmare anticipation of impending "catastrophe"; and necessary labor multiplies, foiling hope of harmony between thought
and action, between "the scholar" and "the yeoman," making
time for thought more limited and thought itself more "clod-
dish" (pp. 38, 66).

27. See Edwin Fussell, *Frontier: American Literature and the American West* (Princeton, Princeton University Press, 1965), pp. 123–24,
352–53.

It is during the climactic moments preceding and following Zenobia's death, however, when the forces of delay and disruption, of conflict and muddlement converge, that the Blithedalers' design actually becomes an "exploded scheme" (p. 9). Having returned to the town for a brief interlude, Coverdale goes again to the Blithedale farm, hoping to find "something real." But he finds instead only a scene so deserted as to suggest that Blithedale life "had been nothing but dream-work and enchantment." Whereupon, in the interior of the wood, he finds his heroic enterprisers, his "grave associates," in "masquerading trim" (pp. 206, 210). The Coverdale of the peep-holed hermitage and the open-windowed hotel—the Coverdale who previously has sought veiled mystery—turns and flees from a scene that belies the Blithedalers' devotion to seriousness of purpose and simplicity of arrangement. Whereupon he finds, on arrival at Eliot's pulpit, not release, but the concluding moments of a scene of conflict, a scene that undermines the group's search for idyllic harmony. Zenobia's dark "history" —"the true nature of her mysterious connection with Westervelt"—and her "purposes" toward Hollingsworth, together with Hollingsworth's purposes toward her and whatever "plot" there had been "against Priscilla," here join Hollingsworth's abuse, in service to the "design" or "project" in which he has "embodied" himself, of the Blithedale experiment—and in consort produce intense drama (pp. 215, 133, 218). The combined pressure of these forces, having inspired this scene, lead in turn to Zenobia's death. Uncertainty, especially of motive and meaning, remains to haunt the world of the novel. Even in the penultimate epiphany, we see most of what we see darkly. But neither the catastrophe of Zenobia's death nor the collapse of the Blithedale experiment is hidden.

During Coverdale's tale of the fate of Blithedale and Hollingsworth, as clarification comes, veils multiply, interlacing clarification and mystery. Hawthorne uses Coverdale's mixing of these elements, however, not merely to stress the specious aspects of Coverdale's clarification but also to prepare for true uncovering and genuine disclosure. The illumination achieved in *The Blithedale Romance* is not finally the work of any one character. Only when Coverdale and Hollingsworth join with the yeoman Silas Foster to search the "broad, black, inscrutable depth" of the midnight river is the full reality of the novel disclosed (p. 232).

In opposition to the basic assumptions of all its characters (in opposition to Old Moodie's plan, Hollingsworth's design, the Blithedalers' experiment, and Coverdale's attempts, through compilation of simple description and manipulation of "mysterious arrangement," to coerce meaning), the reality of Hawthorne's novel remains stubbornly problematic. Only in a moment of genuine crisis do Coverdale and Hollingsworth transcend their characteristic limitations. In the novel's last scene, to be sure, each man has turned again to self-absorption: Coverdale is again "only a poet," a comic, apologetic failure primarily concerned with justifying himself and his conduct by substituting disclosure of the small secret of his love for Priscilla for confrontation with the big mysteries he has fled, and Hollingsworth, once absorbed in the "higher" and "wider" sphere of "the great object of [his] life," is preoccupied with his own guilt and disillusionment (pp. 6, 7, 218, 57). In the painful search for Zenobia's body, however, Coverdale's and Hollingsworth's roles are suddenly revised and in some measure even curiously reversed: Coverdale seats himself "in the stern, with the paddle," while Hollingsworth sits "in the bows, with the hooked pole"; Coverdale "manage[s]" the action, while Hollingsworth probes the "inscrutable" blackness of the river (p. 232).

What happens in this scene is not that Coverdale has given up interpretation; it is rather that he has ceased to substitute his task for involvement: his posture has become a stance, and so has been revised. Faced with countless signs and little certain significance, Coverdale characteristically observes with detachment in order to be free to impose meaning and assign significance. He habitually addresses the Blithedale drama not in the tone of a responding chorus but peremptorily; he uses technique as a means of arbitrary assignment rather than as a mode of rendering and developing and thereby discovering meaning. Nor, of course, does Hollingsworth in his probing of the black water relinquish his activistic bias. But for the first time he makes action a mode of discovery rather than a means of self-assertion. Faced with an imperfect world, Hollingsworth has sought neither to perceive nor to serve the order being worked out around him; he has endeavored, rather, to force his own notion of order upon life. Giving way to his instinct for radical improvisation, he has used his talent for ordering activity to serve his own design. But after Coverdale becomes "the helmsman," and then quietly lets "the boat drift," or slowly paddles it "up stream," again to suffer "it to glide," and after Silas Foster begins his search, Hollingsworth becomes more tentative and explorative (pp. 232–33).

> Silas Foster plied his rake manfully, poking it as far as he could into the water, and immersing the whole length of his arm besides. Hollingsworth at first sat motionless, with the hooked-pole elevated in the air. But, by-and-by, with a nervous and jerky movement, he began to plunge it into the blackness that upbore us. (p. 233)

Even after Hollingsworth touches and pulls forth "the perfect horror" that "the bottom of the river" yields up, ambiguity remains. Zenobia's body, having "grown rigid in the act of struggling," suggests both "terrible inflexibility" and terrible motion. It is a "marble image" of mortal agony. Moreover, having died with knees bent as well as hands clenched, Zenobia suggests, in addition to agony and struggle, "the attitude of prayer" (pp. 234–35). The midnight search for Zenobia thus reinforces the complexity of the reality rendered in *The Blithedale Romance*. But it also discloses the peculiar aspect of both Hollingsworth's and Coverdale's inadequacies: it suggests that Hollingsworth has brought to the ordering of life an uncompromising devotion to perfection more appropriate to artistic pursuits, and that Coverdale has brought to art as interpretation an ironic, qualified commitment more suitable to the pursuit of order in life.

Given his genuine talent for ordering life, Hollingsworth's retreat to the distinctly unreal world of Blithedale must be seen as anticipating that betrayal of self and world that culminates in his effort to subvert the Blithedale experiment to his own ends. Similarly, having accepted the task of interpreting the fate of Hollingsworth and Blithedale, having committed himself to making of the "Knot of Dreamers" something that "shall really deserve to be called poetry" (p. 14), Miles Coverdale uses the dramatic scenes he observes to avoid encounters he dreads. One suggestive fact is the frequency with which he arrives late for dramatic scenes; he almost always is unable quite to hear climactic interchanges or quite to see dramatic encounters. A second is that when heard words seem to him dangerously "mysterious" he simply resolves "that to no mortal" will he "disclose" them (pp. 104–05). What is even more telling, however, is that, faced with a problematic situation, Coverdale becomes a connoisseur of the problematic: by seeing mystery everywhere—even in fireplaces—he appears to seek his truths; but by citing, in a careless, lightly ironic mood, and even in a clownish and playful tone, a multitude of minor mysteries, he is able to circumvent encounter with the more ominous forms mystery takes in his world. Coverdale's sensed relation to Westervelt is not unwarranted: the perverse cynicism with which Westervelt multiplies and manipulates mystery is not unlike Coverdale's tendency to substitute frequent, easy citation for profound, concentrated encounter. Coverdale's posture works, however, contrary to his intent, to enforce encounter with the truth he fears; it actually serves the end he intends it only to appear to serve. Despite himself, Coverdale creates moments in which mystery's darkness refuses longer to be repressed, moments in which need overcomes fear. With his own dramatic logic, Coverdale comes first to "dream" of the darkness he flees, then to stumble upon dramatic exchanges, and then to discover the final catastrophe of Zenobia's death. The logic of his career leads him into events in which the novel's manifold complexities of motive and intent, design and action, result and meaning, culminate.

Through Coverdale's talent for analogy and generalization, Hawthorne links the Blithedale experiment to the "high enterprise" of the New England Puritans (p. 117). Hawthorne's Hollingsworth is a direct descendant of Hawthorne's Endicott (see p. 214). But he is even more distinctly the nineteenth-century American as reformer, a type Hawthorne knew well, especially as a result of his experience at Brook Farm.[28] Similarly, the Blithedale experiment represents a kind of "paradigm" of America as a social experiment. By suggesting "some deep meaning, most worthy of interpretation," however, Hawthorne's Brook Farm experience moved him not only to his own act of imaginative interpretation, through which he made Hollingsworth and Blithedale what they are, but also to creation of a poet-narrator as interpreter. In response, as it were, to a potential paradigm of American experience, Hawthorne created a narrator who became "an obvious surrogate for the American writer" as failed poet.[29]

Coverdale's failure points beyond itself, of course, to Hawthorne's limited achievement. The measure of the difficulty that Coverdale faces in becoming poet-interpreter of the problematic story of Hollingsworth and Blithedale is the subtlety of Hawthorne's rendering of Coverdale's failure. *The Blithedale*

28. On the Brook Farm experiment and its context, see Alice Felt Tyler, *Freedom's Ferment: Phases of American Social History from the Colonial Period to the Outbreak of the Civil War* [1944] (New York, Harper & Brothers, 1962), pp. 175–84.

29. Fussell, p. 124.

Romance is only in part the troubled story of the failed scheme
and plan that dominate its action. It is also the story of the
failed effort of its narrator to make dramatic poetry of that
action. Which is to say that in *The Blithedale Romance* Hawthorne discovered a fictional mode that enabled him to do at
least partial justice to the different dramas enacted by his man
of design and his man of interpretation. Later Henry James
and F. Scott Fitzgerald were to create more diverse, more profound, and more engaging characters of design and interpretation and were, in the process, in rediscovering the fictional
mode discovered by Hawthorne, to create works of art more
perfectly achieved as well as more compelling.

8 Extension of the Form: Henry James, and Fitzgerald's *The Great Gatsby*

> *And as imagination bodies forth*
> *The form of things unknown, the poet's pen*
> *Turns them to shapes, and gives to airy nothing*
> *A local habitation and a name.*
>
> William Shakespeare, A Midsummer
> Night's Dream

> *If thou didst ever hold me in thy heart,*
> *Absent thee from felicity awhile,*
> *And in this harsh world draw thy breath in pain,*
> *To tell my story.*
>
> William Shakespeare, Hamlet

Near the end of his life, Henry James entered upon a dual summing-up. First, from 1907 to 1909, in the Prefaces, he engaged in a prolonged interpretation of his fiction as the work of a lifetime. Later, from 1913 to 1916, he worked on an unfinished interpretation of the growth of his imagination. Separated by several years and inspired by different events, these endeavors assumed different forms. Taken together, however, they illuminate the origin and direction of James' preoccupation with design and interpretation.

In the autobiographical phase of his final interpretive efforts, James uses "imagination and memory" to endow with order the story of his life as a "man of imagination."[1] That story is

1. Henry James, *A Small Boy and Others* [1913] and *Notes of a Son and Brother* [1914], F. W. Dupee, ed., *Henry James: Autobiography* (New York, Criterion, 1956), pp. 4, 455.

shaped in its early stages by tension between the young brothers, William and Henry. William is a denizen of the exalted
"region" of "Experiments": endowed with the "capability" experiments require, William finds in the "region of their performance" his "natural sphere."[2] The young Henry, on the other
hand, seems to the older Henry "scarce even" to have known
"what Experiments were," nor ever to have been permitted
their region to explore. Left only with a memory of "a sense of
peeping into" William's region "to a thrilled effect," and with
the memory of having known "promptly" that "of course [he]
couldn't do" experiments himself, the older, interpreting Henry
James sketches his younger, observing counterpart diligently
at work to explore and exploit his attenuated and altogether
enforced role.[3] Watching "the small boy dawdle and gape"
before "chance feasts," the older James sees his younger self
become "at any rate master of [his] short steps, such as they
were." The "liberty of range and opportunity of adventure"
seized upon by the small boy move James not only to withhold
"no grain of . . . sympathy," nor merely to "wonder" at one so
"foredoomed" yet free, but also to see in his younger self a convenient image or warning—"the very pattern and measure"—
"of all that was to be." The dawdling creature had of course
"to go without many things"—"as all persons do in whom contemplation takes so much the place of action"; but "in the years
that came soon after, and that in fact continued long," he was
nonetheless to enjoy "the so far from showy practice of wondering and dawdling and gaping."[4]

What defines the contrast between William and Henry, at
least as the older Henry James renders it, is not so much simple
tension between thought and action as tension between different modes of thought, different kinds of action. In the realm

2. James, *A Small Boy and Others,* p. 15.
3. Ibid., pp. 15–16.
4. Ibid., pp. 16–17. Cf. *Notes of a Son and Brother,* p. 586.

of experiments, thought as well as action has legitimate place. What is threatened by the glamour and ostensible superiority of William's realm, of the world closed to his younger dawdling brother, is proper acknowledgment of the legitimacy of the world open to the dawdler. As a creature of imagination, as one "whose faculty for application" is all and only in his "imagination" and "sensibility," is the younger Henry merely "the sport" of a special "fate," or is he "the creature" of a special "force"?[5]

It is in response to this query that the older James goes on to picture his younger self as he moves beyond dawdling toward the labor of art. In his young counterpart's need "To feel a unity, a character and a tone in [his] impressions," in his need "to feel them related and all harmoniously coloured," the older James discovers what alone turns the "wondering and dawdling and gaping" spectator into an artist. In feeling that need, at least as James renders it, the younger James has also "positively to face the aesthetic, the creative, even, quite wondrously, the critical life and almost on the spot to commence author."[6]

James' highest achievement as an artist consisted, of course, neither in his life nor in the "subtle, if not . . . monstrous," effort "to write the history of the growth of [his] imagination," but in the fiction that was the primary fruit of his creative and critical life. And that fiction was, on one level, consummated in his Prefaces, where, in the form of notes on the continuity of his endeavor as an artist, he endeavored again to do those

5. James, *A Small Boy and Others*, p. 8, and *Notes of a Son and Brother*, p. 455.

6. James, *Notes of a Son and Brother*, p. 253, and *A Small Boy and Others*, p. 17. Cf. the following: "To live *in* the world of creation—to get into it and stay in it—to frequent it and haunt it—to *think* intently and fruitfully—to woo combinations and inspirations into being by a depth and continuity of attention and meditation—this is the only thing" (Matthiessen and Murdock, eds., *The Notebooks of Henry James*, p. 112).

"things" that through the whole of his life he had "done."[7]
James had of course in his Prefaces to tell the story of his
stories work by work. Yet, as Laurence Holland has stressed,
James' story of his stories has a shape all its own.[8] Again and
again in the Prefaces we confront three interrelated dramas.

There is, first, James' tracing of "the paradoxical intercon-
nection of masterly success and artistic failure"—his tracing
of the relation "between the vivid revival in memory" of his
"ambitious intentions" for his novels and his "disappointing
recognition that these ambitions had not been fully achieved,
even in the novel [he] thought his best."[9] Earlier in his career,
in 1881, James had talked confidently both of "the definiteness,
the unerringness" of the longings of his early, "untried years"
and of his having done very much what he "wanted to do" (he
had recently completed *The Portrait of a Lady*). But in the
years that came soon after (especially in his attempt to put "into
execution the most cherished of all [his] projects—that of
beginning to work for the stage") James learned much about
defeat. Before the day of his Prefaces, to be sure, triumph
again had undone failure, but James was never again to speak
as easily as he had in 1881 of "success" stretching "back a
tender hand to its younger brother, desire."[10] By 1907, when
he turned to interpret the "plan" behind *Roderick Hudson*,
which he had once innocently "supposed" himself to have
"achieve[d]" (p. 7), he worked with more adequately mixed
notions of failure and success.

The second defining drama of the Prefaces derives from

7. Blackmur, ed., *The Art of the Novel*, pp. 47, 4, 347. All page
references in the text of this section of this chapter are to this
edition of James' "Critical Prefaces."

8. Laurence B. Holland, *The Expense of Vision: Essays on the
Craft of Henry James* (Princeton, Princeton University Press, 1964),
p. 156.

9. Ibid.

10. Matthiessen and Murdock, eds., *Notebooks*, pp. 35–37.

what James called "the law of some rich passion . . . for extremes" (p. 31). As the Prefaces, and indeed the later pages of *A Small Boy and Others,* make clear, James was drawn not only to dawdling and gaping but also to experimenting and building. The Prefaces accordingly retell the story of tension between an architectural principle and a "law of fructification."[11] On one side James is a man of "design[s]" and "plan[s]" and "scheme[s]."[12] His classicism, his commitment to deliberate craftsmanship and conscious mastery of technique, entail love of "plotting and planning and calculating." Again and again his "artistic rage" makes itself felt in his effort to carry out his "design." "The dramatist," James says, "has verily to *build,* is committed to architecture, to construction at any cost" (pp. 31, 109).[13] According to a commitment that, at least as he depicts its derivation in his autobiographical writings, was prior, however, the James of the Prefaces is dedicated to imaginative passion; and, given the logic of James' mind, that passion implies obedience to "the law of fructification"—according to which the man of imagination must accept *"all* life" and cultivate each "germ" until it realizes itself.[14] The basic question has always, James says, to come back to the quality of "the artist's prime sensibility," for that sensibility is "the soil" from which the germs given him must derive their nourishment: "The quality and capacity of that soil" determine its ability to permit a germ of experience to " 'grow' with due freshness and straightness" into a new "vision of life" (p. 45; see pp. 47–54).

11. Ibid., p. 111.
12. See e.g. Blackmur, ed., *The Art of the Novel,* pp. 30, 109, 144, 214, 57, 76, 136, 330; cf. p. 186.
13. Note James' use of Ibsen's phrase "the master-builder," Blackmur, ed., *The Art of the Novel,* p. 123.
14. Matthiessen and Murdock, eds., *Notebooks,* p. 111. Blackmur, ed., *The Art of the Novel,* p. 45. Cf. *A Small Boy and Others,* pp. 8, 15–17.

The tensions James develops between his plans and his achievements, on one side, and between his architectural principle and his organic principle, on the other, are within the Prefaces related tensions. James knew that in each case "one's plan, alas, [was] one thing and one's result another" (p. 296). Yet because he had learned to trust not only his sensibility but fiction as a medium, he had also learned to "trust" each donnée to "show" him what it could and would become (p. 53). Despite the discrepancies between his plans and his achievements—despite, that is, his failure simply to achieve what he had attempted—he discovers, in the process of living over the general adventure of his compositions, not only that "buried secrets" and hidden "intentions" lie behind the "so beautifully tangled . . . web" of his work, but also that "the design" of the whole has been "more or less realised" (pp. 11, 345, 228–29). Ironically, the "singular things" that, in the move from envisaged design to realized artifact, have somehow "happen[ed]" have served rather to complete than to mar the work (p. 152). As James finally sees it, therefore, it is only by committing "himself in both directions" at once—to discovery as well as construction—that the artist can hope "To put all that is possible of [his] idea into a form and compass that will contain and express" each of its "delicate adjustments" and the whole of its "exquisite chemistry" (pp. 31, 87).

The third and most inclusive drama defining the Prefaces springs from James' careful effort to interrelate "the compositional problem" (p. 319) defined by his own dual commitment with the various moral problems confronting his protagonists. Repeatedly he insists that the adventures of his protagonists parallel and are analogous with his own technical adventure in rendering them. What he calls, in his last Preface, "the religion of doing" (p. 347) embraces both the action rendered within his works—that is, his characters' efforts to do—and his action in making those works.

A few of the characters who most directly correspond to

James' architectural, constructive passion are artists. But the constructive urge also moves characters to efforts directly to order life. In *The Spoils of Poynton,* for instance, Mrs. Gereth's plan for keeping Poynton is an extension of her original effort, in consort with her husband, to build it: it represents conscious, concerted opposition to the "stupid work" of "clumsy Life" (p. 121); whereas life is "all inclusion and confusion," her endeavor is "all discrimination and selection" (p. 120). Which is to say that her planned action within the novel corresponds to James' constructive action in making the novel—in arranging "the blocks quarried in the deeps of his imagination" (pp. 120–22).[15]

The danger implicit in Mrs. Gereth's constructive passion—that of "making confusion worse" (see p. 143)—shapes the role played by the novel's dawdling spectator, Fleda Vetch. In *The Spoils of Poynton,* as elsewhere, the texture of James' fictional world "positively provokes, all around, a mystic solicitation, the urgent appeal, on the part of everything, to be interpreted and, so far as may be, reproduced" (p. 59). James' own imaginative passion accordingly is also refracted through characters whose passion centers on perception rather than construction, characters who respond to muddlement and complexity—to "the displayed tangle of human relations," the "abyss of ambiguities," "the muddle of fate," and "the much-mixed world" (pp. 63–64, 76)—with efforts to see and understand. Fleda Vetch represents what was for James an "accepted habit": the habit of "dealing with" his "subject-matter" and " 'seeing [his] story' " through a "concrete deputy or delegate" who "contributes to the case mainly a certain amount of criticism and interpretation of it" (pp. 327–28; cf. pp. 63–65).

Like Rowland Mallet in *Roderick Hudson* (1875), Fleda is

15. The Preface to *The Spoils of Poynton* is found in Blackmur, ed., *The Art of the Novel,* pp. 119–39. As the reader will note from the references in the text, however, I have, in discussing this novel as a "representative" case, drawn from several of James' Prefaces.

often "bedimmed and befooled and bewildered, anxious, rest-
less, fallible" (p. 16; cf. p. 70); but like the Prince and the
Princess in *The Golden Bowl* (1904) she is appointed and
obliged to see and know and make out, virtually to represent
to herself "everything that concerns us" (p. 329). Despite its
limitation, furthermore, Fleda's role implicates her deeply in the
total adventure of the novel (see p. 16). Given "the *constant*
force[s]" (including Mrs. Gereth's efforts to preserve and extend order) that make "for muddlement," Fleda's "effort really
to see and really to represent is no idle business" (see p. 149).
For in her efforts to see and represent she not only shares Mrs.
Gereth's ordering activity but also participates in the "muffled
majesty" of James' dual, constructive and creative, passion. In
short, like the Prince and Princess of *The Golden Bowl,* Fleda
for James is "a compositional resource . . . as well as a value
intrinsic" (pp. 328–29).

By interlacing experimentation and dawdling, constructive
passion and imaginative passion, action and interpretation,
James managed to satisfy his "rich passion . . . for extremes"
(p. 31); and he also managed to honor what he saw as his own
enduring urge: "the question," he said, "has ever been for me
but of wondering and, with all achievable adroitness, of causing
to wonder" (p. 254). Under the proper pressure, interpretation could become not base apology for failed designs, nor
"barren commentary" on barren failure, nor "mere gaping
contrition" for deeds undone, but a mode of wondering and a
way of causing to wonder—a way, in fine, of enriching the
"effective interest" of "the facts retailed and the figures introduced," a way of discovering and representing the "finest
and most numerous secrets" of a donnée, a way of achieving
"exemplary" unity and radiance (pp. 327–28, 346, 348).

Two basic fictional patterns, both having to do with America's relation to Europe, emerged from James' prolonged ex-

perimentation and exploration of design and interpretation. In one an entrepreneur, such as Christopher Newman, that "superlative American" and "born experimentalist," journeys to Europe to acquire "everything" that is peculiarly European.[16] James' experimentalists are strong, of course, on the side of life; they get on well in the region of active experimentation. In scope of vision, range of ambition, and depth of resource, as well as in terms of being placed in a consummate work of art, they reached their apotheosis in Adam Verver.

Adam Verver is moved by a grand design: he wants to enrich his community by building in it an edifice capable of meeting all its needs and longings.[17] Behind the enormously rich texture of the language of the novel—behind the efforts waged by James' Prince and Princess to see and know, to penetrate and untangle, and behind the Princess' grand effort beautifully to redo her world—there lies the "majestic scheme" of Adam Verver *(23,* 210).

> It had n't merely, his plan, all the sanctions of civilisation; it was positively civilisation condensed, concrete, consummate . . . a house from whose open doors and windows, open to grateful, to thirsty millions, the higher, the highest knowledge would shine out to bless the land. In this house, designed as a gift primarily to the people of his adoptive city and native State, the urgency of whose release from the bondage of ugliness he was in a position to measure—in this museum of museums, a palace of art which was to show for compact as a Greek temple was

16. *Novels and Tales of Henry James, 2,* 26, 33. Subsequent references in the text of this section of this chapter are to this edition of James' fiction. The reader should note that in this section in each case the italicized number refers to volume, not to page.

17. It is interesting to note that Adam Verver retains two troubled memories from his past, one centering on his first wife and the other on a rebuff at the door of the house of his aspirations. Cf. Jay Gatsby and Thomas Sutpen. See Holland, p. 354.

> compact, a receptacle of treasures sifted to positive sanc-
> tity, his spirit to-day almost altogether lived, making up,
> as he would have said, for lost time and haunting the
> portico in anticipation of the final rites. *(23,* 145)

Adam Verver's "strange scheme" is born in part of his "attribu-
tion of power"—his knowledge that "he had force" because
"he had money"; and in part of his felt kinship with all the
builders of America *(23,* 144, 131). Time itself seems to him
to have decreed that for him "acquisition of one sort" will be
the "perfect preliminary to acquisition of another." In "com-
parative blindness," he has all along been preparing to serve
one "supreme idea" *(23,* 144).

Tied and interwoven with America's past and present, Adam
Verver of American City becomes a surrogate for his land.

> He had had to *like* forging and sweating, he had had to
> like polishing and piling up his arms. They were things
> at least he had had to believe he liked, just as he had be-
> lieved he liked transcendent calculation and imaginative
> gambling all for themselves, the creation of "interests"
> that were the extinction of other interests, the livid vul-
> garity even of getting in, or getting out, first. *(23,* 144)

Such had of course been "far from really the case"; only the
growth of his "supreme idea" for building a concrete, con-
densed, consummate embodiment of civilization, a monument
to man's effort to humanize his world and himself, had made
possible for him the pretense of liking livid vulgarity *(23,* 144).

Strangely, however, Adam Verver's monument to life—his
tribute to man's effort to order his existence—is to be "a palace
of art." Adam Verver is going to build a new and more perfect
Louvre in America. The "structure" which his "imagination"
envisages, and to which he gives himself with all possible
patience and piety, is to be "a monument to the religion he

wished to propagate, the exemplary passion, the passion for perfection at any price" *(23,* 145–46).

In his devoted effort to achieve perfection through planned action, Adam Verver is representative. The flawed Golden Bowl finally becomes an image not only of the marriages and affairs of the novel but also of the various plans, including Adam Verver's, that inspire the novel's action. In the mixed motion of the novel, Adam Verver's majestic plan at times fades. But the action derives, complexly to be sure, from it, and finally returns to it.[18] Adam Verver is the instigator, as it were, of the novel's action; its pope and king, president and author (see *23,* 205, 292–93).

The perfection to which Verver devotes himself is approached and completed, however, only when Maggie, as interpreter and representer of her world, enters upon the work of redoing. By altering and rearranging the tangled relations that define her world, Maggie is able simultaneously to acknowledge radical flaw and to retain devotion to perfection. Through her redirected, recomplicated, redoubled devotion, the marriages are restored and her father's dedication to his design is renewed.[19] The unity thus achieved is of course tense; and it is paid for with sacrifice. But it is unity that transcends division. No one and nothing is simply lost: Charlotte's departure with Adam Verver for America no longer represents a burial or a doom, but a great opportunity—she joins in renewal of his purpose, and together they go forth to represent "the arts and the graces to a people languishing afar off and in ignorance" *(24,* 357).

In contrast to James' experimentalists, his passionate pilgrims lack capacity for experimentation; they embody abundance—enormous potential wealth, enormous capacity and longing for life—that they know not how to realize. They ac-

18. See *23,* 210–11, 214–16, 220–25, 131, 170–71, 125–28.
19. See *24,* 25–26, 33, 145.

cordingly journey to Europe, when they do not go simply to see,[20] not to possess Europe but to be possessed and realized and saved by it. It is in another of the late works, *The Wings of the Dove,* in the person of Milly Theale, that James' pilgrims attain their apotheosis.

Although "the possibilities" shine "out of Milly" *(19,* xx), she is dying of an unspecified malady that manifests itself in simple yet acute need of saving form. "Her possibilities are quite plain," Kate Croy remarks. "I should n't care for her if she had n't so much. . . . [And] I should n't trouble about her if there were one thing she did have. . . . She has nothing" *(20,* 51–52). What is required is form capable of expressing each of Milly's possibilities and the whole of her "exquisite chemistry" *(7,* xiii). Milly is potentially too rich actually to possess anything; she is all too much "the heir[ess] of all the ages" to be an actual child of any. Thus balked of her inheritance—as an enormously rich yet curiously dispossessed princess, as a wandering heiress-heroine in search of an author—she goes to Europe, hoping there to discover (or to be discovered by) someone capable of giving expression to her enormous wealth. In her effort to realize everything within her, in her effort to wrest from her shrinking hour all that she possibly can of life, thus absolutely to live, she must depend upon "the aid of others" *(19,* ix, viii).

To the struggle not to betray what she is, Milly is completely devoted. She wants to redeem "possible great chances . . . neglected, possible great moments" missed *(19,* 287). Yet because she is so "devoted," she also is perilously "exposed"; because her wealth cries out not to be wasted, because she yearns so to live, Milly can "but fall somehow into some abysmal trap." Moreover, because she is what she is, she inevitably

20. James' passionate pilgrims (see "A Passionate Pilgrim" [1871]) frequently go simply "to appreciate." Insofar as they seek "to make" Europe their "own," they do so imaginatively; they want "to take intellectual possession" only (see *11,* xix; cf. *23,* 145; and *2,* xv).

constitutes for others "a complication as great as any they might constitute" for her *(19,* ix-x).

By exuding abundance—as a veritable incarnation of the unrealized abundance of America—and by making her plea for aid, Milly moves others to action. Her own need is matched by the equally intense yet very different needs of the world into which she comes. As Kate quickly sees, all of London will inevitably adore and want Milly *(19,* 228, 282). The sly maneuvering of Lord Mark, the gossipy planning of Susan Stringham, and the careful scheming of Maude Lowder evolve under the pressure of peculiar "interests" and "motives"; to each Milly becomes "a complication" *(19,* viii-ix).[21] But it is to Kate Croy, who all instinctively is mortal foe to waste, that Milly becomes the great, the final complication.

Even before Milly descends upon her world, Kate Croy has begun to give shape to her design. She wants with Merton Densher to find new and rich harmony. Together they have discovered within and between themselves genuine affection and "a precious unlikeness." They want to marry: they want to couple "her pure talent for life" with his talent "on the side of the mind," his mastery of the mysterious realm of consciousness *(19,* 50; *20,* 176). Marriage, however, the union they seek, lies "somehow before them like a temple without an avenue." The "great ugliness" is the want "of means sufficient" to enable them to consummate their union and reach their temple *(19,* 59, 62).

As one whose talent is for life, as one endowed with cleverness and blessed with an instinct for tactics and strategy, Kate must accept responsibility for bringing them to their proper temple without loss. Through her "scheme" she must "work" Densher in "with other and alien things" and yet "pay no price" *(19,* 61–62). The danger of course, as Kate puts it, is

21. See R. W. B. Lewis, "The Vision of Grace: James's *The Wings of the Dove," Modern Fiction Studies,* 3 (1957), 39.

that "of doing something base." But, as one to whom power "was the last thing . . . [to be] treated as a mystery," and as one gifted with a "mastery of fitnesses," she cannot shirk the task: "I shall sacrifice nobody and nothing," she says, "and that's just my situation, that I want and that I shall try for everything" *(19,* 175; *20,* 315; *19,* 72).

Feeling herself also appealed to for participation in Milly's drama, Kate responds with "superior diplomacy" *(19,* xix). Through her plan and her game,[22] she will save Milly from loss, enabling her to live, fully if briefly; yet at the same time, indeed in the same motion, she will provide for her own marriage to Densher. Kate is born to "handle" life not only because she loves its beautiful show, but because she loves "the beauty" of what she sees in her plan. Her plan has about it "high colour" and "great style" because she clings "to some saving romance in things" *(20,* 114, 30; *19,* 74, 72): "only believe in me," she tells Densher, in words echoed by every author of design, "and it will be beautiful" *(20,* 19).

Milly alone finally defines her world; the story is her story, the book her book. Densher's last act of interpretation must therefore be his endeavor to "understand her" *(20,* 403). Milly defines her world, however, not by controlling either its action or its language but by a dispensation in which she becomes her own author. With one supreme, unobserved act, and one supreme, unread epistle, she redefines the whole of her world. In the meantime, the world given Milly to redefine is itself being defined, in considerable measure, by the juxtaposition of Kate's plan with Merton's effort, as James puts it in his *Notebooks,* to read Kate's "game."[23]

Driven by her own strong will, Kate initiates an action she cannot control; she becomes herself the victim as well as the somewhat "brutal" instrument of forces she sets in motion yet

22. Matthiessen and Murdock, eds., *Notebooks,* pp. 172–73.
23. Ibid.

cannot direct. Kate is betrayed in part by her own "habit of anticipation"—her tendency to simplify "in advance" *(19, 182;* see *20,* 323). But she is betrayed too by her dark past, the unspoken horror of her origins as represented by her father, Lionel Croy, and by present acts, especially Lord Mark's, of petty revenge. In short, incongruous elements and conflicting desires twist Kate's efforts to order and liberate and save.

Merton Densher accordingly is left with beautiful plan turned "dreadful game" to read *(20,* 347). Densher's life within the world of the novel corresponds to his role in its structure: as one whose talent is for perceiving and understanding rather than acting and performing, he is an observer and interpreter. Not only does he submit to Kate's direction—"He would do as *she* liked . . . he would be . . . deeply diplomatic" *(19,* 75). He even permits himself to be handled by her—he submits "to her management of him," accepting the "postponed and relegated," the "so extremely manipulated state" to which she "beautifully" reduces him *(20,* 175–76). But in the process he makes the task of reading his own. Because it is "so extraordinarily special to Kate," Merton shrinks "from the complications involved in judging" and interpreting "Kate's design" *(20,* 77). But he finally must judge and interpret it—not only because of his own need to see and know, nor merely because he must make us see, but because, like Milly, Kate needs not "to be liked" but "to be judged" *(19,* 252).

Kate's design accordingly remains an unarticulated "game" until, in Book VIII, Densher performs his appointed task. "Don't think," Kate says, that "I'll do *all* the work for you. If you want things named you must name them." Densher, who "had quite, within the minute, been turning names over," sees promptly the one that "stared at him there dreadful" as the only one "that properly fitted. 'Since she's to die I'm to marry her?' " *(20,* 225), he asks. After Kate has repeated his words, Densher continues to spell out her game: "So that when her death has taken place I shall in the natural course have money?" With it out before him, finally phrased and again repeated, even elaborated—and we shall be free, Kate adds—Densher knows that this plan—"all along"—was all and "only" what Kate had "meant" *(20,* 225).

Densher's interpretation is an inquiry into the meaning and significance of Kate's design. That design is in turn, however, a response both to the deep need Kate feels and to the straining abundance Milly embodies. Densher accordingly must address himself not simply to the design Kate pursues but to the problem Milly poses: which is to say that Densher's interpretation is more than interlaced with Kate's design; in essential motive, by being a response to the problem that Milly poses as well as to the game that Kate plays, Densher's interpretive endeavor is analogous to Kate's active endeavor.

Milly is "the American girl": in Mrs. Stringham's phrase, she is "a mine of something precious" and mysterious and beautiful, a mine that needs only to be worked to "yield a treasure." She represents "the freedom of all the centuries," the possibility of "high style and state," the possible conjunction of the whole of art and life *(20, 215; 19,* 126; *20,* 174, 185), and yet, in Kate's no less accurate assessment, Milly "has nothing" *(20,* 52). The "possible but forbidden life," the "beautiful fictions and priceless arrangements," that Milly represents yet cannot realize correspond to the "everything" that Kate and Densher seek *(20,* 147, 298). That life is, indeed, not only beauty but meaning itself. Early in the novel we learn that Kate senses the presence in her family's history of "words and notes without sense" and, then, "no words nor any notes at all." Kate is determined that "the broken sentence" which is her heritage and her life will be made whole, that it will "end with a sort of meaning" *(19,* 4, 6). Kate's design is her effort to achieve that meaning. Not unlike Kate's, Milly's heritage is fragmented. She is the sole "survivor of a general wreck," "the last broken link" from a past defined by "high extravagance of speculation and dissipation" *(19,* 241, 174). In contrast to Kate, of course, Milly knows only how to languish and long, not how to seek the "bright sound" and "bright colour" she wants. Yet strangely, by seizing upon "some complete use of her [unrealized wealth] . . . as a counter-move to fate," she succeeds in doing what Kate fails to do: she manages to bless her broken world *(20,* 294, 142; *19,* 73).

In his effort simultaneously to judge "Kate's design" and to "understand" Milly *(20,* 77, 403), Densher attains a significant part of the meaning he pursues. Having read Kate's design and having called it by its proper name, he is prepared to learn from Milly of sounds that lie beyond "the inevitable sounds of life," beyond the real and hampered state of man. He learns imaginatively and "extraordinarily" to fill in and refine the meaning of the "faint far wail" of Milly's unread letter *(20,* 396; see *2,* xvi).

Although it is ennobled and enriched by her unperceived act and unread epistle, Milly's world is not simply redeemed. The order sought and the freedom pursued are achieved only in the novel, only in art, not in the life it represents and translates. The beauty Milly embodies remains haunted by "the great smudge of mortality . . . the shadow of pain and horror" *(20,* 298–99). The fictions and arrangements Milly suggests are "full of a poetry" never fully and simply to be her world's; she speaks, and must speak, "with an ironic smile of a possible but forbidden life" *(20,* 147).

Milly's triumph, though genuine, accordingly is paradoxical. On two occasions she becomes herself. With "the aid" of her "painted sister" in "the wonderful Bronzino" things melt "together" in "magnificent maximum, the pink dawn of an apotheosis" *(19,* 220, 228, 217). Later, in her rented palace, by becoming "embodied poetry," Milly is able independently to acquit herself "as hostess": across the room over which she presides she sends to Kate and Densher "all the candour of her smile, the lustre of her pearls, the value of her life, the essence of her wealth" *(20,* 217, 214, 229). But this victory is also fleeting. Amid "stretches of . . . gallery paved with squares of red marble, greasy now with the salt spray," amid the "bright sound" and "bright colour" of the city of flowing streets and shifting moods, an asylum for centuries to refugees, the place of art as artifact, Milly's rented Venetian palace changes. Having become the scene of her triumph, it becomes the scene of betrayal—and thereby an image not only of Milly's life but of Europe and its people, of man and his world: "the whole place, in its huge elegance, the grace of its conception and the beauty of its détail, was more than ever like a great drawing-room, the drawing-room of Europe, profaned and bewildered by some reverse of fortune" *(20,* 261, 294).

To become herself—to conquer fate and overcome the profaning, bewildering work of fortune—Milly must make the scene of betrayal the scene also of supreme triumph. From her profaned palace she writes and dispatches her letter and then becomes her book. Yet because she remains "disconcerting poetry" her triumph remains troubling *(20,* 184). The perfect order and beauty sought by Kate Croy and Merton Densher and strained toward by Milly Theale finally stand as at once possible and forbidden, a temple somehow forever without an avenue. The order and beauty sought in life are attained only in art, which, as Milly sees when she confronts her "painted sister," endures and yet is "dead," exists but is not alive. Through the beauty of her "characteristic poetry" *(19,* 228, 221, 194), Milly enables, as it were, her book to exist. But her book, in contrast, gives her life very different from the life that within it we see her seek. Kate Croy and Merton Densher come finally to stand, forever changed, forgiven, and blessed, under Milly's wings. But they are redeemed—their world is made whole—only at great expense and supreme sacrifice, and only through an act that cannot directly be observed and a letter that can never directly be read—an act and letter that come in the novel as an image of "something dreamed and missed, something reduced, relinquished, resigned: the poetry, as it were, of something sensibly *gone.*"[24]

The Golden Bowl and *The Wings of the Dove* represent "expert violations" of the interpreted design.[25] Given, first, the very basic role the distinction between experimenters and dawdlers played for James, second, the very complex relationship he saw between experimenters and dawdlers and between each of them and his own artistic endeavors, third, the very vigorous imagination with which he was blessed, and fourth, the very deep devotion he brought to artistic exploration, such violations were inevitable: design and interpretation would necessarily proliferate and intermingle, be turned and changed.

In 1925, in a letter to F. Scott Fitzgerald, T. S. Eliot called *The Great Gatsby* "the first step that American fiction has taken since Henry James."[26] In the story of the interpreted design, Eliot's contention is sound. Like Henry James, William Dean Howells and Theodore Dreiser were committed to literary art as "representation." But they tended, far more than James, to delimit representation: they thought art essentially a means of describing, and in that limited sense of representing, what they took to be order prior to it and meaning independent of it.[27]

24. I have borrowed here from *The Spoils of Poynton;* see *Novels and Tales, 10,* 249.

25. See R. W. B. Lewis, *The American Adam: Innocence, Tragedy, and Tradition in the Nineteenth Century* (Chicago, University of Chicago Press, 1955), p. 155.

26. T. S. Eliot, Letter to F. Scott Fitzgerald, December 1925, in Edmund Wilson, ed., *The Crack-Up* [1945] (New York, New Directions, 1956), p. 310.

27. See Gordon Haight, "Realism Defined: William Dean Howells," *Literary History of the United States,* ed. Robert E. Spiller and others (rev. ed. New York, 1953), pp. 879–98. Kenneth S. Lynn, *Dream of Success: A History of the Modern American Imagination* (Boston, Little,

In terms of the stories told, the contrast between James on one side and Howells and Dreiser on the other was crucial. Like James, Howells and Dreiser were drawn to stories of men of design. Their stories of such men tend, moreover, in good American fashion, to treat plans for founding dynasties, constructing mansions, and building financial empires. Even more than James, both Howells and Dreiser implicitly acknowledge that, in an increasingly acquisitive society, the American penchant for designs had come increasingly to center either on acquiring "a million a year" or on constructing emblems of wealth.[28] But like James in *The Bostonians,* which in the tradition of *The Blithedale Romance* has to do with a design for reform, Howells and Dreiser characteristically told stories of designs, not of interpreted designs. Silas Lapham and Frank Cowperwood have as much claim as Hollingsworth or Adam Verver to stand as representative American builders. Indeed, since they do not share place with men of interpretation—with surrogates for the interpreting artist—Lapham and Cowperwood are given preeminence not ordinarily given men of design. What in Howells' and Dreiser's stories is all important is the fate of designs; what is at stake is the possibility of meaningful action. Only in the most implicit, the most oblique and necessary way—that is, only by virtue of the presence of the work of art itself—is stress given either to the possibility that designed action, having failed, will require completion in poetry, or to the possibility that interpretive endeavors (like works of art) may also fail.

Brown, 1955). Kazin, *On Native Grounds,* pp. 3–90. F. O. Matthiessen, *Theodore Dreiser,* American Men of Letters Series (New York, Sloane, 1951). Lionel Trilling, "Reality in America," *The Liberal Imagination,* pp. 1–19.

28. See *Novels and Tales of Henry James, 17,* 485; and Henry James, *The American Scene,* ed. W. H. Auden (New York, Scribner, 1946), pp. xxv, 135–38. See also Newton Arvin, "Henry James and the Almighty Dollar," *Hound and Horn, 7* (1934), 434–43.

F. Scott Fitzgerald began his career in the tradition of Howells and Dreiser. "Winter Dreams" (1922) focuses on Dexter Green's effort, through appeal to his slightly absurd vision of Judy Jones' beauty, to overcome the dismal spring and desolate winter of his world. Like Howells in *The Rise of Silas Lapham* and Dreiser in *The Financier* and *The Titan,* Fitzgerald himself is the only interpreter in "Winter Dreams," just as he had been in *This Side of Paradise* (1920).[29]

In "The Diamond as Big as the Ritz" (1922), Fitzgerald reintroduces into American fiction the interpreting narrator, or what James previously had termed a "concrete deputy or delegate" who "contributes to the case mainly a certain amount of criticism and interpretation of it."[30] The story centers on a family—the Washingtons of Montana—who are directly descended from George Washington and Lord Baltimore and who are engaged in corrupt and insatiable ravaging of their new world. But by telling the story through a visiting interpreter, John T. Unger of Mississippi, Fitzgerald was able to move beyond his other engagements—in, for example, *The Beautiful and Damned* (1922) and *The Vegetable* (1922)—with perversions of American dreams toward *The Great Gatsby* (1925), his most perfectly achieved work of art.

As an image of what Americans have made of America, "The Diamond as Big as the Ritz" is altogether bleak. It bespeaks loss of faith, if not in the possibilities, at least in the actualities of American life. *The Great Gatsby* is permeated with corruption and contains, in the valley of ashes, Fitzgerald's starkest image of the New World as waste land. Yet the story of Jay Gatsby is finally far less grim than the story of the Washingtons. Gatsby's "incorruptible" version of "the last

29. See *This Side of Paradise* (New York, Scribner, 1920), p. 304; and *All the Sad Young Men* (New York, Scribner, 1926), p. 57. See Arthur Mizener, *The Far Side of Paradise: A Biography of F. Scott Fitzgerald* (Boston, Houghton Mifflin, 1951), Chap. 5.

30. Blackmur, ed., *The Art of the Novel*, pp. 327–28.

and greatest of all human dreams"—the dream of a new and perfect life in a new and perfect world—serves, as several critics have noted, to relieve grimness.[31] It does not, however, in itself represent relief; it makes relief possible. The whole of Gatsby's story, including both his dream and his absurd plan for realizing it—his plan for procuring a fortune, a mansion, and a bride—is redeemed from corruption and waste, from failure and absurdity only through Nick Carraway's effort imaginatively to interpret and render it. The first four paragraphs of the novel prepare us for the form the novel's unfolding is to take. In the first three paragraphs, the narrator, Nick Carraway, introduces himself—he is, we learn, a self-conscious and self-critical narrator as well as a spectator; in the fourth paragraph he introduces the subject of his narrative, Jay Gatsby—who is, we learn, a builder as well as a dreamer. Carraway's small cottage on the edge of Gatsby's spacious estate suggests the role he is to play within the novel: the role of observer and spectator, critic and interpreter of a scene and an action dominated by Gatsby.

Gatsby represents, Carraway tells us, "everything for which I have an unaffected scorn." Yet because he has found in Gatsby "some heightened sensitivity to the promises of life"—"a romantic readiness"—and because of the curious way Gatsby "turned out . . . at the end," Carraway has not been able not to tell Gatsby's story. Having watched Gatsby pursue "his dream" with "unwavering devotion," Carraway knows that Gatsby has lived in faith that man can shape his life at will, compelling it to yield the meaning he needs (pp. 2, 110). Carraway accordingly knows that Gatsby has become what he has become through his "extraordinary gift for hope"—his extraor-

31. *The Great Gatsby* (New York, Scribner, 1925), pp. 155, 182. All page references in the text of this section of this chapter are to this work. See Marius Bewley, "Scott Fitzgerald's Criticism of America," *Sewanee Review, 62* (1954), 223–46; and Edwin Fussell, "Fitzgerald's Brave New World," *English Literary History, 19* (1952), 291–306.

dinary faith that through devoted action he not only can shape the future but can "fix" the "terrible mistake" that mars the past (pp. 2, 111, 131). Moved as he is by faith in observing closely and "reserving judgments," Carraway is drawn to seek purpose in the "purposeless splendor" and meaning in the problematic fate that define Gatsby's life (pp. 1, 79). Unlike Gatsby's faith, which leaves him vulnerable to destruction (see p. 137), Carraway's faith renders him vulnerable to despair: to loss of "interest in the abortive sorrows and short-winded elations of men" (p. 2) and loss of faith in the effort "to save . . . fragment[s]" of "dead dream[s]" (pp. 153, 135). If in Gatsby, Fitzgerald dramatizes the peculiar beauty and vulnerability of one dedicated to actualizing dreams, in Carraway he dramatizes the peculiar beauty and vulnerability of one dedicated to finding meaning in the "undefined consequence" of an action (p. 64).

Behind Gatsby there is a history of dislocation and alienation, the attendants, as it were, of the experience of immigration, and thus of the very process of Americanization. But behind him there also is an imagined history. On one side, he is James Gatz, the son of "shiftless and unsuccessful farm people." On the other, he is Jay Gatsby, the child of "his Platonic conception of himself," the heir to a history almost wholly "invented." Unable in the presence of abundance—of mansions in the town and yachts upon the lake—to accept dislocation and deprivation, "his imagination" has created an identity— ✓ a "conception"—to which he remains "faithful to the end" (pp. 98–99).

James Gatz' attempt to become Jay Gatsby, his attempt to live out of his invented history, is one part of his attempt to realize his "unutterable" dream (p. 112). Given his world, his dream, despite its "gaudiness," is necessary. At times its vitality almost overwhelms him, almost reduces him to a mere embodiment of its impulse; and at times he almost fatally betrays it by making devotion to it service not to beauty but to

the "vast, vulgar, and meretricious" (pp. 98–99). From outset
to end, he just misses "being absurd" (p. 48).[32] Yet both his
conception of himself and his dream survive everything. To its
curiously actual yet unreal world, Gatsby's dream comes as "a
deathless song"; in its own way it is so "absolutely real" that it
changes everything it touches "into something significant, elemental, and profound" (pp. 97, 46–47). Though altogether
unactual, it is its world's primary source of positive good, its
primary hope of overcoming the "foul dust" and the "valley
of ashes" (pp. 2, 23–24).

Before it is finally rendered "incorruptible," however, Gatsby's particular version of "the last and greatest of all human
dreams" becomes a "dead dream" and leads to "grotesque"
"nightmare" (pp. 155, 182, 135, 164). And it does so because,
in the design through which Gatsby attempts to actualize it, it
is wed to "perishable breath" and mortal mansion. In entering
the round world of time-space, it falls victim to the "accidental" and ends in "holocaust" (pp. 112, 162–63).

In its earliest recorded form, Gatsby's effort to express "his
unutterable visions" (p. 112) takes the form of a "SCHEDULE"
(a direct descendant of Benjamin Franklin's) copied on a
flyleaf of "a ragged old copy of a book called *Hopalong Cas-
sidy."* The schedule itself is intended to enforce industry and
frugality, to foster physical, mental, and moral growth, and to
encourage development of social graces and personal cleanli-
ness—"No wasting time"; "No more smokeing or chewing";
"Bath every other day"; "Practice elocution, poise and how to
attain it" (p. 174). Later, goaded by loss of Daisy—to whom he
has "felt [himself] married"—and by knowledge that the "terrible mistake" of her marriage with the wealthy Tom Buchanan
is a result of his being poor, Gatsby turns his dream into a

32. Note that the quoted phrase applies specifically to Gatsby's voice,
and cf. p. 174, where we learn that Gatsby's first schedule includes practicing elocution.

design that dictates a precise course of action. On one side he will pursue "his phantom millions"—he will accumulate a prodigious fortune and procure a colossal mansion. On the other he will pursue Daisy, to whom, as an embodiment of ideal beauty, he commits himself as "to the following of a grail" (pp. 131, 149).

Although it culminates in his own death, Gatsby's effort to turn dream to design and design to actuality provides the key to understanding his story. When Carraway first realizes that Gatsby's mansion is situated across the bay from Daisy's home not by "strange coincidence" but by design, the whole of Gatsby's life begins to take form and to demand interpretation anew. "He came alive to me," Carraway says, "delivered suddenly from the womb of his purposeless splendor" (p. 79).

The "romantic speculation" and "bizarre accusations" that Gatsby evokes from all sides represent responses to the rich mystery, the problematic ambiance, in which he moves (pp. 44, 65). Gatsby takes "satisfaction" in these "legends" and "inventions"—reports, for instance, that he is a murderer, a German spy, a gangster, a nephew to Von Hindenburg, and a nephew or cousin of Kaiser Wilhelm (pp. 44, 61, 33)—not simply because he prizes notoriety, but because he longs to be interpreted (p. 98; cf. p. 67). What seems to Nick Carraway, who doesn't "like mysteries" (p. 72),[33] most to demand interpretation, however, is that Gatsby's design itself ends in ironic failure: that Gatsby's effort to right the moment of affront at the door of Daisy's "beautiful house" leads to more humiliating defeat at the more vulgar hands of Tom Buchanan; that Gatsby's effort to establish a grand mansion ends with an "empty" house that speaks only of "huge incoherent failure"; and that Gatsby's effort to have Daisy in order that she may reign as queen in his mansion ends not merely in unsuccess but

33. See p. 37 and note that Carraway is generally very fastidious. He likes "to leave things in order" (p. 178).

in his death at the hands of a confused and outraged stranger (pp. 148, 181).

Nick Carraway's interpretation of Gatsby's fate involves more, however, than an inquiry into what went wrong in Gatsby's plan. In all Gatsby says and does, despite "his appalling sentimentality," there is an echo of "an elusive rhythm, a fragment of lost words" heard long ago. What accordingly is required of Carraway is that he define what lies behind Gatsby's design; and it is with this, as we shall see, that Carraway ends. Gatsby's sentimentality and silence together represent the residue of a dream for which his design is not an adequate correlative. Although it becomes his "ancestral home," although it corresponds to his invented history and is itself the work of a failed "plan to Found a Family," Gatsby's colossal mansion is not commensurate with his needs. Similarly, despite the vitality of Gatsby's vision of her, Daisy remains, or at least again becomes, a curiously beautiful fraud of a hopelessly corrupt world. Only in Carraway's interpretation is the fullness of Gatsby's dream recovered (pp. 112, 154, 89).

Carraway's effort to interpret Gatsby is for the most part rather simple. In some moments he simply discredits what is false: he explodes "wild rumors" and clears away "misconceptions" just as, before leaving the mansion for the last time, he erases "an obscene word" that some unknown boy has scrawled on its white steps (pp. 102, 181). In other moments he records what he has directly observed or reports, either directly or indirectly, what he has heard or been told. In his most characterstic moments, however, he redeems failed action by endowing it with narrative order. The first party Gatsby gives in the "blue gardens" and grounds of his glowing mansion is rich in sound and color: while the orchestra plays "yellow cocktail music," the air comes "alive with chatter and laughter" that strain to become an "opera" (pp. 39–40; cf. p. 82). The "few [invited] guests" mingle with strangers who simply come, and together they become a "sea-change of faces" in search of the host no one knows (pp. 40–41; cf. p. 45). For a moment, when Gatsby first appears, the scene achieves what it has all along been striving for: it becomes "something significant, elemental, and profound." But the moment flees. Order promptly gives way to "dissension" and ends in the "violent confusion" of "harsh, discordant din" (pp. 47, 52, 54). Only when, as the party is ending, Carraway looks "back" does Gatsby's failed party become something more than a weird collection of strangers and curiosity-seekers. Indeed Gatsby himself survives the confused "sound of his still glowing garden" and overcomes the "sudden emptiness" of his mansion only because Carraway sees and renders him standing under a "wafer of a moon." Only in Carraway's narrative is Gatsby able paradoxically to stand at once in "complete isolation" and as a perfect "figure of the host" (p. 56).

Finally, however, Carraway is forced, before he can recount Gatsby's past, to mix speculation with data, and before he can reconstruct the events leading up to Gatsby's death, to become both an imaginative interpreter and a detective.[34] The only adequate image of the "unquiet darkness" of Gatsby's world, the only adequate measure of the deep desolation that exists for Carraway to redeem, is the "desolate" "valley of ashes"—the "fantastic farm where ashes grow like wheat into ridges and hills and grotesque gardens; where ashes take the forms of houses and chimneys and rising smoke and, finally, with a transcendent effort, of men who move dimly and already crumbling through the powdery air" (pp. 22–23). Above this radically mortal world, in which the mixed motion of time carelessly changes all that men are and all that they do, there brood the grotesque, faded "eyes of Doctor T. J. Eckleburg," just as above the "waste land" of Gatsby's world there brood

---

34. See Thomas Hanzo, "The Theme and the Narrator of *The Great Gatsby*," *Modern Fiction Studies*, 2 (1956–57), 183–90.

the eyes of Nick Carraway (pp. 23–24).[35] Unlike that of its synecdoche, however, the juxtaposition that defines the structure of the novel is neither specious nor sterile. In contrast to the soiled words and corrupted motives of the advertisement, Carraway's vision participates in the same "creative passion" we see in Gatsby's action. In the interim—"in the meantime," the "in between time"—world of *The Great Gatsby,* Carraway's interpreting vision is all we have (p. 97). It is not to be confused, as George Wilson confuses Eckleburg's "persistent stare" (see pp. 24, 160), with divine vision, but it does arrange and deepen, recapture and relate.

It is in his most fully interpretive moments—when he accepts the burden of imaginative reconstruction, when, in short, he plays the role Fitzgerald planned for Cecilia in his unfinished novel, *The Last Tycoon*—that Carraway most clearly functions as a deputy of the artist.[36] Only in such a moment, moreover—that is, only when he is presenting the events of the day following Tom Buchanan's effectual defeat of Gatsby and Daisy's accidental killing, with Gatsby's car, of Tom's mistress, in picturing Gatsby waiting for a call from Daisy, a call that could revive hope for his miscarried design—is Carraway able to attribute to Gatsby something approaching tragic illumination.

> No telephone message arrived . . . I have an idea that Gatsby himself didn't believe it would come, and perhaps he no longer cared. If that was true he must have felt that he had lost the old warm world, paid a high price for living too long with a single dream. He must have looked

35. See Milton Hindus, "The Eyes of Dr. T. J. Eckleburg," *Boston University Studies in English, 3* (1957), 22–31. See also Mizener, Chap. 9.

36. See *The Last Tycoon,* ed. Edmund Wilson (New York, Scribner, 1941), p. 140: "I shall grant myself the privilege, as Conrad did, of letting her [my narrator] imagine the actions of the characters."

up at an unfamiliar sky through frightening leaves and shivered as he found what a grotesque thing a rose is and how raw the sunlight was upon the scarcely created grass. A new world, material without being real, where poor ghosts, breathing dreams like air, drifted fortuitously about . . . [sic] like that ashen, fantastic figure gliding toward him through the amorphous trees. (p. 162)

When the ashen figure has come and killed the drifting ghost, when the holocaust is complete, all that remains is for Carraway to show why, despite all that is maudlin about him and despite the end he meets, Gatsby is worth more than the whole of the "rotten" world that destroys him (p. 154).

The "creative passion" lying behind Carraway's effort to clear up each "tremendous detail" of Gatsby's life and fate enables him to render Gatsby's dream "incorruptible" (pp. 97, 129, 155). Carraway delivers Gatsby from mere "notoriety" and "wild rumors"; he completes him and makes him great. In themselves Gatsby's bizarre parties, his failed efforts to establish community, remain spectacular yet incoherent anthologies of celebrities and outcasts. In themselves the characteristically hidden scenes in which he approaches Daisy and seems to near realization of his design know no consummation (pp. 98, 102). In Carraway's imaginative translation, however, the man who has been left in "complete isolation" becomes the perfect figure of the host, and the mansion that has become a splendid mausoleum becomes again a mansion, its temporary inhabitant's true "ancestral home" (pp. 56, 154).

Carraway's triumph derives from his ability to stand both "within and without" the action he narrates—his ability to be a participant yet a "watcher in the darkening streets"—his ability to give himself, like James' dawdlers, to always "looking up and wondering . . . simultaneously enchanted and repelled by the inexhaustible variety of life" (p. 36). By suffering within, by understanding and relating the whole of what he sees, not simply to his own life, nor merely to his country's history but to all human endeavor, Carraway brings rich order to Gatsby's story. Having enabled Gatsby to stand under a "wafer of a moon" on the white steps of his mansion, overlooking "blue" grounds and "glowing garden," as a veritable icon "of the host" (pp. 56, 182; cf. 154), Carraway moves on to become a lyric poet. The "valley of ashes" and "the inessential houses" of the Sound together "melt away until" the valley of ashes and the green breast of the new world are coherently related and Gatsby's story (to borrow and reverse the phrase Gatsby himself has used in dismissing any possible love between Tom and Daisy) becomes not in the least "just personal" (pp. 23, 182, 152). We accordingly see behind Gatsby's dream an old vision and hear behind his voice "a fragment of lost words" heard long ago; we become aware that "the old island" once had been the "fresh, green breast of the new world," and that the "vanished trees, the trees that had made way for Gatsby's house, had once pandered in whispers to the last and greatest of all human dreams." In response to "something commensurate to his capacity for wonder"—pulsed on the edge of a vast, empty continent of an open and new world, confident in all innocence, believing "in the green light, the orgiastic future" of perfection, man then had dared to respond, as Gatsby later was to respond, with wonder at the distance he had come and with faith that he now would live his dream (pp. 112, 182). Thus near to success—thus invited and enticed with pandered whispers by his world—he had dared to move beyond dreaming his dream to an attempt to live it. Because of the beauty of his dream and the heroism of his effort to move beyond it, Gatsby can be made great. Yet because he has so dared only to see the vanishing trees give way, not to a city of man, but to a valley of ashes, not to the marriage and mansion envisaged, but to "huge incoherent failure" (p. 181), he can be made great only through reconstituting interpretation, reordering art.

9 Apotheosis of the Form: Faulkner's *Absalom, Absalom!*

> *Follow, poet, follow right*
> *To the bottom of the night,*
> *With your unconstraining voice*
> *Still persuade us to rejoice;*
>
> *With the farming of a verse*
> *Make a vineyard of the curse,*
> *Sing of human unsuccess*
> *In a rapture of distress . . .*
>
> W. H. Auden, "In Memory of
> W. B. Yeats"

Unlike Hawthorne, Melville, and James, F. Scott Fitzgerald was able to interlace action and interpretation without making interpretation itself a source of intense drama. Action in *The Great Gatsby* is deeply problematical, but understanding, at least for the interpreting deputy of the author, is made easy. For William Faulkner's interpreting deputies, understanding is almost impossible. No less than his men of action, Faulkner's interpreters speak only with the authority of failure: they are partial, failed narrators.[1]

1. Like Hawthorne and Melville, Faulkner was fascinated with failure. See Robert A. Jelliffe, ed., *Faulkner at Nagano* (Tokyo, Kenkyusha, 1956), pp. 3, 4, 6, 37–38, 68, 161; Jean Stein, Interview with William Faulkner, *Paris Review, 4* (1956), 28–52; F. L. Gwynn and Joseph L. Blotner, eds., *Faulkner in the University* (Charlottesville, University of Virginia Press, 1959), pp. 84, 271, 277.

In *Knight's Gambit,* in the story "Monk," Faulkner sketches the situation that characteristically confronts his narrators. Charles Mallison, Faulkner writes, is troubled by the "clowning of circumstances," by "ciphers" that refuse to "add up." In order "to bridge . . . inconsistencies" and get at the logic of Monk's story, Mallison must become both an incipient detective and an incipient artist. If he is "to make something out of . . . the nebulous and inexplicable material" given him, he must use "the nebulous tools of supposition and inference and invention." "Monk" accordingly becomes the story of its narrator as well as its subject; it derives much of its limited force from the drama with which Faulkner invests the interpretive act. Charles Mallison does what he does in troubled faith that through interpretation "the paradoxical and even mutually negativing" aspects of Monk's life "can be juxtaposed and annealed . . . into verisimilitude and credibility."[2]

Faulkner's most powerful working out of the genre of which "Monk" is a minor instance is *Absalom, Absalom!*[3] The cen-

2. *Knight's Gambit* (New York, Random House, 1949), pp. 49–50, 39. See William Van O'Connor, *The Tangled Fire of William Faulkner* (Minneapolis, University of Minnesota Press, 1954), pp. 135–45; and esp. Michael Millgate, *The Achievement of William Faulkner* (London, Constable, 1966), pp. 150–64. The lines quoted from "Monk" have, of course, mainly to do with the interpretive side of *Absalom, Absalom!* For Faulkner's first engagement directly with the design side of *Absalom, Absalom!,* see Faulkner's unpublished short story "The Big Shot," in the Faulkner papers at the University of Virginia, as discussed in Millgate, pp. 159–60. In this story we have an earlier version of the affront scene in *Absalom, Absalom!* that I discuss below, and we have born of this affront to a small boy an "unflagging dream." As Millgate, who was the first critic to discover the relevance of "The Big Shot" to the core of Sutpen's story, shows, this story does for one side of *Absalom, Absalom!* very much what "Monk" does for the other.

3. Faulkner ranked *Absalom, Absalom!* second to *The Sound and the Fury* in terms of the anguish experienced in producing it. But whereas *The Sound and the Fury* unfolds as interpretations of the story and fate of Caddy, a static and largely passive figure who is

tral action of *Absalom, Absalom!* flows from Thomas Sutpen's
attempt "to establish a dynasty"; it is the story of a man who,
in an effort to leave something "to represent his own blood, his
own passion," sought to make "himself a king" and found "a
line of princes."[4] In the first half of the book (its first five sec-
tions) most of the relevant facts are given, many in the first
pages. But since a few facts are missing, even those available
outstrip understanding: they are, as one character puts it, "just
incredible."[5] Gradually we come to see *Absalom, Absalom!* as
the story of a man who—with the innocence of Oedipus and
the resolution of Ahab—has made pursuing his "design" the
sole business of his life. The story itself unfolds, however, as a
series of complexly entangled and variously imaginative responses to the presence of riddle and the offense of incredi-
bility. The people who tell Sutpen's story represent man in his
aspect of bafflement. Together they re-create, from "a few old
mouth-to-mouth tales," a story of people dimly seen, people
"who once lived and breathed" and "in whose living blood and
seed we ourselves," the interpreters and the inhabitants of their
world, "lay dormant and waiting" (pp. 100–01). To each of its
interpreters, Sutpen's story presents itself as a "jigsaw puzzle
picture" whose "integers" appear always to be "waiting, almost
lurking, just beyond his reach, inextricable, jumbled, and un-
recognizable yet on the point of falling into pattern which would
reveal to him at once, like a flash of light, the meaning of his
whole life" (p. 313). Haunted by mystery, and even more by
the sense of its imminent resolution, of almost touching, from
moment to moment, *the* answer, Faulkner's characters truly

---

not directly present, *Absalom, Absalom!* unfolds as interpretations of
the story and fate of a dynamic and enormously active man.

4. Gwynn and Blotner, pp. 35, 98, 198.

5. *Absalom, Absalom!* [1936] (New York, Random House, 1951),
p. 100. All page references in the text of this chapter are to this edition
of *Absalom, Absalom!*, a later impression of the first edition.

are doomed. Their interpretive role represents what is for them
the only possible response to bafflement.

The focus of *Absalom, Absalom!* accordingly is dual. On
one side there is the story of Sutpen's effort to realize his grand
design: the action of the novel centers on the various "phase[s]"
(p. 41) of Sutpen's Franklinesque "schedule" (p. 264). On the
other side there are the characters Faulkner got "out of the
attic" of his imagination to tell Sutpen's story.[6] In retrospect at
least, Sutpen's action and "secret end" appear always to have
been "inexplicable and incredible" to those around him (pp.
38–39). His interpreters' task is to construct not a mansion but
a story; they must form, out of the fragments available to them,
a coherent account of the origin, purpose, character, and fate
of Sutpen's design.[7]

Like the novel's focus, both its physical and temporal settings
are dual. The scene of most of its action is Yoknapatawpha
County, Mississippi; the scene of most of its interpretation is
Cambridge, Massachusetts. The novel stretches, moreover,
from the early nineteenth century to the early twentieth, from a
time when Yoknapatawpha was "still frontier" (a time when
"bold ruthless" men endeavored "where and when" they "could
and wanted to" to conquer the wilderness and build mansions),
through a period of war and devastation to a time of contemplation (a time when men meditate upon their ruined land's gutted
mansions and ravaged fields).[8]

Through its strange structure and its dual focus, *Absalom,
Absalom!* reaches beyond Thomas Sutpen, not only to those
touched by his life, nor merely to those compelled to measure
his fate and weigh his story, but to an illimitable context of
relevance: to the "hinterland" and the "wilderness"; to the
South's "unavoidable" rendezvous with "catastrophe" (p. 74),

6. Gwynn and Blotner, p. 73.
7. See Harvey Breit, Introduction, *Absalom, Absalom!*, p. ix; and
Ilse D. Lind, "The Design and Meaning of *Absalom, Absalom!*," *PMLA*,
70 (1955), 887–912.
8. Gwynn and Blotner, pp. 37, 3.

the United States' "destiny" (p. 118), and "two doomed" races' complexly mixed fate (p. 114); to Hamlet, whom Faulkner links to his interpreters, and Faustus, whom he links to his man of design (pp. 174, 178); to the fall of Rome and the crumbling of Jericho (p. 271); and, in and through all, to "the folly" and "the fate" of man (pp. 87, 377).[9]

The dual struggle of man in *Absalom, Absalom!*—Sutpen's effort to master his world and his interpreters' effort to define that effort—is in one sense doomed: Faulkner's characters move "from abysmal and chaotic dark" to "eternal and abysmal" blackness, from uncomprehending undefeat to defeat so final that its very "finality" is not only "irrevocable" but "unplumbable." In their effort to understand no less than in their effort to act, they labor in "iron and impregnable dark" (pp. 171, 173, 360). Haunted by the "sonorous defeated names" of the past, troubled by the "lonely and foredoomed" men of the present, and fearful of the future "oblivion to which we are all doomed," they know that neither action nor "inquiry" and "amazed speculation" will suffice (pp. 12, 167, 129, 33, 43). "Do you understand it?" asks one investigating, speculating interpreter of another. "I dont know," is the reply; "Yes, of course I understand . . . I dont know." "Yes," the questioner remarks, "You dont know" (p. 362).

9. It seems to me that, however strange it may be, Faulkner found in the story of the South—in its "long and quite un-American experience with poverty," in its experience with "frustration, failure, and defeat," and in its preoccupation with "guilt" and "the reality of evil" (Woodward, *The Burden of Southern History*, pp. 17–21)—not barriers but links between the South and the modern world. It accordingly seems to me wrong to identify Sutpen either strictly with the South or strictly with non-Southern American characteristics. See the discussion in Cleanth Brooks, *William Faulkner: The Yoknapatawpha Country* (New Haven, Yale University Press, 1963), pp. 426–28. See also Olga W. Vickery, *The Novels of William Faulkner: A Critical Interpretation* (rev. ed. Baton Rouge, Louisiana State University Press, 1959), pp. 93–94; and Hyatt H. Waggoner, *William Faulkner: From Jefferson to the World* (Lexington, University of Kentucky Press, 1959), pp. 165–66.

Faulkner's characters are not simply doomed, however, for there is within them a "bitter and implacable reserve of undefeat." Together they stand as "author and victim" of a thousand catastrophes, and to the end their fates remain "strange, contradictory and bizarre; not quite comprehensible" (pp. 11, 89, 14). But their struggle is not as a result merely catastrophic. Since without them nature, the "very Environment itself," is as "soundless Nothing," it proves, if not malleable, something less than indomitable. And since even more recalcitrant history belongs to them, since it is the myth they live and make, and in living and making, constantly remake, it proves to be for them somehow "meaningful" as well as "indecipherable" (pp. 258, 8, 101).

During the unfolding of his story, through Quentin Compson, we hear Sutpen speak of his "design"—to "accomplish" which, he remarks, "I should require money, a house, a plantation, slaves, a family—incidentally of course, a wife" (p. 263). Long before we hear Sutpen's self-explanation (to General Compson, Quentin's grandfather), however, we see him as creator. As the novel opens, Sutpen comes to us, through Miss Rosa Coldfield as told to Quentin Compson, as a creator descending out of nowhere upon the amazed world of Yoknapatawpha. From outset to end, Sutpen is "slave" to a single "fixed goal" (pp. 34, 53). In company with his "wild blacks" and his "captive [French] architect," whom he has armed "in bloodless paradox" with "shovels and picks and axes," the tools of "peaceful conquest," Sutpen directs the conquering of a "hundred square miles of tranquil and astonished earth." "Immobile, bearded and hand palm-lifted," he brings "out of the soundless Nothing" a mansion of "castlelike magnificence" surrounded by "formal gardens and promenades": with "the up-palm immobile and pontific," by saying *Be Sutpen's Hundred* like the oldentime *Be Light,*" he "create[s] the Sutpen's Hundred" (pp. 8–9, 38–39).

So central is Sutpen to his world that, as the twin interpreters, Quentin Compson and Shreve McCannon, suggest, it takes him "to make" all the rest (p. 262). Yet, although he is a creator, although he embodies the stuff of which the makers of civilizations are made, Sutpen creates neither himself nor his story. Within this peculiar historical novel, the hero owes his narrated life, the only dimension of his life to escape oblivion, to the willingness of his interpreters variously, and often reluctantly, to say, Be Sutpen. He comes to us only indirectly and only because he is prodigiously destructive—only because his action leads to devastation so absolute and far-reaching that he, his descendants and acquaintances, and their descendants and acquaintances are moved to interpretation.

In some measure, Sutpen commands interpretation because he is so vain that he contrives "somehow to swagger even on a horse" and because he is so ruthless that "anyone could look at him and say, Given the occasion and the need, this man can and will do anything" (pp. 16, 46; italics omitted). But Sutpen's grandeur derives ultimately neither from his vanity and ruthlessness nor from his courage and endurance—courage that makes his spirit "indomitable" even in the face of "final defeat" and endurance that enables him to bear more than anyone "believed any bones and flesh could or should . . . be asked to stand" (pp. 167, 163, 254). What does most to account for the aura of "ascendancy" surrounding Sutpen is his "unflagging" dedication (pp. 37–38). Sutpen is set apart in some measure by his violation of local mores (by his being ruthless, Faulkner later remarked, without "pretense to be anything else");[10] but he is set apart even more by his reposed and visionary gaze. For like Ahab's, Sutpen's gaze is that of a man who has survived a "solitary furnace experience"—a man who has "fought through," "at enormous cost," not mere "normal hardship," but every "added and unforeseen" calamity—and who yet has emerged, on the far side of failure, consecrated to the task of realizing his "wild braggart dream" (pp. 32–33, 165–66).

10. Gwynn and Blotner, p. 80; cf. p. 35.

Sutpen's commitment to his dream makes him gigantic. He does what he does in part "in order to live with himself for the rest of his life." But far from being narrowly personal, his commitment resembles Jay Gatsby's and even recalls Adam Verver's.[11] Sutpen too carries with him memory of affront—memory of having been rebuffed at the door of the house of his aspirations; and he too has responded, first by conceiving a "compelling dream," and then by turning it into articulated and pursued "design" (pp. 166, 240). In all that he does, of course, as was the case with Hollingsworth, there is the self writ large. By sheer force of will he fathers children who are "replicas of his face." But even Miss Rosa, his most implacable foe and damning interpreter, insists that he did not "voluntarily undertake the hardship and privation of clearing virgin land and establishing a plantation in a new country just for money." Whether his effort to realize his defined purpose must finally be viewed as the "dark avocation" of a demon or as the work of a courageous builder, Sutpen clearly is driven (and handicapped) by longing that transcends the desire to acquire, longing born of "stubborn and amazed outrage," longing for vindication (pp. 23, 17, 72, 174).

The one whose vindication Sutpen seeks is an expanded version of the small, ragged boy he himself has been—the small boy we see dismissed at the door of a grand mansion and denied acknowledgment of an "errand" accepted and run in "good faith." Sutpen's response to rebuff and affront, his determination to get "what they have"—the land and slaves and fine house—"that made them do what [that] man did" to that boy, transcends personal vindication, however, precisely because the boy he has been has become for him a "boy-symbol" (pp. 233, 238, 261). Sutpen does what he does, though of course in the end ironically, in behalf of family and forebears —indeed, in behalf of all the violated and insulted: all whose

11. See above n. 17, Chap. 8.

"labor" is "brutish and stupidly out of all proportion to its reward"; all who have been left "forlorn nameless and homeless lost" children; and all who have been "brutely evacuated into a world without hope or purpose for them" (pp. 236, 267, 235). In seeking to build a house that will "accept and retain human life," he acts somehow that all affronted men may together be "riven forever free from brutehood" (pp. 85, 261).[12]

The primary source of bafflement and therefore the primary occasion of interpretation in *Absalom, Absalom!* is the expanse of the "holocaust" Sutpen authors in seeking his complex vindication. Prior to the death of his wife, Ellen Coldfield, and to the unfolding of the fates of his "doomed children," prior to the destruction of his "doomed house" and to the disclosure of his own inglorious end—not only as "a sonless widower, barren of that posterity" he had most wanted, but as the somewhat corpulent, haggling owner of a "little store"—Sutpen evokes "inquiry" and "speculation" (pp. 18–19, 375, 155, 281, 33, 43). The not only "violent" but ironic end to which his "allotted course" leads makes him not only a "final and complete affront" to man, but also the subject of "reports and rumors," legends and stories about "who" he was, "where . . . he came from," and "why" (pp. 11, 14, 44, 17).

Among Sutpen's several interpreters, Quentin Compson is focal. He shares the labor of interpretation with others—with his Harvard roommate, Shrevlin McCannon, as well as with his grandfather, his father, and Miss Rosa Coldfield; but he alone links the interpreters and interlaces their interpretations. Like Nick Carraway in *The Great Gatsby,* like the various observers in James' works, and like Miles Coverdale in *The Blithedale Romance,* Quentin Compson defines the perimeter from which we view the novel's central figure and action.

Quentin's task is his by inheritance. Not only is he a descendant of one of the "bold ruthless" early settlers of Mississippi

12. See Gwynn and Blotner, pp. 97–98, 198, 35.

who sought to establish "a princely line";[13] he also, through his father and grandfather, is the inheritor of Sutpen's story. In addition, his task is his by appointment. He has been designated by Miss Rosa Coldfield, who is herself a compulsive interpreter of Sutpen as well as "the county's poetess laureate." "So maybe you will enter the literary profession," she says to Quentin, "as so many Southern gentlemen and gentlewomen too are doing now and maybe some day you will remember this and write about it. . . . Perhaps you will even remember kindly then the old woman who made you spend a whole afternoon sitting indoors and listening while she talked about people and events you were fortunate enough to escape yourself." Quentin feels the burden of his heritage and appointment. He knows that Miss Rosa wants Sutpen's story told—that she has told him so that he can tell "people whom she will never see and whose names she will never hear" (pp. 9–11). But he is moved by more than heritage and appointment; he makes the task of interpretation his own.

What we see at work in Quentin's prolonged and finally compulsive narrative effort is, on one side, his conviction that Sutpen's story is significant—his conviction, that is, that understanding of Sutpen's story will illuminate not only the past but the present; and is, on the other, faith that through interpretive telling "the paradoxical and even mutually negativing" aspects in Sutpen's story "can be juxtaposed and annealed . . . into verisimilitude and credibility"[14]—his faith, that is, that narrative technique is a mode of understanding, is a discovering and ordering tool. In Quentin's and Shreve's joint effort at reconstruction and translation, a mode of creative activity very different from the one that inspires Sutpen's action is at work.

13. Ibid., p. 3. Note that, at least in Faulkner's discussion, "failure" also links Quentin's family to Sutpen.
14. *Knight's Gambit*, p. 39.

They stared—glared—at one another. It was Shreve speaking, though . . . it might have been either of them and was in a sense both: both thinking as one, the voice which happened to be speaking the thought only the thinking become audible, vocal; the two of them creating between them, out of the rag-tag and bob-ends of old tales and talking, people who perhaps had never existed at all anywhere, who, shadows, were shadows not of flesh and blood which had lived and died but shadows in turn of what were . . . shades too. (p. 303)

Having incited his roommate to interpretation, Quentin enters with him into a game of creation—a game at once synthetic, in its piecing together of disparate interpretations, and inventive, in its supplying of scenes and filling of gaps, and imaginative, in its constructing of a whole. In the only way they know and with the only tools given them, Quentin and Shreve try to do justice simultaneously to "the parched earth's agony" and to "the imponderable and aloof stars" of man's aspiration (p. 362). Neither of them, as Faulkner later observed, "look[s] at truth" steadily and "intact." But through them their maker tells us what we need to know of their world.[15]

Even before he arrives in Yoknapatawpha, Sutpen is behind with his "schedule": already he has neared realization of his design only to see it crumble before his eyes; already he is haunted by wasted labor that he has found impossible to incorporate into his design (see p. 264). Through its first three "phase[s]," Sutpen's second attempt to realize his design goes well. He manages, in contrast to Hollingsworth, to erect his grand edifice. Within a few days after his arrival, he secures land which he names "as if it had been a king's grant in unbroken perpetuity from his great grandfather"; and within two years, through the "quiet and unflagging fury" of his dedication, he erects a mansion and breaks and plants his land (pp. 41, 16,

15. Gwynn and Blotner, pp. 273–74. Cf. pp. 73, 75.

38). Ensconced in "baronial splendor," in "the largest edifice in the county, not excepting the courthouse itself," Sutpen enters the "second phase" of his plan: he waits; for three years he makes no move. Then, with the town watching "in shocked amazement," he lays "deliberate siege to the one man in the town with whom he could have . . . nothing in common." Through some obscure use of Mr. Coldfield's position as a small merchant, Sutpen obtains imported chandeliers, rugs, mahogany, and crystal for his mansion. Whereupon, having furnished his mansion, he *procures* a wife. Despite open opposition from the community, Sutpen marries Ellen Coldfield (pp. 39, 41–42; cf. p. 43).

Having become a bridegroom on schedule, "almost five years to the day from that Sunday morning when he rode into town," Sutpen is prepared to begin his dynasty. For a brief time life continues to yield to his design. To his marriage with Ellen Coldfield are born two children, a son, Henry, and a daughter, Judith. Then, as "the biggest single landowner and cotton-planter in the county," and with "his plantation . . . running smoothly," Sutpen begins "within ten years of the wedding" to act "a role of arrogant ease and leisure" (pp. 48, 72).

As Sutpen nears his "triumphant coronation," however, his life begins to disintegrate. Like Gatsby's, Sutpen's mansion is only briefly the scene of life. In sinister fulfillment of Thoreau's warning, Sutpen's grand edifice becomes a "rotten mausoleum," a scene, first, of repeated deaths, and later, of Henry's prolonged effort to die. The land of his plantation shrinks and falls fallow, he dies, and finally his mansion burns. Only his longing for posterity is fulfilled, and that only with grim irony: in the end, as Shreve puts it, there is "One nigger Sutpen left," and he is an idiot (pp. 102, 350, 378).

Even before the final working out of his fate, Sutpen himself is moved to interpretation. He has stood at the door of his mansion—at the door he had "planned" as part of his vindica-

tion of the affronted boy-symbol—there to order his own un-
acknowledged son away; and in that moment he has "felt and
heard the design—house, position, posterity and all—come
down like it had been built out of smoke." Given ruins and
decay, doom and final defeat, Sutpen becomes his own interpreter. In his interpretation, moreover, he combines "patient
amazed recapitulation" with query (pp. 267, 263; cf. p.
163). "You see," he is quoted as having said to Quentin's
grandfather, "I had a design in my mind. Whether it was a
good or a bad design is beside the point; the question is, Where
did I make the mistake in it, what did I do or misdo in it,
whom or what injure by it to the extent which this [devastation]
would indicate" (p. 263).

Sutpen's effort at interpretation is short and unsuccessful;
he achieves no tragic illumination. But his query recalls the
question lying behind the Puritan jeremiad, and his concern
for his "mistake" recalls Franklin's concern with his *errata*.
He manages, moreover, through his plea for interpretation, "to
designate" his interpreters as "the presiding augur[s] of his
own disaster" (p. 62). Long before Sutpen's own move toward
interpretation, however, Sutpen's nameless French architect
anticipates, in spirit and intent, Sutpen's interpreters. His
"gaunt face" and his "eyes desperate and hopeless but indomitable too, invincible too," make the small Frenchman the
proper architect of the Sutpen mansion (p. 257). Since he is
"an artist" as well as "a good architect," however, and since
he is "a casual and bitterly disinterested spectator" as well as
a "condemned and conscientious ghost," he manages, beyond
designing Sutpen's mansion, to prepare for the labor later to be
performed by Sutpen's interpreters (p. 38).

Early in the novel we learn through Quentin of the architect's effort to salvage one part of Sutpen's design. In "single-
handed" battle "the little grim harried foreigner"—dressed "in
his formal coat and his Paris hat"—curbs the "dream of grim
and castlelike magnificence at which Sutpen obviously aimed."

And in vanquishing "Sutpen's fierce and overweening vanity
or desire for magnificence or for vindication or whatever it
was," the architect "create[s] of Sutpen's very defeat the victory which, in conquering, Sutpen himself would have failed
to gain" (pp. 38–39). Like the interpreters who follow him, the
architect does what he does in part for himself, in part perhaps
for Sutpen, but in part, too, for the planned castle of grim magnificence: because it is inspired by Sutpen's effort to bring
order out of soundless nothing, his desire to shelter "human
life," the planned castle is worth changing into a mansion (p.
85).[16] In the end, of course, after it has become a mausoleum
and a fire-gutted ruin, the mansion must be again redeemed.
But in his effort to create of Sutpen's defeat the sought victory,
the architect begins what Quentin and Shreve are to complete.

Miss Rosa Coldfield is the child of a heritage moral, legalistic, and, in its "vindictive mysticism," even distinctly religious. From her "barren youth" in the Coldfield home—"an
overpopulated mausoleum," Shreve terms it—to her lonely
death, her life is "without rhyme or reason or hope of reward"; she is a victim, from womb to grave, of some dark,
uncertain game of "savage time" (pp. 82, 144, 176). But her
"grim haggard amazed voice" bespeaks more than the ac-
cumulated "impotent yet indomitable frustration" of all her
years; she is Sutpen's "grim and implacable unforgiving" foe
(pp. 7, 14).

Behind her insistence that Sutpen is a "fiend blackguard and
devil"—"the evil's source and head"—resides a memory of
affront so gross that she cannot bring herself to name it. From
her we learn that her "life was destined to end on an afternoon
in April forty-three years" before she summons Quentin to
hear her story and receive her commission (pp. 15, 18).

16. Note that after he has failed in his effort to escape from Sutpen's
Hundred, the architect is capable of a gesture so charged that it
"seemed to gather" and grind to dust and fling away "all misfortune
and defeat that the human race ever suffered" (pp. 257–58).

Through other interpreters, we learn that on that wounded April day the hurrying Sutpen withdrew an already accepted proposal of marriage, suggesting instead, in words that left Miss Rosa "rigid and precarious with rage" and "outrage," "that they try it first and if it was a boy and lived, they would be married" (pp. 279, 284).

Miss Rosa's fate has been fixed in part by this "mortal affront"—which recalls the affront Sutpen has suffered, the affront in avenging which he does, among other things, what he does to Miss Rosa. But she also is driven by less personal offense. She has been doomed to endless, compulsive interpretation of Sutpen by "the final and complete affront" of his death at the hands of Wash Jones (pp. 177, 14). She adjudges Sutpen's death by scythe "final outrage and affront" because she knows, Shreve suggests, that from beyond the "symbolic shape" of the scythe, Sutpen, "even though dead, even when earth itself declined any longer to bear his weight," will return as king to mock and jeer "at her" (pp. 177–78).

The interpretation with which Miss Rosa emerges from the furnace of her own experience is a demonology. She believes, as Shreve surmises and summarizes, that Sutpen is an incarnation of evil itself—that "this Faustus, this demon, this Beelzebub," at least from time antedating his descent with his "twenty subsidiary demons" upon Yoknapatawpha, has been a deliberate devotee of devastation, a prince of darkness (p. 178). Like her older sister Ellen, Miss Rosa views things "in a state very near hysteria." But what most mars her interpretation is not that she informs it with the "logic- and reason-flouting quality of a dream" (pp. 54, 22), but rather that in it she is persistently simplistic. Facing a problematic story and lacking essential information (such as Sutpen's reasons for opposing Judith's marriage to Charles Bon), she imposes a neat demonology: she attributes Sutpen's opposition to Judith's marriage to the caprice of a demon; and she attributes the devastation Sutpen has wrought to the machinations of doom. She and her family have been decreed by fate to be victims of a "fatality and curse" for which Sutpen has been the agent. In payment for some crime of her "father or his father" before him, her family has been "cursed to be instruments" not only of Sutpen's destruction, but of their own (p. 21; cf. p. 68).

Through her demonology, Miss Rosa manages to wring meaning from her family's tale of woe; and she is able, in addition, at last to explain to her own satisfaction "why God let us [the South] lose the War: that only through the blood of our men and the tears of our women could He stay this demon and efface his name and lineage from the earth" (p. 11, italics omitted). But her understanding is neither fully reliable nor fully liberating. Miss Rosa finally makes minimal peace with her heritage. She enters the names—"Mr. Coldfield's own, and Charles Bon's and even Sutpen's" (p. 82)—in the family Bible. But she remains sentenced creature as well as author of an "ogre-world" ruled by dark forces (p. 21). Only in a few scattered moments—when she enters the names in the Bible and tries, late in life, to help Henry Sutpen—does she move beyond preoccupation with the "man whom she could neither forgive nor revenge herself upon" (p. 13). In the end she must rely upon others to find the freeing interpretation she cannot attain.

Mr. Compson is not given to hysteria or dream. He is a citizen of the village and a creature of reasonableness. He is free, moreover, from felt affront; he is an interpreter by virtue of his having been born a son of General Compson. But like Miss Rosa, Mr. Compson, in his early and independent interpretation, forces the information available to him into a specious pattern; which is to say that he too forecloses, that he too, as it were, compels rather than makes meaning.

In contrast to Miss Rosa's consistent demonology and despite his own calm reasonings, Mr. Compson is at times inconsistent—with regard, for instance, to the time Judith and Charles Bon have together (compare pp. 99, 101). Furthermore, despite both his gift for allusion and analogy (see p. 62) and his rich sources of information, he ends in simplification. The test again has to do with Sutpen's opposition to Judith's marriage. Deprived of knowledge of Charles Bon's parentage (unaware, that is, that Bon's father is Thomas Sutpen and that Bon's mother is a woman Sutpen has put aside because she is part Negro, unaware, in short, that problems of incest and miscegenation surround the projected marriage), Mr. Compson concocts an hypothesis: Henry has murdered Bon because Bon was "at least an intending bigamist." Out of moralistic, even legalistic regard for ceremony, Henry (in Mr. Compson's reconstruction) demands that Bon renounce the octoroon he has married in a "meaningless" ritual; and when Bon continues to refuse, Henry kills him (pp. 90, 117–18).

Mr. Compson's efforts to construct scenes and motives are intertwined with the other interpretations, and are in themselves timid and inadequate. They prepare, however, for far bolder imaginative work. Together Quentin and Shreve reconstruct, out "of the rag-tag and bob-ends of old tales and talking," the major stages and scenes of Sutpen's rise and fall (p. 303).

In their effort to see what has happened and to find out what is hidden (see p. 303; compare pp. 370–71, 364–65), Quentin and Shreve meet with considerable success. "If I had been there," Quentin feels at one point, "I could not have seen it this plain" (p. 190; italics omitted). Together they "see" Sutpen conceive his design and attempt, by marrying Eulalia Bon, to realize it. They see him discard his son, Charles Bon, and his wife, Eulalia Bon; and they hear him attribute his action to his wife's "misrepresentation" of her race, which he accepts as making her and their child incompatible with "his entire design" (pp. 262–63). "I found," Sutpen is quoted as having said, "that she [my wife] was not and could never be, through no fault of her own, adjunctive or incremental to the design which I had in mind, so I provided for her and put her aside," not "hastily" but deliberately, and only after having "explained how this new fact rendered it impossible that . . . [she] and [the] child be incorporated in my design," and only after having "made to the fullest what atonement lay in my power for whatever injury I might have done" (pp. 240, 264, 273).

Having learned of Sutpen's initial failure, Quentin and Shreve are prepared for the collapse of his second effort at execution. For they are prepared to see his discarded wife and disinherited son become principal and agent in events that finally bring Sutpen face to face with dilemma and failure. During his first effort at "building toward [his] design," Sutpen has been forced to choose between "absolute and irrevocable negation of the design" and "holding to [his] original plan for the design" (p. 273). But in his second effort, he is left with no viable choice. Quentin and Shreve see him telling General Compson how he "had been tricked" by his first marriage and how, in the effort to extricate himself from the consequences of that trick, he had become even more entangled. Finally he is left "Sitting there and moralizing on the fact that, no matter which course he chose, the result would be that that design and plan to which he had given fifty years of his life had just as well never have existed at all" (p. 272).

Through such seeing and hearing, Quentin and Shreve prepare for another imaginative leap: they become one with Henry Sutpen and Charles Bon. In the cold New England night of interpretation, they so enter the story that there are present in their room "now not two of them but four, the two . . . not individuals now yet something both more and less than twins" (p. 294). Concomitantly, in the days when Charles Bon and Henry Sutpen journey across the South to their final, fateful confrontation, Shreve and Quentin are present: "So that now it was not two but four of them riding the two horses through the dark . . . four of them and then just two—Charles-Shreve and Quentin-Henry" (p. 334).

Through the reenactments that follow the imaginative leap Quentin and Shreve make, we see Henry learn of Charles Bon's parentage—learn, that is, first of the incest and then of the miscegenation that marriage between Judith and Bon implies. Increasingly, Quentin and Shreve act for Henry and Bon. At crucial points their acting is all we have: "So it's the miscegenation, not the incest, which you cant bear," "Bon" says to "Henry." "You will have to stop me, Henry." But "You are my brother." "No I'm not. I'm the nigger that's going to sleep with your sister. Unless you stop me, Henry." And then, "Do it now, Henry" (pp. 356–58).

Quentin and Shreve thus rehearse for us the scenes that seal Sutpen's fate. Through them we see Henry kill Bon. And through them we see that what is left after Charles Bon's death is, on one side, devastation, and on the other, an expended creator. The Sutpen who returns from war is at once "impotent and furious." His "indomitable willing" and "undefeat" remain; but he is nothing more than a "mad impotent old man," an "ancient varicose and despairing Faustus" left clinging in "vain" to a "dream of restoring his Sutpen's Hundred"—to a dream of something "remembered and . . . lost" (pp. 180–84).

Together Quentin and Shreve move beyond bafflement; they construct a plausible story. Looking behind what is given them, they create a human reality commensurate with that given—a reality dense and mixed enough to do justice to the "facts." They make the uncertain difficult move from "fact" to meaningful human truth. Yet despite their achievement, they at times are haunted, like Miss Rosa, by seeing "closed" doors they cannot open and by hearing "echo[es] . . . not the shot[s]" (p. 150). Furthermore what they end with is finally too simply a romantic, melodramatic love story.

Within the world of *Absalom, Absalom!*, neither historical interpretation, even when genuinely imaginative, nor spasmodic fiction will suffice. Working "in the darkness," Quentin and Shreve know that they "dont know" whether they "understand." On one side, they are too easily satisfied with official recounting. It is neither the "flipness, the strained clowning" nor the improvising in their game that limits their interpretation. What they create is "probably true enough" (pp. 362, 280, 335). They are finally, if strangely, too academic: "the cold room" of their interpretation is "not only dedicated to . . . but set aside for" that "best of ratiocination which after all was a good deal like Sutpen's morality"—"the old logic, the old morality which had never yet failed to fail him"—and even like "Miss Coldfield's demonizing" (pp. 279–80). To the end the two of them cling to a "code of logic and morality," to a "formula and recipe of fact and deduction," that forces them to stand "back to back as though at the last ditch, saying No to Quentin's Mississippi shade" (pp. 275, 280).

It accordingly is from what Quentin and Shreve see, not from what they understand, and it is through two other creations of the grand interpreter, Faulkner himself, that we are able to move beyond the story of Sutpen to principles that illuminate the shadowy world of *Absalom, Absalom!* In a letter containing the only words surely his, Charles Bon writes to Judith Sutpen about men driven by hunger and want.

> say we merely needed ammunition. And imagine us, the scarecrows with one of those concocted plans of scarecrow desperation . . . ; and we (the scarecrows) bringing it off with a great deal of elan . . . ; imagine, I say, the prey and prize, the ten plump defenseless sutlers' wagons, the scarecrows tumbling out box after beautiful box . . . clawing at the boxes . . . opening them at last and finding— What? Stove polish. Gallons and gallons and gallons of the best stove polish. (p. 130)

Charles Bon writes his story of the ironically got plenitude of stove polish with the selfsame stove polish; "at least," he notes, "we have stove polish. We have plenty of it. We have too much." By converting stove polish into ink, Bon redefines the

failure of his plan and thereby manages to "extract some ultimate essence" out of his plight. He finds in his undefeat—in
his refusal to "become inured to hardship and privation," in
his insistence upon redefining failure—a source of renewal of
faith "not in human nature perhaps but at least in man" (p.
130). In tone and content, Bon's letter is the work of a child
of Sutpen's design. It not only suggests that man's "scarecrow
desperation" moves him to "concocted plans"; it also suggests
both the need and the method man has for overcoming the
defeat with which such plans must finally meet.

In giving Bon's letter to Quentin's grandmother, Judith also
speaks as a child of Sutpen's design.

> "Yes," Judith said. ". . . Read it if you like or dont read
> it if you like. Because you make so little impression, you
> see. You get born and you try this and you dont know
> why only you keep on trying it and you are born at the
> same time with a lot of other people, all mixed up with
> them, like trying to, having to, move your arms and legs
> with strings only the same strings are hitched to all the
> other arms and legs and the others all trying and they
> dont know why either except that the strings are all in
> one another's way like five or six people all trying to make
> a rug on the same loom only each one wants to weave his
> own pattern into the rug." (p. 127)

Like the world it renders, the prose is in travail. Through
words that keep on striving, each separate yet a part of the
whole, each in its place yet in motion, we are given a world in
which men, with other men and without choice, "get born" into
a given natural and temporal context and yet must live and
strive. It is, moreover, a world whose only pattern is the crazy-
quilt of all man's disparate efforts to make patterns: "each
one wants to weave his own pattern into the rug; and it cant
matter, you know that, or the Ones that set up the loom would
have arranged things a little better, and yet it must matter be-

cause you keep on trying or having to keep on trying" (p. 127).

Judith's words provide both an image of her world and a definition of the tension that defines it—tension between the "it cant" and the "it must" of meaning and order. But they also suggest why Sutpen, despite his considerable talent for life, despite his courage and devotion and his "alertness for measuring and weighing event against eventuality, circumstance against human nature," must fail. He is doomed, not by sheer arrogance or ruthlessness, nor simply because Thoreau's responsible nature must inevitably tire of him and turn and destroy him, "as if [it] held a balance and kept a book and offered a recompense . . . even if man did not," nor even because the "obliterating rake" of history or the "rusty scythe" of time demand and work his destruction (pp. 53, 251, 148, 177). What does most to account for his undoing is his complex innocence.[17] For it is his innocence that supports his absurd faith that with nothing but "courage" (which "he knew he had") and "shrewdness" (which "he believed he could learn") he can realize his design and thereby inform his life with purpose and meaning (p. 244). And it is his innocence that inspires his absurd sense of non-involvement in the human "maelstrom of faces and bodies"—his absurd assumption that he can do what he wants to do without inflicting injury to the persons, labors, or dreams of other men extensive enough to "indicate" failure (pp. 206, 263). Too innocent either to recognize that his affront to Miss Rosa has made her forever his foe or to anticipate that his affront to Eulalia Bon will move her to

17. See Brooks, *William Faulkner*, pp. 296–97, on Sutpen's innocence. See also Brooks's earlier article *"Absalom, Absalom!: The Definition of Innocence,"* *Sewanee Review, 59* (1951), 543–58. Cf. my discussions above of "absolute man" (n. 40, Chap. 2; n. 16 and n. 17, Chap. 4). See Arthur M. Schlesinger, Sr., "What Then Is the American, This New Man?," *American Historical Review, 48* (1943), 225–44. Note too General Compson's advice to Charles Bon's son—you "must go away," he says. "Whatever you are, once you are among strangers, people who dont know you, you can be whatever you will" (p. 204).

Do we know it was a planned revenge?

planned revenge, Sutpen is undone by a series of affronts to man
—affronts he ironically makes in the name of man affronted.
Acting in faith very much like the faith attributed to Miss Rosa's
aunt—that one's "intentions and actions" can have no "result[s]
other than" those one foresees and seeks—Sutpen creates
around him an "atmosphere of grim embattled conspiracy and
alliance"; and yet he fails even to suspect, until it is too late,
that he is "an embattled foe." Indeed, to the end he remains
"a foe who [does] not even know that [he is] embattled"—
who does not know that stubborn earth and intractable history
are allied against him, who does not understand that he is entangled in the efforts of affronted others to redeem their lives
by weaving pattern into the emerging fabric of existence (pp.
55, 63).

Sutpen's demise—the defeat prepared and promoted by his
innocence—also derives, however, from his uncritical acceptance of his society's clichés regarding life and man, his dependence upon its abstractions regarding success and race.
Sutpen's whole design is controlled by simplistic imitation:
given no adequate "analogy" with which "to compare and
gauge" the significance of the injury done him at the door of
the mansion, he settles for imitation (p. 234). He determines,
as Faulkner later remarked, not to become "more compas-
sionate or more honest," but to become "as rich as" the man
who has affronted him, to be "as big as [that man] was on the
outside."[18] Later, when he learns that Eulalia Bon has mis-
represented her race, he accepts his society's artificial and
"absolute caste system" (p. 345). And in so doing, by his own
act of designating her incompatible with his design, he makes
her an enemy of it.

By accepting his society's definitions without revision, Sutpen fails his world, dooming himself to a life defined by affronts
that redouble desperation and inspire new designs. In addition

18. Gwynn and Blotner, p. 35.

to the affronts by which he makes Miss Rosa an implacable foe and an ordering demonologist, he offends both of his sons and both of his wives. From the moment when he puts Eulalia Bon "aside" because she is part Negro to the moment when he puts Milly Jones aside because her child by him is a daughter rather than a son, from the moment when he refuses to acknowledge Charles Bon to the moment when he betrays Wash Jones, who trusted him because he was "brave" and kills him because of his betrayal, Sutpen moves from affront to affront. Having been forced by Thomas Sutpen's dismissal of Charles Bon to repudiate his birthright, Henry Sutpen is moved first to a "design" of his own, then to murder, and finally to prolonged waiting for his own death (pp. 247, 284, 335; see p. 89). Only after years of silent, motionless waiting in the Sutpen mausoleum, as though "already a corpse," and only after he has told Quentin what must be told, is Henry free to die in the fire that destroys Sutpen's mansion. Charles Bon, by virtue of his father's initial repudiation and repeated denial, is doomed to live in "fearful intensity of need" of recognition: he lives without a "visible father" in the "limbo" into which Sutpen has evacuated him (pp. 373, 327, 313, 124).

Far more than his sons, however, it is his wives that Sutpen moves to plots of their own. In putting Eulalia Bon aside and in reducing Ellen Coldfield to an object "incidentally of course" to be procured, Sutpen outrages the one and "corrupts" the other (pp. 263, 72; see p. 240). Long before Sutpen's design has worked itself out to its violent end, Eulalia Bon has learned, at least as Shreve and Quentin see her, deliberately to avenge affront, and Ellen Coldfield has learned to engineer life.

With "almost unbearable unforgiving" and with furious "will for revenge," Eulalia Bon becomes "implacable" in her "plotting and planning." By "shaping and tempering" and "grooming" her son, she makes him the instrument of her "plotting" (pp. 297–300, 306). When he journeys into Sutpen's Mississippi, Charles Bon goes as the prepared agent of his mother's plan for confusing and undoing the design for which Sutpen has sacrificed her. Indeed, according to Shreve and Quentin, even Eulalia Bon's lawyer devises a "design"—for blackmailing Sutpen—of which Bon is to be the instrument.[19]

In contrast to Eulalia Bon, who becomes Sutpen's foe, Ellen Coldfield ostensibly becomes his ally. But by placing her in a "complementary shell" where she must forever remain "a stranger," by subordinating her to his design, Sutpen "corrupt[s] Ellen in more ways than one." She becomes all too much his ally. Through "planned and arranged and executed" campaigns, she seeks to fill the vacancies in the life of the Sutpen mansion (pp. 138, 72, 321). Wherefore she becomes the matchmaker of the courtship that is Sutpen's undoing.

> She spoke of Bon as if he were three inanimate objects in one, or perhaps one inanimate object for which she and her family would find three concordant uses: a garment which Judith might wear . . . a piece of furniture which would complement and complete the furnishing of her house and position, and a mentor and example to correct Henry's provincial manners and speech and clothing. (p. 75; cf. p. 321)

With even deeper irony, Ellen precedes Thomas Sutpen in using Henry as her instrument. In engineering the courtship between Bon and Judith, she makes Henry the agent of her matchmaking; she uses him to win Judith for Bon and Bon for Judith (see pp. 103, 97–99).

Ellen's engineering effort ends with failure, leaving her "spent amazed and uncomprehending" (p. 106). But it plays a significant role in creating within Sutpen's world a conspiracy of counterdesigns. Even when he stands so near realization that he begins to act his "role of arrogant ease and leisure," his own created world stands arrayed against him (see p. 72). In the final, fatal confrontation between Henry and Charles

19. See pp. 300–01, 306–07, 312, 331.

Bon, between man "doomed and destined to kill" and man doomed and destined to die, there are conjoined not only Sutpen's wives' plans—the one for revenge and the other for wholeness—but the destructive countermoves to which they have reduced Sutpen. The confluence of his wives' designs finally forces Sutpen to "turn square around and run . . . the fiance out of the house and . . . the son out of the house," then to reclaim Henry from his wife's matchmaking, and finally "so [to] corrupt, seduce and mesmerize" Henry that he does "the office of the outraged father's pistol-hand" (pp. 91, 179).

What is made clear in the process by which Sutpen is brought to participate in the destruction of his own design is a principle of proliferation of plans and designs—a principle that derives from and has to do with the nature of man's effort in *Absalom, Absalom!* to order nature and history. In his dual effort to master "the maelstrom of unbearable reality"—in his "solitary" struggle with "the stubborn yet slowly tractable earth," in his effort to make "the land of the earth" sustain rather than "destroy" him, and in his "solitary" struggle with the change wrought by "time," in his effort to order the "corridor of [his] doomed and tragic" history, the corridor through which echo defeated names of the fall of Rome and the crumbling of Jericho (pp. 150, 162, 12, 112, 271)—man in *Absalom, Absalom!* is forced by "scarecrow desperation" (pp. 129–30) to author designs (pp. 150, 189). Whereupon, faced with the "holocaust" to which his designs have led, he responds with "some indomitable desperation of undefeat" by authoring interpretations (pp. 19, 189).

Absalom, Absalom! is structured, beyond the juxtaposition of a man of design and a man of interpretation, by the juxtaposition of design and interpretation as such. As designs proliferate, interpretations multiply, making the novel an imitation of human minds and imaginations as well as human wills in action. Its language and action are assimilated to a recurring pattern—of affront leading to design, design leading to action, action leading to failure (as well as to new affronts and new designs), failure leading to inquiry, and failed inquiry leading to imaginative interpretation.

The devastation Sutpen authors is reclaimed in part within the novel by Judith. Strong like her father, she nonetheless retains "the soft virtues" he sacrifices (see p. 154). She is able not only to expiate (see p. 370) but to live with enduring compassion and love. Of Charles Bon, she says simply "I love, I will accept no substitute; . . . if happy I can be I will, if suffer I must I can" (p. 121; italics omitted). She brings Bon's "wife" to visit his grave and sends to New Orleans for Bon's son. Moreover, having first accepted she later partially revises her society's definition of race; at least as Quentin and Shreve see her, she finally accepts Bon's son. Though she (at least presumably) never knows Bon to be her father's son and though she never actually becomes Bon's wife, she nevertheless ends the series of front-door affronts by accepting Bon's son into the Sutpen mansion. She is not able to redeem the tortured life of Charles Etienne de Saint Velery Bon; but having asked him to call her "Aunt Judith," she dies nursing him. Toward Thomas Sutpen, the father whose heritage is doom, she unfailingly acts with compassion. In her action as well as in her words to Mrs. Compson, Judith acknowledges both man's complex entanglement with man and man's complex fate—the fate of being caught and held in tension between the "it cant" and the "it must" of meaning, yet of being called to struggle, to try and keep on trying.[20]

Judith's action in itself, however, surely is incommensurate with the devastation amidst which she struggles. If we are to understand how it is possible in *Absalom, Absalom!* to be "kilt" without being "whupped" (p. 187; cf. pp. 184, 280) —how it is possible for those who are dead yet to remain "not only indifferent but impervious" to death and even to be-

20. See Brooks, *William Faulkner*, pp. 303–05, to whose discussion of Judith I am indebted.

come "somehow a thousand times more potent and alive" (p. 280)—we must look beyond Judith and the tension she defines (and partially makes, in her action, creative) first to the re-claiming and ordering responses of the interpreters, and then to the novel itself.

It is through his interpreters that Faulkner brings order out out chaos, art "out of the rag-tag and bob-ends of old tales and talking" (p. 303). It is through them, moreover, that he links the story of Thomas Sutpen, first, to the "wilderness" and "hinterland," then to the fate of the Old South, and finally to the "destiny of the United States," the vanishing of Rome, and the crumbling of Jericho (pp. 74, 21, 118, 271). But even Quentin and Shreve stop short of full, freeing understanding. To the end they "dont know" whether they hate the South of Sutpen's story (pp. 362, 378). Their narrative efforts or, more specifically, their verbal efforts, are limited, furthermore, because, like the tombstones of which Judith speaks (in con-cluding her description of man's endeavors "to weave . . . pat-tern into the rug" of his existence), they "cant ever die or perish" (p. 128). They bring order rather to man's apprehen-sion and measure of his life than to his life itself. Only by re-maining content to make nothing happen can Quentin and Shreve, as interpreters, hope to prevail over man's condition and fate, and thereby replenish "faith in human misfortune and folly." In short, they must seek a victory that lies not prior to defeat but after it—a victory born of "indomitable desperation of undefeat" and sustained by determination, beyond "the murdering and the folly, to salvage at least from the humbled indicted dust something anyway of the old lost enchantment of the heart" (pp. 302, 189, 150). Only out of ruins can they con-struct a new story, only out of tragedy, a new triumph.[21]

The work of interpretation that is refracted through the partial and confused efforts of Miss Rosa Coldfield and Mr.

21. Cf. Jelliffe, pp. 156–57.

Compson and mirrored in the synthetic, speculative, imaginative efforts of Quentin and Shreve culminates in the poetic effort of the novelist. It is, in brief, through Faulkner's effort to bring order to the lost lives of his men of design and interpretation, through his effort to give pattern and meaning to the action and the thought of Yoknapatawpha, that the story of Sutpen and his interpreters is transformed into art and thereby redeemed, like the staff of Thoreau's artist of Kouroo, from time itself. In Faulkner's novel alone are "the paradoxical and even mutually negativing anecdotes in [this piece of] the history of the human heart . . . juxtaposed and annealed by art into verisimilitude and credibility."[22] Only in the created world of Yoknapatawpha can tension between the "it cant" and the "it must" of meaning and order be at once honored and harnessed; only therein do harmony and rhythm and wholeness and radiance preside over and inform man's varied attempts in action and thought to weave pattern into the fabric of his existence and, in so weaving, to create life out of mere existence. Under the touch of Faulkner as failed poet, the failure met by Sutpen's design merges with what are, in themselves, failed interpretations; yet from that unlikely union there comes forth poetry of language and action, of word and image and character and incident. It is "mere" poetry, a created and human song "of human unsuccess" sung "in a rapture of distress."[23] But it is poetry of "such mixed motion and such imagery" that the disorder wrought by designed action becomes emerging form, and the barrenness of failed interpretations a thousand things.[24]

22. *Knight's Gambit*, p. 39. Cf. Faulkner's depiction of the resistance of history to understanding, of disorder to interpretation, of reality to art with James Joyce's development in *Ulysses* of "tension between paradigm and reality" and of the "resistance of fact to fiction" (Frank Kermode, *The Sense of an Ending: Studies in the Theory of Fiction* [New York, Oxford University Press, 1967], p. 113.)

23. Auden, "In Memory of W. B. Yeats," p. 143.

24. Wallace Stevens, "The Rock," *Collected Poems,* p. 527.

Bibliography

The following bibliography includes works of essentially four kinds: first, the sources of my study; second, works of criticism and scholarship that have influenced my apprehension and measure of those sources; third, sources I have touched rather than explored and in which the themes of this study might further be developed; and fourth, secondary works that develop those themes along different lines or in different directions, including a few very important works that have appeared since my study was first completed. I have omitted here a few works that are mentioned in my notes but that are only tangentially related to my central concerns. The organization of the bibliography, with the possible exception of the first category, "General Critical Studies," in which I include only those works relevant to more than one of the study's three major parts, should speak for itself.

GENERAL CRITICAL STUDIES

Brownell, W. C., *American Prose Masters*, New York, Scribner, 1909.

Carpenter, Frederic I., *American Literature and the Dream*, New York, Philosophical Library, 1955.

Feidelson, Charles, Jr., *Symbolism and American Literature*, Chicago, University of Chicago Press, 1953.

Fiedler, Leslie A., *Love and Death in the American Novel* [1960], rev. ed. New York, Stein and Day, 1966.

Fussell, Edwin, *Frontier: American Literature and the American West*, Princeton, Princeton University Press, 1965.

Hoffman, Daniel G., *Form and Fable in American Fiction*, New York, Oxford University Press, 1961.

Hoffman, Frederick J., *The Mortal No: Death and the Modern Imagination,* Princeton, Princeton University Press, 1964.

Jones, Howard Mumford, *Ideas in America,* Cambridge, Mass., Harvard University Press, 1944.

—— *The Theory of American Literature,* Ithaca, Cornell University Press, 1948.

Kaul, A. N., *The American Vision: Actual and Ideal Society in Nineteenth-Century Fiction,* Yale Publications in American Studies, 7, New Haven, Yale University Press, 1963.

Lawrence, D. H., *Studies in Classic American Literature,* New York, Thomas Seltzer, 1923.

Lewis, R. W. B., *The American Adam: Innocence, Tragedy, and Tradition in the Nineteenth Century,* Chicago, University of Chicago Press, 1955.

Matthiessen, F. O., *American Renaissance: Art and Expression in the Age of Emerson and Whitman,* New York, Oxford University Press, 1941.

Mumford, Lewis, *The Golden Day: A Study in American Experience and Culture* [1926], Boston, Beacon Press, 1957.

Parrington, Vernon Louis, *Main Currents in American Thought,* 2 vols. New York, Harcourt, Brace, 1927.

Pearce, Roy Harvey, *The Continuity of American Poetry,* Princeton, Princeton University Press, 1961.

Poirier, Richard, *A World Elsewhere: The Place of Style in American Literature,* New York, Oxford University Press, 1966.

Rourke, Constance, *American Humor,* New York, Harcourt, Brace, 1931.

Smith, Henry Nash, *Virgin Land: The American West as Symbol and Myth* [1950], New York, Vintage, 1957.

Trilling, Lionel, *The Liberal Imagination: Essays on Literature and Society* [1950], Garden City, New York, Doubleday, 1957.

Wilson, Edmund, ed., *The Shock of Recognition: The Development of Literature in the United States Recorded by the Men Who Made It,* 2 vols. Garden City, New York, Doubleday, Doran, 1943.

Winters, Yvor, *Maule's Curse: Seven Studies in the History of American Obscurantism,* Norfolk, Conn., New Directions, 1938.

Part One: Literary and Historical Background

Introduction and Chapter 1: THE INTERPRETED DESIGN AS A
PROSE FORM

Abrams, M. H., *The Mirror and the Lamp: Romantic Theory and
the Critical Tradition,* New York, Oxford University Press,
1953.

Barth, Karl, *From Rousseau to Ritschl,* trans. Brian Cozens, The
Library of Philosophy and Theology, London, S C M Press,
1959.

Blackmur, R. P., *The Double Agent: Essays in Craft and Elucida-
tion,* New York, Arrow, 1935.

Burke, Kenneth, *The Grammar of Motives,* New York, Prentice-
Hall, 1945.

—— *The Philosophy of Literary Form: Studies in Symbolic Action* [1941], 2d ed. Baton Rouge, Louisiona State University
Press, 1967.

Čapek, Mileč, *The Philosophical Impact of Contemporary Physics,*
Princeton, Princeton University Press, 1961.

Forster, E. M., *Two Cheers for Democracy,* London, Edward
Arnold, 1951.

Frye, Northrop, *Anatomy of Criticism: Four Essays,* Princeton,
Princeton University Press, 1957.

—— *The Educated Imagination,* Bloomington, Indiana University Press, 1964.

—— *Fables of Identity: Studies in Poetic Mythology,* New York
Harcourt, Brace, 1963.

Handlin, Oscar, *The Uprooted: The Epic Story of the Great Migrations that Made the American People,* Boston, Little, Brown,
1951.

Heller, Erich, *The Disinherited Mind,* New York, Meridian, 1959.

Hirsch, Eric Donald, *Validity in Interpretation,* New Haven, Yale
University Press, 1967.

Krieger, Murray, *The New Apologists for Poetry,* Minneapolis,
University of Minnesota Press, 1956.

—— *A Window to Criticism: Shakespeare's Sonnets and Modern
Poetics,* Princeton, Princeton University Press, 1964.

Langer, Susanne K., *Philosophy in a New Key: A Study in the Symbolism of Reason, Rite, and Art,* New York, Mentor, 1948.

Malraux, André, *The Psychology of Art,* trans. Stuart Gilbert, London, Chatto and Windus, 1948.

—— *The Voices of Silence,* trans. Stuart Gilbert, Garden City, New York, Doubleday, 1953.

Maritain, Jacques, "Poetry's Dark Night," *Kenyon Review, 4* (1942), 149–59.

Merk, Frederick, *Manifest Destiny and Mission in American History,* New York, Knopf, 1963.

Miller, J. Hillis, *The Disappearance of God: Five Nineteenth-Century Writers,* Cambridge, Mass., Harvard University Press, 1963.

Niebuhr, Reinhold, *The Irony of American History,* New York, Scribner, 1952.

Russell, Bertrand, "The Free Man's Worship" [1903], *Mysticism and Logic and Other Essays* (London, Allen and Unwin, 1917), pp. 46–57.

Schlesinger, Arthur M., Sr., "What Then Is the American, This New Man?" *American Historical Review, 48* (1943), 225–44.

Schorer, Mark, "Technique as Discovery," *Hudson Review, 1* (1948), 67–87

Stevens, Wallace, *The Necessary Angel: Essays on Reality and the Imagination,* New York, Knopf, 1951.

Tocqueville, Alexis de, *Democracy in America* [1835–1840], trans. Henry Reeve, ed. Phillips Bradley, 2 vols. New York, Vintage, 1954.

Urban, Wilbur M., *Language and Reality: The Philosophy of Language and the Principles of Symbolism,* London, Allen and Unwin, 1939.

Whitehead, Alfred North, *Science and the Modern World,* New York, Mentor, 1948.

Wimsatt, William K., Jr., *The Verbal Icon: Studies in the Meaning of Poetry,* Lexington, University of Kentucky Press, 1954.

Woodward, C. Vann, *The Burden of Southern History,* New York, Vintage, 1961.

Chapter 2: THE ORIGINS OF DESIGN: ASPECTS OF THE COLONIAL
EXPERIENCE; AND *Chapter 3:* THE ORIGINS OF INTERPRETATION:
THE PURITAN JEREMIAD AS A LITERARY FORM

Primary Works

Arber, Edward, and A. G. Bradley, eds., *The Travels and Works
of Captain John Smith,* 2 vols. London, 1910.
Belcher, Joseph, *The Singular Happiness,* Boston, 1701.
Bradford, William, *Of Plymouth Plantation, 1620–1647,* ed.
Samuel E. Morison, New York, Knopf, 1952.
Buckingham, Thomas, *Moses and Aaron,* New London, 1729.
Bulkeley, Peter, *The Gospel-Covenant,* London, 1646.
Burnham, William, *God's Providence in Placing Men,* New London, 1722.
Burton, John, *A Sermon Preach'd before the Trustees for Establishing the Colony of Georgia in America,* London, 1733.
Dana, James, *Two Discourses,* New Haven, 1801.
Danforth, Samuel, *A Briefe Recognition of New-Englands Errand
into the Wilderness,* Cambridge, Mass., 1671.
Davenport, John, *A Sermon Preach'd at the Election . . . 1669,*
Boston, 1670.
Forbes, Allyn B., ed., *The Autobiography of Thomas Shepard,
Publications of the Colonial Society of Massachusetts,* 27 (1927–
30), 345–400.
Higginson, John, *The Cause of God and His People in New-
England* [1663], in *Elijah's Mantle,* Boston, 1722.
Hosmer, James K., ed., John Winthrop, *Journal: History of New
England, 1630–1649,* 2 vols. New York, Scribner, 1908.
Hubbard, William, *The Happiness of a People,* Boston, 1676.
[Johnson, Edward] *A History of New-England,* London, 1654.
Mather, Cotton, *Magnalia Christi Americana; or, the Ecclesiastical
History of New-England* [1702], 2 vols. Hartford, 1853–55.
Mather, Increase, *The Day of Trouble Is Near,* Boston, 1674.
—— *A Discourse concerning the Uncertainty of the Times,* Boston, 1697.
[Mather, Increase] *Necessity of Reformation,* Boston, 1679.
Mitchel, Jonathan, *The Great End and Interest of New-England*
[1662], in *Elijah's Mantle,* Boston, 1722.

—— *Nehemiah on the Wall in Troublesom Times,* Cambridge, Mass., 1671.

Montgomery, Robert, *A Discourse concerning the Design'd Establishment of a New Colony to the South of Carolina* [1717], *American Colonial Tracts Monthly,* Vol. I (1897–98), No. 1.

Oakes, Urian, *The Sovereign Efficacy of Divine Providence,* Boston, 1682.

Prince, Thomas, *The People of New-England,* Boston, 1730.

Radin, P., ed., *An Impartial Inquiry into . . . the Province of Georgia* [1741], *Occasional Papers,* California State Library, Reprint Series No. 13, San Francisco, 1940.

Shepard, Thomas, "Election Sermon, 1638," *New England Historical and Genealogical Register, 24* (1870), 361–66.

—— *A Treatise of Liturgies,* London, 1653.

[Stephens, Thomas] *The Castle-Builders; or, the History of William Stephens . . . A Political Novel,* London, 1759.

Stoughton, William, *New-Englands True Interest,* Cambridge, Mass., 1670.

Tailfer, Pat., and others, with Comments by the Earl of Egmont, *A True and Historical Narrative of the Colony of Georgia* [1740], ed. Clarence L. Ver Steeg, Athens, University of Georgia Press, 1960.

Ward, Nathaniel, *The Simple Cobler of Aggawam in America,* London, 1647.

Webb, John, *The Government of Christ Considered and Applied,* Boston, 1738.

Wigglesworth, Michael, "God's Controversy with New-England" [written in 1662; first published in 1873], *Proceedings of the Massachusetts Historical Society, 12* (1871–73), 83–93.

Willard, Samuel, *The Character of a Good Ruler,* Boston, 1694.

Winthrop Papers, 6 vols. to date, Boston, Massachusetts Historical Society, 1929–.

Secondary Works

Adams, Henry, "Captain John Smith," *North American Review, 104* (1867), 1–30.

Ahlstrom, Sydney E., "Theology in America: A Historical Survey," *Religion in American Life,* ed. J. W. Smith and A. L. Jamison, Vol. II: *The Shaping of American Religion,* Princeton, Princeton University Press, 1961.

Andrews, Charles M., *The Colonial Period of American History,* 4 vols. New Haven, Yale University Press, 1934–37.

Bancroft, George, *History of the United States from the Discovery of the American Continent,* 10 vols. Boston, 1834–74.

Boorstin, Daniel J., *The Americans: The Colonial Experience,* New York, Random House, 1958.

—— *The Lost World of Thomas Jefferson* [1948], Boston, Beacon Press, 1960.

Crane, Verner W., *The Southern Frontier, 1670–1732,* Durham, North Carolina, Duke University Press, 1928.

Emerson, Ralph Waldo, "The Young American," *The Complete Works of Ralph Waldo Emerson,* ed. Edward W. Emerson (Centenary Edition, 12 vols. Boston, Houghton Mifflin, 1903–04), *1,* 361–95.

Haroutunian, Joseph, *Piety versus Moralism: The Passing of the New England Theology,* New York, Holt, 1932.

Heimert, Alan, "Puritanism, the Wilderness, and the Frontier," *New England Quarterly, 26* (1953), 361–82.

James, Henry, Sr., "Democracy and Its Issues," *Lectures and Miscellanies* (New York, 1852), pp. 1–49.

Love, W. D., *The Fast and Thanksgiving Days of New England,* Boston, 1895.

Miller, Perry, *Errand into the Wilderness,* Cambridge, Mass., Harvard University Press, 1956.

—— *The New England Mind: From Colony to Province,* Cambridge, Mass., Harvard University Press, 1953.

—— *Orthodoxy in Massachusetts, 1630–1650,* Cambridge, Mass., Harvard University Press, 1933.

Morgan, Edmund S., *The Puritan Dilemma: The Story of John Winthrop,* Library of American Biography, Boston, Little, Brown, 1958.

Morison, Samuel Eliot, *Builders of the Bay Colony,* Boston, Houghton Mifflin, 1930.

Niebuhr, H. Richard, *The Kingdom of God in America,* Chicago, Willett, Clark, 1937.

Ong, Walter J., *Ramus: Method and the Decay of Dialogue,* Cambridge, Mass., Harvard University Press, 1958.

Schneider, Herbert W., *A History of American Philosophy,* Columbia Studies in American Culture, 18, New York, Columbia University Press, 1946.

Smith, John E., *The Spirit of American Philosophy,* New York, Oxford University Press, 1963.

Turner, Frederick Jackson, *The Frontier in American History,* New York, Holt, 1920.

Tyler, Moses Coit, *History of American Literature, 1607–1765* [1878], New York, Crowell-Collier, 1962.

PART TWO: DESIGN, INTERPRETATION, AND THE DRAMA OF
SELF-PORTRAITURE

General

Morgan, Edmund S., *Visible Saints: The History of a Puritan Idea,* New York, New York University Press, 1963.

Pascal, Roy, *Design and Truth in Autobiography,* London, Routledge and Kegan Paul, 1960.

Sayre, Robert F., *The Examined Self: Benjamin Franklin, Henry Adams, Henry James,* Princeton, Princeton University Press, 1964.

Chapter 4: ANTICIPATIONS OF AN AUTOBIOGRAPHICAL FORM:
EDWARDS' *Personal Narrative* AND FRANKLIN'S *Autobiography*

Primary Works: Jonathan Edwards

Austin, S., ed., *The Works of President Edwards,* Worcester Edition, 4 vols. New York, 1844.

Dwight, Sereno E., ed., *The Works of President Edwards: With a Memoir of His Life,* 10 vols. New York, 1829.

Miller, Perry, ed., *Images or Shadows of Divine Things,* New Haven, Yale University Press, 1948.

—— "Jonathan Edwards on the Sense of the Heart," *Harvard Theological Review, 41* (1948), 123–45.

Personal Narrative, in Samuel Hopkins, *The Life and Character of . . . Jonathan Edwards,* Northampton, Mass., 1804.

Primary Works: Benjamin Franklin

The Autobiography of Benjamin Franklin, ed. Leonard W. Labaree and others, New Haven, London, Yale University Press, 1964.

Labaree, Leonard, and others, eds., *The Papers of Benjamin Franklin,* 7 vols. to date, New Haven, Yale University Press, 1959–.

Smyth, Albert H., *The Writings of Benjamin Franklin,* 10 vols. New York, Macmillan, 1905–07.

Van Doren, Carl, ed., *Benjamin Franklin's Autobiographical Writings,* New York, Viking, 1945.

Primary Works: Thomas Shepard

Forbes, Allyn B., ed., *The Autobiography of Thomas Shepard, Publications of the Colonial Society of Massachusetts, 27* (1927–30), 345–400.

Secondary Works

Baumgarten, P. R., "Jonathan Edwards: The Theory Behind His Use of Figurative Language," *PMLA, 78* (1963), 321–25.

Becker, Carl, "Benjamin Franklin," *Dictionary of American Biography, 6* (1931), 585–98.

Chinard, Gilbert, "The Apotheosis of Benjamin Franklin," *Proceedings of the American Philosophical Society, 99* (1955), 440–73.

Crane, R. S., "Anglican Apologetics and the Idea of Progress, 1699–1745," *Modern Philology, 31* (1934), 273–306, 349–82.

Farrand, Max, Introduction, *Benjamin Franklin's Memoirs: Parallel Text Edition,* Berkeley and Los Angeles, University of California Press, 1949.

Jones, Howard Mumford, "American Prose Style: 1700–1770," *Huntington Library Bulletin, 6* (1934), 115–51.

Labaree, Leonard W., Introduction, *The Autobiography of Benjamin Franklin,* New Haven, Yale University Press, 1964.

Lovejoy, A. O., "The Parallel of Deism and Classicism," *Modern Philology, 29* (1932), 281–99.

Meister, Charles W., "Franklin as a Proverb Stylist," *American Literature, 24* (1952), 157–66.

Miller, Perry, "From Edwards to Emerson," *New England Quarterly, 8* (1940), 589–617.

—— Introduction, Jonathan Edwards, *Images or Shadows of Divine Things,* New Haven, Yale University Press, 1948.

—— *Jonathan Edwards,* New York, William Sloane, 1949.

Murdock, Kenneth B., *Literature and Theology in Colonial New England,* Cambridge, Mass., Harvard University Press, 1949.

Sanford, Charles L., "An American Pilgrim's Progress," *American Quarterly, 4* (1954), 297–310.

Shea, Daniel B., Jr., "The Art and Instruction of Jonathan Edwards's *Personal Narrative," American Literature, 37* (1965), 17–32.

Smith, John E., Introduction, Jonathan Edwards, *The Religious Affections,* New Haven, Yale University Press, 1959.

Van Doren, Carl, *Benjamin Franklin,* New York, Viking, 1938.

Wector, Dixon, "Poor Richard: The Boy Who Made Good," *The Hero in America* (New York, Knopf, 1941), Chapter 4.

Wright, Louis B., "Franklin's Legacy to the Gilded Age," *Virginia Quarterly Review, 22* (1946), 268–79.

Chapter 5: EXTENSION OF THE FORM: THOREAU'S *Walden*

Primary Works

Bode, Carl, ed., *Collected Poems of Henry Thoreau,* New York, Packard, 1943.

Harding, Walter, and Carl Bode, eds., *The Correspondence of Henry David Thoreau,* New York, New York University Press, 1958.

Miller, Perry, ed., *Consciousness in Concord: The Text of Thoreau's Hitherto "Lost Journal," 1840–1841,* Boston, Houghton Mifflin, 1958.

The Writings of Henry David Thoreau, Walden Edition, 20 vols. Boston, Houghton Mifflin, 1906.

Secondary Works

Aaron, Daniel, *Men of Good Hope: A Story of American Progressives,* New York, Oxford University Press, 1951.

Beach, Joseph W., *The Concept of Nature in Nineteenth-Century English Poetry,* New York, Macmillan, 1936.

Canby, Henry S., *Thoreau,* Boston, Houghton Mifflin, 1939.

Channing, William E., *Thoreau, the Poet-Naturalist,* rev. ed. Boston, Goodspeed's Book Shop, 1902.

Cook, R. L., *Passage to Walden,* Boston, Houghton Mifflin, 1949.

Emerson, Ralph Waldo, "Thoreau," *Atlantic Monthly, 10* (1862), 239–49.

Harding, Walter, *A Thoreau Handbook,* New York, New York University Press, 1959.

Hyman, Stanley, "Henry Thoreau in Our Time," *Atlantic Monthly, 178* (1946), 137–46.

Paul, Sherman, *The Shores of America: Thoreau's Inward Exploration,* Urbana, University of Illinois Press, 1958.

Shanley, J. Lyndon, *The Making of Walden,* Chicago, University of Chicago Press, 1957.

Chapter 6: APOTHEOSIS OF THE FORM: HENRY ADAMS' *Education*

Primary Works

Adams, Brooks, ed., *The Degradation of the Democratic Dogma,* New York, Macmillan, 1919.

"Buddha and Brahma: A Poem," *Yale Review, 5* (1915–16), 82–89.

Cater, Harold Dean, ed., *Henry Adams and His Friends: A Collection of His Unpublished Letters,* Boston, Houghton Mifflin, 1947.

The Education of Henry Adams [1907], Boston and New York, Houghton Mifflin, 1918.

Ford, Worthington C., ed., *A Cycle of Adams Letters, 1861–1865,* 2 vols. Boston and New York, Houghton Mifflin, 1920.

—— *Letters of Henry Adams, 1858–1918,* 2 vols. Boston and New York, Houghton Mifflin, 1930–38.

History of the United States during the Administrations of Thomas

Jefferson and James Madison, 9 vols. New York, 1889–91.
Mont-Saint-Michel and Chartres [1904], Boston and New York, Houghton Mifflin, 1913.

Secondary Works

Adams, Brooks, "The Heritage of Henry Adams," introduction to *The Degradation of the Democratic Dogma,* New York, Macmillan, 1919.
Blackmur, R. P., "Henry Adams: Three Late Moments," *Kenyon Review, 2* (1940), 14–26.
—— "Henry and Brooks Adams: Parallels to Two Generations," *Southern Quarterly Review, 5* (1939), 308–34.
—— "The Novels of Henry Adams," *Sewanee Review, 51* (1948), 281–304.
Folsum, James K., "Mutation as Metaphor in *The Education of Henry Adams," English Literary History, 30* (1963), 162–74.
Glicksberg, Charles I., "Henry Adams and the Modern Spirit," *Dalhousie Review, 27* (1947), 299–309.
Hume, Robert A., *Runaway Star: An Appreciation of Henry Adams,* Ithaca, Cornell University Press, 1951.
—— "The Style and Literary Background of Henry Adams, with Attention to *The Education of Henry Adams," American Literature, 16* (1945), 296–315.
Jordy, William H., *Henry Adams: Scientific Historian,* New Haven, Yale University Press, 1952.
Levenson, J. C., *The Mind and Art of Henry Adams,* Boston, Houghton Mifflin, 1957.
Samuels, Ernest, *The Young Henry Adams,* Cambridge, Mass., Harvard University Press, 1948.
—— *Henry Adams: The Middle Years,* Cambridge, Mass., Harvard University Press, 1958.
Smith, Bernard, "The Quest for Beauty," *Forces in American Criticism* (New York, Harcourt, Brace, 1939), pp. 220–29.
Stevenson, Elizabeth, *Henry Adams: A Biography,* New York, Macmillan, 1956.
Stone, James, "Henry Adams's Philosophy of History," *New England Quarterly, 14* (1941), 538–48.

Wright, Nathalia, "Henry Adams's Theory of History: A Puritan Defense, " *New England Quarterly, 58* (1945), 204–10.

PART THREE: DESIGN, INTERPRETATION, AND THE ART OF FICTION

General

Bewley, Marius, *The Complex Fate: Hawthorne and Henry James,* London, Chatto and Windus, 1952.

—— *The Eccentric Design: Form in the Classic American Novel,* New York, Columbia University Press, 1959.

Chase, Richard, *The American Novel and Its Tradition,* Garden City, New York, Doubleday, 1957.

Kazin, Alfred, *On Native Grounds: An Interpretation of Modern American Prose Literature,* New York, Reynal and Hitchcock, 1942.

Kermode, Frank, *The Sense of an Ending: Studies in the Theory of Fiction,* New York, Oxford University Press, 1967.

Lynn, Kenneth S., *Dream of Success: A History of the Modern American Imagination,* Boston, Little, Brown, 1955.

Chapter 7: DEFINITION OF A FICTIONAL FORM: HAWTHORNE'S *The Blithedale Romance*

Primary Works: Hawthorne

Charvat, William, and others, eds., *The Centenary Edition of the Works of Nathaniel Hawthorne,* 3 vols. to date, Columbus, Ohio State University Press, 1962–.

Lathrop, George P., ed., *The Complete Works of Nathaniel Hawthorne,* Riverside Edition, 12 vols. Boston, 1883.

Pearson, Norman Holmes, ed., The French and Italian Notebooks by Nathaniel Hawthorne, unpublished Ph.D. dissertation, Yale University, 1941.

Stewart, Randall, ed., *The American Notebooks by Nathaniel Hawthorne,* New Haven, Yale University Press, 1932.

—— *The English Notebooks by Nathaniel Hawthorne,* New York, Modern Language Association of America, 1941.

Primary Works: Melville

Moby-Dick, ed. Charles Feidelson, Jr., The Library of Literature, New York, Bobbs-Merrill, 1964.

Secondary Works

Arvin, Newton, *Hawthorne* [1929], New York, Russell and Russell, 1961.

Blair, Walter, "Color, Light, and Shadow in Hawthorne's Fiction," *New England Quarterly, 15* (1942), 74–94.

Cowley, Malcolm, "Hawthorne in the Looking-Glass," *Sewanee Review, 56* (1948), 545–63.

Crews, Frederick C., "A New Reading of *The Blithedale Romance," American Literature, 29* (1957–58), 147–70.

—— *The Sins of the Fathers: Hawthorne's Psychological Themes,* New York, Oxford University Press, 1966.

Curl, Vega, *Pasteboard Masks: Fact as Spiritual Symbol in the Novels of Hawthorne and Melville,* Cambridge, Mass., Harvard University Press, 1931.

Davidson, Edward, *Hawthorne's Last Phase,* New Haven, Yale University Press, 1949.

Feidelson, Charles, Jr., "*The Scarlet Letter," Hawthorne Centenary Essays,* ed. Roy Harvey Pearce (Columbus, Ohio State University Press, 1964), pp. 31–77.

Fussell, Edwin, "Neutral Territory: Hawthorne on the Figurative Frontier," *Hawthorne Centenary Essays,* ed. Roy Harvey Pearce (Columbus, Ohio State University Press, 1964), pp. 297–314.

Hall, Lawrence S., *Hawthorne, Critic of Society,* New Haven, Yale University Press, 1944.

Howe, Irving, *Politics and the Novel,* New York, Meridian, 1957.

James, Henry, *Hawthorne,* English Men of Letters Series, London, 1879.

—— "Nathaniel Hawthorne," *Library of the World's Best Literature,* ed. Charles Dudley Warner (30 vols. New York, 1896–98), *12,* 7053–61.

Leavis, Q. D., "Hawthorne as Poet," *Sewanee Review, 59* (1951), 179–205, 426–58.

Levin, Harry, *The Power of Blackness: Hawthorne, Poe, Melville,* New York, Knopf, 1958.

More, Paul Elmer, "The Solitude of Nathaniel Hawthorne," *Shelbourne Essays,* First Series, New York, Putnam, 1904.

Pearce, Roy Harvey, "Hawthorne and the Twilight of Romance," *Yale Review, 37* (1947–48), 487–506.

——, ed., *Hawthorne Centenary Essays,* Columbus, Ohio State University Press, 1964.

Stewart, George R., "The Two *Moby-Dicks,*" *American Literature, 25* (1954), 417–48.

Stewart, Randall, Introduction, *The American Notebooks by Nathaniel Hawthorne,* ed. Randall Stewart, New Haven, Yale University Press, 1932.

—— *Nathaniel Hawthorne: A Biography,* New Haven, Yale University Press, 1948.

Trollope, Anthony, "The Genius of Nathaniel Hawthorne," *North American Review, 129* (1879), 203–22.

Turner, Arlin, "Hawthorne and Reform," *New England Quarterly, 15* (1942), 700–14.

Van Doren, Mark, *Nathaniel Hawthorne,* American Men of Letters Series, New York, William Sloane, 1949.

Waggoner, Hyatt H., *Hawthorne,* Cambridge, Mass., Harvard University Press, 1955.

Watters, R. E., "Melville's 'Isolatoes,' " *PMLA, 60* (1945), 1138–48.

Chapter 8: EXTENSION OF THE FORM: HENRY JAMES, AND FITZGERALD'S *The Great Gatsby*

Primary Works: Henry James

The American Scene, ed. W. H. Auden, New York, Scribner, 1946.

Blackmur, R. P., ed., *The Art of the Novel: Critical Prefaces by Henry James,* New York, Scribner, 1934.

Dupee, F. W., ed., *Autobiography,* New York, Criterion, 1956.

Edel, Leon, ed., *The American Essays of Henry James,* New York, Vintage, 1956.

—— *The Future of the Novel,* New York, Vintage, 1956.

—— *Selected Letters of Henry James,* New York, Farrar, Straus and Cudahy, 1955.

Lubbock, Percy, ed., *The Letters of Henry James,* 2 vols. London, Macmillan, 1920.

Matthiessen, F. O., ed., *Stories of Writers and Artists,* New York, New Directions, n.d.

Matthiessen, F. O., and Kenneth B. Murdock, eds., *The Notebooks of Henry James,* New York, Oxford University Press, 1947.

The Novels and Tales of Henry James, New York Edition, 26 vols. New York, Scribner, 1907–17.

The Sacred Fount, New York, Scribner, 1901.

Primary Works: F. Scott Fitzgerald

All the Sad Young Men, New York, Scribner, 1926.

The Beautiful and Damned, New York, Scribner, 1922.

Flappers and Philosophers, New York, Scribner, 1921.

The Great Gatsby, New York, Scribner, 1925.

Tales of the Jazz Age, New York, Scribner, 1922.

This Side of Paradise, New York, Scribner, 1920.

The Vegetable, or From President to Postman, New York, Scribner, 1923.

Wilson, Edmund, ed., *The Last Tycoon,* New York, Scribner, 1941.

Secondary Works

Arvin, Newton, "Henry James and the Almighty Dollar," *Hound and Horn, 7* (1934), 434–43.

Beach, Joseph W., *The Method of Henry James,* New Haven, Yale University Press, 1918.

Beebe, Maurice, and Jackson R. Bryer, "Criticism of F. Scott Fitzgerald: A Selected Checklist," *Modern Fiction Studies, 7* (1961), 82–94.

Bewley, Marius, "Scott Fitzgerald's Criticism of America," *Sewanee Review, 62* (1954), 223–46.

Bishop, John Peale, "The Missing All," *Virginia Quarterly Review, 13* (1937), 107–21.

Blackmur, R. P., "Henry James," *Literary History of the United*

States, ed. Robert E. Spiller and others (rev. ed. New York, Macmillan, 1953), pp. 1039–64.

Dupee, F. W., *Henry James,* The American Men of Letters Series, New York, William Sloane, 1951.

———, ed., *The Question of Henry James,* New York, Holt, 1945.

Edel, Leon, *Henry James,* 3 vols. Philadelphia, Lippincott, 1953–62.

——— and Dan H. Laurence, eds., *A Bibliography of Henry James,* rev. ed. London, Hart-Davis, 1961.

Fussell, Edwin, "Fitzgerald's Brave New World," *English Literary History, 19* (1952), 291–306.

Haight, Gordon, "Realism Defined: William Dean Howells," *Literary History of the United States,* ed. Robert E. Spiller and others (rev. ed. New York, Macmillan, 1953), pp. 879–98.

Hanzo, Thomas, "The Theme and the Narrator of *The Great Gatsby,*" *Modern Fiction Studies, 2* (1956–57), 183–90.

Hindus, Milton, "The Eyes of Dr. T. J. Eckleburg," *Boston University Studies in English, 3* (1957), 22–31.

Hoffman, Frederick J., ed., *The Great Gatsby: A Study,* New York, Scribner, 1962.

Hoffman, Frederick J., *The Twenties: American Writing in the Postwar Decade,* New York, Collier, 1962.

Holland, Laurence B., *The Expense of Vision: Essays on the Craft of Henry James,* Princeton, Princeton University Press, 1964.

James, Henry, *Hawthorne,* English Men of Letters Series, London, 1879.

Lewis, R. W. B., "The Vision of Grace: James's *The Wings of the Dove,*" *Modern Fiction Studies, 3* (1957), 33–40.

Lubbock, Percy, *The Craft of Fiction,* New York, Scribner, 1921.

Matthiessen, F. O., *Henry James: The Major Phase,* New York, Oxford University Press, 1944.

Miller, James E., Jr., *The Fictional Technique of Scott Fitzgerald,* The Hague, Netherlands, Martinus Nijhoff, 1957.

Mizener, Arthur, *The Far Side of Paradise: A Biography of F. Scott Fitzgerald,* Boston, Houghton Mifflin, 1951.

Novell-Smith, Simon, ed., *The Legend of the Master,* London, Constable, 1948.

Turnbull, Andrew, *Scott Fitzgerald,* New York, Scribner, 1962.

Ward, J. A., *The Imagination of Disaster: Evil in the Fiction of Henry James,* Lincoln, University of Nebraska Press, 1961.

Wilson, Edmund, ed., *The Crack-Up* [1945], New York, New Directions, 1956.

Wilson, Edmund, *The Triple Thinkers,* New York, Harcourt, Brace, 1938.

Chapter 9: APOTHEOSIS OF THE FORM: FAULKNER'S *Absalom, Absalom!*

Primary Works: William Faulkner

Absalom, Absalom! [1936], New York, Random House, 1951.

Collins, Carvel, ed., *William Faulkner: Early Prose and Poetry,* Boston, Little, Brown, 1962.

—— *William Faulkner: New Orleans Sketches,* New Brunswick, N.J., Rutgers University Press, 1958.

A Green Bough, New York, Smith and Haas, 1935.

Gwynn, F. L., and Joseph L. Blotner, eds., *Faulkner in the University,* Charlottesville, University of Virginia Press, 1959.

Jelliffe, Robert A., *Faulkner at Nagano,* Tokyo, Kenkyusha, 1956.

Knight's Gambit, New York, Random House, 1949.

The Marble Faun, Boston, The Four Seas, 1924.

"Nobel Prize Address," *The Faulkner Reader,* New York, Random House, 1954.

Stein, Jean, Interview with William Faulkner, *Paris Review, 4* (1956), 28–52. Reprinted in Malcolm Cowley, ed., *Writers at Work: The "Paris Review" Interviews,* New York, Viking, 1959, pp. 119–41.

Secondary Works

Backman, Melvin, "Faulkner's Sick Heroes: Bayard Sartoris and Quentin Compson," *Modern Fiction Studies, 2* (1956), 95–108.

Beebe, Maurice, "Criticism of William Faulkner: A Selected Checklist with an Index to Studies of Separate Works," *Modern Fiction Studies, 2* (1956), 150–64.

Breit, Harvey, Introduction, *Absalom, Absalom!* [1936], New York, Random House, 1951.

Brooks, Cleanth, *"Absalom, Absalom!:* The Definition of Innocence," *Sewanee Review, 59* (1951), 543–58.

—— "History, Tragedy, and the Imagination in *Absalom, Absalom!," Yale Review, 52* (1963), 340–51.

—— *William Faulkner: The Yoknapatawpha Country,* New Haven, Yale University Press, 1963.

Brumm, Ursula, "Wilderness and Civilization: A Note on William Faulkner," *Partisan Review, 22* (1955), 340–50.

Cowley, Malcolm, Introduction, *The Portable Faulkner,* New York, Viking, 1946.

—— "William Faulkner's Legend of the South," *Sewanee Review, 53* (1945), 343–61.

Daniel, Robert W., *A Catalogue of the Writings of William Faulkner,* New Haven, Yale University Library, 1942.

Edmonds, Irene C., "Faulkner and the Black Shadow," L. D. Rubin, Jr., and R. D. Jacobs, eds., *Southern Renascence: The Literature of the Modern South,* Baltimore, Johns Hopkins University Press, 1953, pp. 192–206.

Flint, R. W., "Faulkner as Elegist," *Hudson Review, 7* (1954), 246–57.

Hoffman, Frederick J., and Olga Vickery, eds., *William Faulkner: Two Decades of Criticism,* East Lansing, Michigan State University Press, 1951.

Howe, Irving, *William Faulkner: A Critical Study,* New York, Random House, 1952.

Kazin, Alfred, "Faulkner in His Fury," *The Inmost Leaf* (New York, Noonday, 1959), pp. 257–73.

Lind, Ilse Dusoir, "The Design and Meaning of *Absalom, Absalom!," PMLA, 70* (1955), 887–912.

Longley, John L., Jr., *The Tragic Mask: A Study of Faulkner's Heroes,* Chapel Hill, University of North Carolina Press, 1963.

Magny, Claude-Edmonde, "Faulkner ou l'inversion théologique," *L'Age du roman américain* (Paris, Editions du Seuil, 1948), pp. 196–243.

Meriwether, James B., "William Faulkner: A Check List," *The Princeton University Library Chronicle, 18* (1957), 136–58.

Millgate, Michael, *The Achievement of William Faulkner,* London, Constable, 1966.

Miner, Ward L., *The World of William Faulkner,* Durham, Duke University Press, 1952.

O'Connor, William Van, *The Tangled Fire of William Faulkner,* Minneapolis, University of Minnesota Press, 1954.

Sewall, Richard B., *"Absalom, Absalom!," The Vision of Tragedy* (New Haven, Yale University Press, 1959), pp. 133–47.

Thompson, Lawrance, *William Faulkner: An Introduction and Interpretation* [1963], New York, Holt, Rinehart and Winston, 1967.

Vickery, Olga W., *The Novels of William Faulkner: A Critical Interpretation,* Baton Rouge, Louisiana State University Press, 1959.

Waggoner, H. H., *William Faulkner: From Jefferson to the World,* Lexington, University of Kentucky Press, 1959.

Warren, Robert Penn, "William Faulkner," *Selected Essays* (New York, Random House, 1958), pp. 59–79.

Index